The Governance of Small States in Turbulent Times

Harald Baldersheim
Jozef Bátora (eds.)

The Governance of Small States in Turbulent Times
The Exemplary Cases of Norway and Slovakia

Barbara Budrich Publishers
Opladen • Berlin • Toronto 2012

All rights reserved. No part of this publication may be reproduced, stored in or introduced into a retrieval system, or transmitted, in any form, or by any means (electronic, mechanical, photocopying, recording or otherwise) without the prior written permission of Barbara Budrich Publishers. Any person who does any unauthorized act in relation to this publication may be liable to criminal prosecution and civil claims for damages.

You must not circulate this book in any other binding or cover and you must impose this same condition on any acquirer.

A CIP catalogue record for this book is available from
Die Deutsche Bibliothek (The German Library)

© 2012 by Barbara Budrich Publishers, Opladen, Berlin & Toronto
www.barbara-budrich.net

ISBN   978-3-86649- 340-7

Das Werk einschließlich aller seiner Teile ist urheberrechtlich geschützt. Jede Verwertung außerhalb der engen Grenzen des Urheberrechtsgesetzes ist ohne Zustimmung des Verlages unzulässig und strafbar. Das gilt insbesondere für Vervielfältigungen, Übersetzungen, Mikroverfilmungen und die Einspeicherung und Verarbeitung in elektronischen Systemen.

Die Deutsche Bibliothek – CIP-Einheitsaufnahme
Ein Titeldatensatz für die Publikation ist bei Der Deutschen Bibliothek erhältlich.

Verlag Barbara Budrich ⓑ Barbara Budrich Publishers
Stauffenbergstr. 7. D-51379 Leverkusen Opladen, Germany

86 Delma Drive • Toronto, ON, Canada
www.barbara-budrich.net

Jacket illustration by disegno, Wuppertal, Germany – www.disenjo.de
Typesetting by Walburga Fichtner, Cologne, Germany
Printed in Europe on acid-free paper by
paper&tinta, Warsaw

Contents

Preface vii

Notes on contributors viii

1. The governance of small states: an introduction 1
   Harald Baldersheim and Jozef Bátora

Security, sovereignty and borders

2. Regional security integration: Nordic and Visegrad
   approaches 19
   Jozef Bátora and Janne Haaland Matlary
3. Strangers at the gate: national policies on migration
   in Norway and Slovakia 38
   Živka Deleva and Leonid Tuzov

Responses to the international financial crisis

4. Economic crisis management: national versus supranational
   responses in Slovakia 63
   Andrej Wertlen
5. Responses to financial crisis through party programs
   in Slovakia: national or europeanized? 79
   Dušan Leška
6. The impact of the economy on governments' electoral
   performance 94
   Hanne Marthe Narud

Political cleavages in flux

7. Social structure and party choice in Norway and Slovakia:
   a loosening of ties? 123
   Oddbjørn Knutsen
8. The appeal of populism 157
   Oľga Gyárfášová and Anders Ravik Jupskås

9. Why are there so few female MPs in Slovak parliaments? 186
Elisabeth Bakke

Institutional transformation

10. Regionalization of governance: testing the capacity
for reform 208
Harald Baldersheim and Ľudmila Malíková
11. Good local governance: What is it?
How can it be promoted? 229
Lawrence E. Rose

Conclusion

12. Prospects for two small countries in a turbulent world 254
Harald Baldersheim and Jozef Bátora

Index 263

Preface

This book is the fruit of cooperation between members of the Department of Political Science at the University of Oslo and political scientists at Comenius University in Bratislava going back to the early 1990s. Less than a year after the Velvet Revolution, Harald Baldersheim spent some time at Comenius University in Bratislava and elsewhere in Slovakia assessing prospects of local governance reforms. Then, between 2001 and 2005, Jozef Bátora worked on his PhD at the Department of Political Science at the University of Oslo with Harald as one of his dissertation advisors. This linkage proved crucial also in the development of the research project "Small European states and the effects of the global financial crisis" financed by Norway´s EEA Grants 2009 – 2011, which provided the framework for the current book. Work on the book involved a number of seminars both in Oslo and in Bratislava, in which the contributors to this volume as well as a number of other academics and practitioners have participated.

There are a number of people and institutions who deserve our thanks. To take the latter first, we would like to thank the Norwegian government for generous support of our application via the EEA Grant Scheme. Besides this book, the result is a fairly high number of students and researchers who went on exchange between our respective institutions in the project period. Existing links were broadened and deepened and the formalization of an Erasmus agreement between our institutes will provide for a steady flow of exchange students of political science between Bratislava and Oslo for years to come. We are grateful for the support provided to this book and the entire research project by Silvia Miháliková, the Dean of the Faculty of Social and Economic Sciences at Comenius University as well as by Lucia Mokrá, the Vice-Dean. We would also like to thank Norway´s ambassador to Slovakia, Trine Skymoen, for her interest in our project activities.

Language editing on the book was done by Peter Glen in Oslo and by Bill Bagatelas in Bratislava. Layout editing was done by Zuzana Hozlárová at IESIR in Bratislava.

Last but not least, Harald would like to thank his wife Anne Kristin for support and encouragement all the time since our first visit to Slovakia during that wonderful spring of 1990, and Jozef would like to thank his wife Zuzana and his two sons Adam and Michal for letting him work late evenings and early mornings.

Oslo and Bratislava, October 2011

The editors

Notes on contributors

Elisabeth Bakke is Associate Professor of Political Science at the University of Oslo
Harald Baldersheim is Professor of Political Science at the University of Oslo
Jozef Bátora is Associate Professor and Director at the Institute of European Studies and International Relations, Comenius University in Bratislava
Živka Deleva is Senior Researcher at the Institute of European Studies and International Relations, Comenius University in Bratislava
Oľga Gyárfášová is Senior Researcher at the Institute of European Studies and International Relations, Comenius University and Senior Researcher at the Institute of Public Affairs (IVO) in Bratislava
Janne Haaland Matlary is Professor of Political Science at the University of Oslo
Oddbjørn Knutsen is Professor of Political Science at the University of Oslo
Dušan Leška is Associate Professor at the Institute of European Studies and International Relations, Comenius University in Bratislava
Ľudmila Malíková is Professor and Director at the Institute of Public Policy at Comenius University in Bratislava
Hanne Marthe Narud is Professor of Political Science at the University of Oslo
Anders Ravik Jupskås is a PhD Candidate in Political Science at the University of Oslo
Lawrence E. Rose is Professor of Political Science at the University of Oslo
Leonid Tuzov is a PhD Candidate at the Institute of European Studies and International Relations, Comenius University in Bratislava
Andrej Wertlen is an Analyst in UBS Zurich and a graduate of the Institute of European Studies and International Relations, Comenius University in Bratislava

Chapter 1
The governance of small states: an introduction

Harald Baldersheim and Jozef Bátora

> What they [small states] have learned to cultivate is an amazing capacity to jump. Although they appear to land on their stomachs, in fact they always land on their feet and retain the ability to jump again and again in different directions, correcting their course as they go along. In a world of great uncertainty and high-risk choices, this is an intelligent response.
>
> Peter J. Katzenstein (1985: 211)

What are the constraints on and the opportunities for governance of small states in an interdependent and increasingly turbulent global setting? How do small states deal with radical changes in the international environment? What is the role of political institutions in facilitating and constraining policy responses to a rapidly changing international environment? What is the role of political leaders in facilitating processes of change, learning, the transferal of ideas, and innovation? How can political leadership contribute to stability in times of change? This book seeks to answer these questions by adopting a comparative perspective on the processes of change and adaptation in the governance of Norway and Slovakia. These two small European states with highly open economies have been exposed to the same set of global turbulences related to post-Cold War changes in the security environment and the global financial crisis that arose in the aftermath of the collapse of the US housing bubble of 2007-2008; they also face internal challenges springing from rapidly rising expectations while demographic shifts place pressure on their welfare systems. Their governance structures and processes are informed by their different politico-administrative cultures, different history and levels of stability of democratic governance structures and, indeed, by their different modes of attachment to the European Union and other regional integration frameworks. These differences and a comparative approach in exploring the questions raised above can shed light not only on the specific forms of adaptation of governance structures in two small European states, but can also generate insights into the role of integration structures in facilitating and constraining change.

Is there anything special about small states?

This book analyzes puzzles of governance and political behavior in two small European countries in a period of global turbulence and domestic pressures. Do small states such as these have any specific advantages in today's world, or are there only disadvantages? Would they be better off growing larger or joining larger states? Judging by the growing literature on small states, the latter course would seem to be the rational one for small states to follow. When reading some of the existing literature in the field, one may well wonder why there are so many small states, and why their number is growing. The overarching argument of this book is that small states may have their problems, but also certain advantages in the world of today.

Nearly half of the world's 200 or so sovereign states have fewer than 5.5 million people. Only around fifty states have more than 20 million people. Slovakia with 5.4 million is ranked as number 110 in terms of population size: Norway, with 4.9 million, is number 114. The number of micro states with a population of fewer than one million is steadily increasing.

The reasons for the somewhat skewed picture of small states may be twofold. First, notions of state conduct and good governance have largely been shaped by the experiences of large, dominant states or super-powers (Steinmetz and Wivel 2010). Second, scholarly interest in small states, such as it is, deals mostly with issues of foreign policy and security. The picture often conveyed is one of serious threats to small states, inadequacies, and a lack of capabilities to pursue own interests (Panke 2010).[1] Furthermore, external challenges are often seen as the prime drivers of domestic politics and institutional change, painting a picture of passive adaptation.

This book seeks to redress this imbalance in two ways. First, it covers a broad array of governance and policy choices in two small European states, ranging from issues of national security to local democracy. Second, it explores the interrelatedness of external and internal adaptation as these connections appear during the turbulences of the first decade of the twenty-first century.

The turbulence of these years presents many parallel challenges to Norway and Slovakia through the series of shocks and aftershocks that sprang from the end of the Cold War, the acceleration of European integration, the financial earthquake of 2008/9, and a pluralization of society and politics on the domestic scene. Before spelling out the challenges inherent in these developments, we turn to a discussion of the specific features of the small state.

---

1   There are exceptions from this analytical pattern, however. Some authors can see small states' advantages and potential in foreign policy making compared to the limitations experienced by great powers (see Egeland 1988).

What is the key to the specific problems of small states: geographic, demographic or economic features, or institutions, resources, and power (Smith, Pace and Lee 2005)? Peter Katzenstein's research into European small states in the post-war period has indicated that the answer might be certain institutional characteristics that gave such small states adaptive prowess. Baldur Thorhallsson (2006) suggests a series of objective features such as population, area, and economic and military capabilities besides more subjective indicators of elite ambitions and perceptions that together determine a state's capacities and vulnerabilities in the international arena. According to this analysis, size is not a fixed feature of a given state, but a variable that may take on differing values over time. We find this a fruitful line of thought but do not wish to take quite as many variables into consideration since several of the indicators discussed by Thorhallsson are probably intercorrelated. We seek to simplify the analysis by focusing on a combination of three features of small states:

- military dependence
- economic openness
- political cost-effectiveness

First, a small state in an environment of larger neighbors has a serious *security problem*. It may solve this by resorting to strategies of hiding (making oneself as innocuous as possible, for example through demonstrations of peacefulness), binding (security through multi-lateral institutions), or finding the support of a Big Brother (Steinmetz and Wivel 2010: 10). The preferred small-state option is that of binding whenever possible. But how do small states act when this option does not work or is of limited relevance, as in today's (in)security environment?

Second, a small state with a (relatively) small economy necessarily has an *open economy* – it has to trade across borders to survive as a developed society. Free trade across national borders is more important to smaller than to larger countries with bigger, differentiated domestic markets. Strategies of *competitiveness* are therefore vital to small states. Such strategies may include monetary policies (e.g. currency and interest rate manipulations), joining regulatory regimes that regulate competition (e.g. the WTO or the EU), or stimulating domestic productivity and innovation. In economic theory, small-state size has often been seen as a disadvantage to growth (e.g. Romer 1986). However, a study by the World Bank a few years back demonstrated the opposite – that small states were better off, with higher rates of growth and higher levels of income and living standards (Easterly and Kraay 1999). A later study, however, found little or no effect of size on the performance of states across a wide array of economic and social indicators (Rose 2006). It may nevertheless be of great interest to investigate how small states react when the very system established to ensure smooth trade across national borders comes to a near standstill, as it came close to doing during the financial crisis of 2007-08.

Third, *political integration* is less costly in small states, but also more vital to national survival. Political integration is about establishing a correspondence between what Dahl and Tufte (1973) term 'citizen effectiveness' and 'system capacity'. The former refers to the citizens' opportunities to formulate and express political demands, the latter denotes the polity's capacity to respond to and meet citizens' expectations. In most democratic polities political parties form the most important channels of political integration, but are of course supplemented by the media, associations, and other actors of civil society. Overall, Dahl and Tufte see citizen effectiveness as greater in small polities, and system capacity as greater in larger polities. Be that as it may, in our view the core issue is *the connection* between the two features of democratic polities, i.e. the processes of political integration. We would contend that political integration is easier to achieve in small polities for numerical as well as for sociological reasons. In small states, for purely numerical reasons, leaders are more accessible to the ordinary public than they are in larger states. The ratio of citizens to leaders in small states makes it more likely that an ordinary citizen knows personally somebody in a political position, or at least "knows somebody who knows somebody". High accessibility makes it more difficult to exclude groups from policy-making. Furthermore, small states are usually more socially and culturally homogeneous than large states; this is not only because of their smallness, but also because they have often been formed by breakaway provinces that felt alienated inside a larger unit because of their difference; both Norway and Slovakia are cases in point. Homogeneity lowers the transaction costs of leadership. The more diverse voter preferences are, the greater the costs of aggregating those preferences (Hiscox and Lake 2002); consequently, the probability of finding a solution that is agreeable to everyone, or at least to very broad segments of society, is lower in large states. Small states are not only easier to integrate politically, they may also function in general in more democratic ways than larger states (Ott 2000). The mechanism of integration characteristic of small states as identified by Peter Katzenstein in a classic study of small-state politics is that of the social partnership of elites across political divides, which again accelerates processes of learning. Partnership is in turn driven by the elites' perception of small-state vulnerability in an unpredictable world (Katzenstein 1985, 2003).

This does not mean that small states are immune to authoritarian features. Although citizens may have easier access to political leaders in small states, it was also pointed out by Dahl and Tufte that the pressure of conformity may be high and the cost of dissent intolerable in small polities (Dahl and Tufte 1973). Less room for social and cultural deviance may provide fertile ground for certain forms of populism. Dag Anckar has followed up this line of thought by asking whether small polities are prone to tyranny by majorities (Anckar 2009). His enquiry is based on a line of reasoning attributed to James Madison who argued that the diversity of large states would ensure circulation of elites and entail a guarantee against permanent rule by one particular faction of society. Thus, cost-effective political integration may be achieved in small states at the price of the suppression of dissent and low elite circulation. However, the empirical investigations actually carried out by Anckar failed to reveal any clear relationship between the size of states and the duration of regimes. There was, in other words, no tendency for the governments of small states to remain in office for overly long periods of time. This general finding does not, of course, rule out the possibility of tyrannies of majorities in our two particular cases. We may therefore reasonably ask to what extent circulation of elites takes place in Norway and Slovakia, whether elites are recruited in a way that makes them representative of the population at large or biased towards particular segments of society, and whether social cleavages are mirrored in elections and representative assemblies.

The findings of higher levels of growth and standards of living in small states suggest, furthermore, that these states are well capable of adapting to changing circumstances and exploit opportunities in their environments. This again may point to a general capacity of flexibility and adjustment favored by certain social features associated with small size, such as social homogeneity and mutual trust. In general, the cost-effectiveness of small-scale politics may allow for *institutional nimbleness*. As their environments change small states may need to adapt and change quickly, too. Survival requires a capacity for institutional innovation and adaptation and encourages a spirit of experimentation. Recent examples include the Nordic free commune experiments of the 1990s (Baldersheim and Ståhlberg 1994), or the political-administrative reforms pioneered by i.a. New Zealand and later known as "New Public Management" (Bouckaert and Pollitt 2004), or adaptations of foreign affairs administrations in small states to the information age (Bátora 2008). Small states may also be less prone to the bureaucratic sclerosis that often characterizes large states. For example, in Europe, small states tend to be ahead of the larger ones in terms of the adoption of e-governance.[2]

But again, an opposing view can be found. Small states may more easily become imbued with clientelism and cronyism, corruption, and nepotism based on acquaintanceships and kinship ties (Gerring and Zarecki 2011). The governance of small states may more easily follow group-think patterns, even over the brink. The mechanics of the 2008 Icelandic banking crisis come to

---

2   Of the five top-ranking European countries in the Global E-Government Development Reports and Surveys in 2005 and 2008, four were small countries.
    http://www2.unpan.org/egovkb/global_reports/index.htm (27.09.11).

mind (Gylfason et al. 2010: 137-165). In contrast, the administration of larger states is necessarily more impersonal and bureaucratic, for better or worse.

All in all, theories about small states are somewhat contradictory and empirical findings support rather divergent conclusions. A "state of the art" such as this makes it even more interesting to examine two particular cases in some detail.

Why compare Norway and Slovakia?

What is the justification for comparing Norway and Slovakia? Apart from being small European countries of roughly the same size, their dissimilarities may be more striking than their similarities. There is of course the similarity in their paths to national independence – peaceful secession and goodbye to a 'big brother': Norway's break with Sweden in 1905, and Slovakia's farewell to its Czech cousin in 1993. Otherwise, Norway can be classified as a *mature*, stable, and rich democracy while Slovakia belongs to the *transitional* democracies (Bakke 2002) with a struggling economy and a GDP per capita at 70 per cent of the EU average. Norway shares, furthermore, a Nordic political culture imbued with an egalitarian spirit (Graubard 1986) and a Protestant ethic (Heidar 2004:23), while Slovakia belongs to the Central European sphere with a predominantly Catholic tradition and a more widespread acceptance of power-distance[3] compared to Norway.

We would argue that these dissimilarities make a comparison all the more interesting. Through our analyses we do not seek *explanations* for outcomes, we seek *examples* of responses and policy choices that two small states make faced with the same sorts of challenges. We do expect these responses to be different, given the different circumstances of the two countries, but presented side by side they may illustrate the range of choices open to, as well as the constraints on, small countries in the contemporary globalized world.

A concept of *system maturity* may highlight the contextual contrasts between the two countries. The concept refers not just to differences between them in terms of the duration of independent statehood, but more precisely to the institutionalization of the state. Deep institutionalization is a process of aculturation, i.e. the development and internalization of norms of conduct that guide actors in ambiguous situations (March and Olsen 1989, Meyer and Rowan 1977), for example in situations in which a written constitution provides no clear answers. Institutionalization takes time and becomes a source

---

3   In the sense of Gert Hofstede's theory of organizational cultures (Hofstede 1984, Hofstede et al. 2010).

of political stability but may also lock actors into scripts that may lose their usefulness in dealing with new challenges. Slovakia's lower level of system maturity in comparison to Norway may therefore not necessarily be a handicap in dealing with the global turbulences of the twenty-first century.

System maturity may be further analyzed in terms of political integration. As mentioned above, integration is about uniting points of view across social segments that may represent opposing interests. Norway has a legacy of corporatism in this regard, as noted by Katzenstein (1985), who saw this as a source of adaptive strength, a feature that eased negotiations between elites representing the various corporations. From the late 1970s onwards, political analysts identified corporatism as a driver of political-administrative segmentation that slowed the required social innovation and adaptation (Egeberg et al. 1978), even to the point of political fragmentation (Trangy and Østerud 2001). Successive Norwegian governments have attempted to cut back on corporatist arrangements, but many of these constructions still stand. Slovakia has fewer such permanent structures of socio-political bargaining and elite consultations, which means that it is less constrained but also less scripted in finding solutions in turbulent situations. Is that a source of adaptiveness or weakness?

The objectives stated for a 1994 volume about Norway and Slovenia (Bucar and Kuhnle 1994) could also serve as guidelines for the present book:

> to provide basic sources of knowledge and information about politics and society in the two countries; to provide analytical perspectives on economic and political challenges of two small European democracies in a European and global setting...; ... to serve as a model for initiating bilateral research cooperation between institutions and individual scholars in two countries... (ibid. pp. vi-vii).

At that point in time the impression was conveyed of both states as well as Europe in general being very much at a crossroads, and the future of European cooperation as well as that of national development being highly uncertain. Interestingly, the same could be said today with equal justification as regards both European integration and security, as well as national developments in Norway and Slovakia, although now, seventeen years on, for quite different reasons.

What are the challenges the two countries are facing at the end of the first and the beginning of the second decade of the twenty-first century?

Interwoven global turbulences

A new (in)security environment

The immediate aftermath of the Cold War and the excitement on the demise of the Soviet empire prompted numerous academics and policy practitioners to declare the victory of democracy and market economic principles: nothing short of a rapid development towards a peaceful global market comprised of friendly democratic societies was expected. Fukuyama's proclamation of the 'end of history' and Gorbachev's idea of a community of freedom and security reaching 'from Vancouver to Vladivostok' captured this spirit. However, despite these expectations and visions, at the onset of the second decade of the twenty-first Century, the world order is highly turbulent and volatile. Turbulences range from a rapidly changing security environment, via the crisis of global financial institutions, to a shifting demography of societies in Europe and elsewhere.

Turbulences in the global security environment relate to at least three factors: denationalized forms of warfare; new kinds of security threats; and, new ways of states' tackling violent confrontations capitalizing upon new types of instruments and actors. Regarding the first factor, most of the conflicts in the last two decades have not been inter-state but intra-state, involving governments in confrontation with non-state actors. Non-state actors such as terrorist networks, drug cartels, and organized crime syndicates have been challenging the dominant position of states and governments as providers of security and holders of the legitimate monopoly on the use of violence (Krahmann 2010). In a Weberian sense, the very foundations of statehood have been severely challenged in places such as Mexico or Colombia, where drug barons have been successfully waging an all-out war against governmental authorities trying to maintain control and an acceptable level of public safety. Similarly, in countries such as Libya or Egypt, the revolutionary movements of the 'Arab spring' have led to the implosion of state structures and the spread of authority to complex constellations of societal groups.

Regarding the second factor, cyber attacks and globally organized terrorist activities represent a new breed of threat for governments. The organized cyber attacks on Estonia in June 2007 or the cyber attack on the electronic network of the Norwegian Nobel Committee in October 2010 show how vulnerable governmental and non-governmental organizations in Western societies have become in confrontation with geographically distant and technologically savvy enemies. As the Estonian case shows, it is difficult to trace a cyber attacker, the sources of cyber attacks may change location globally, and given legal restrictions on action in other countries' territories, it may be close to impossible to orchestrate an adequate response.

As regards the third factor, states such as China have been increasingly prone to cooperating with and sometimes coopting non-state actors who have been involved in carrying out unfriendly activities in relation to foreign societies.[4] As Neumann and Sending (2010) argue, states have not become irrelevant or sidelined by non-state actors; on the contrary, their power and dominance are reasserting themselves in new ways and through new patterns. That, of course, is only the case if states are indeed able to adapt to the rapidly changing security environment. It is more often the case, however, that the extent of the changes and their rapidity represent a crisis of existing notions of how states think about security and, indeed, of how they organize for it. The current crisis of NATO as a key security framework in Europe, and small states' efforts to develop regional security frameworks in the Nordic region and in Central Europe, are examples of this.

The financial crisis: the emergence of a new financial world order?

The international financial crisis that appeared in 2007/2008 shared one feature with the collapse of the Soviet Union: it was predicted by virtually no one, and yet with hindsight it seemed inevitable – the writing was on the wall for all to see. The crisis has, so far, been through two stages and a third stage is underway. The first stage was the near collapse of the international banking system triggered by the fall of the Lehman Brothers Bank, when the U.S. government refused to come to the rescue when the subprime loan bubble burst. This resulted in a paralyzing loss of mutual trust in the banking system since banks depend on loans from each other to finance investments. When banks stopped lending to each other, the whole system came to a near standstill with an ensuing liquidity problem throughout the system. In some countries there was the beginning of a run on banks the like of which had not been seen since the start of the Great Depression eighty years earlier. In some cases bank customers actually began lining up to withdraw their money, the most conspicuous example being the British Northern Rock Bank, which was taken over by the state in 2008. The beginning of the erosion of customer trust forced governments to intervene: first by guaranteeing savings, then by making funds available to banks to enable them to maintain a stream of liquidity to counteract the loss of faith between banks.

The second stage was reached when governments had to find ways of financing the huge rescue funds made available to shore up the banking system. In many cases government spending in this regard entailed budget deficits of unprecedented levels. These deficits were clearly far beyond what the

---

4   See for instance "US experts close in on Google hackers" in *Financial Times*, February 21, 2010 (available at http://www.ft.com/intl/cms/s/0/a6f5621c-1f21-11df-9584-00144feab49a.html#axzz1Rza5s3Fk).

EU would normally find acceptable. Most governments made a point of covering their deficits over a short time period to avoid lower credit ratings in international credit markets. Consequently, governments have sought to tighten their budgets through a combination of strategies such as reduced immediate spending, lowering future welfare obligations, and increased fees and taxes. Reduced spending has entailed, for example, lower pay for government employees, lay-offs, and cuts in job-related perks. Future welfare obligations have been reduced by raising the pension age or lowering the rates of unemployment benefits or social security. Needless to say, this has caused resentment in the population in many countries. Demonstrations and protests have been the order of the day and have been particularly vehement in Greece, France, and Spain.

In the third stage the crisis reached the real economy with reduced demand for goods and services, cuts in production, and rising unemployment. In the U.S., for example, unemployment currently stands at over ten per cent of the workforce. The EU average (27 countries) is 9.6 per cent (as of October 2010); however, the rates vary widely from country to country, with 4.8 in Austria, and nearly 21 per cent in Spain. The unemployment rate in Norway is 3.5, and in Slovakia 14.7 per cent.[5]

Norway and Slovakia are exposed to the impacts of the financial crisis through the dependency of their banks on the international banking systems for financing credits to domestic borrowers. Norway is further exposed through the investments of its sovereign fund in companies around the world; a worldwide recession may be felt through lower rates of return on investments and consequently fewer resources available for public welfare expenditures (around twenty per cent of current spending over the national budget is covered by returns from the sovereign fund, or "the pension fund" as it is known in Norway)[6]. Slovakia's dependence on the automobile-manufacturing industry also means that an international recession may be quickly transmitted to the workforce in the form of lay-offs, and then to public budgets as tax incomes are reduced.

---

5 Source: Eurostat (http://epp.eurostat.ec.europa.eu/tgm/table.do?tab=table&language=en&pcode=teilm020&tableSelection=1&plugin=1), accessed on 5 December 2010).

6 The "expenditure regulation" (*handlingsregelen*) states that no more than four per cent of the returns on the sovereign fund is to be used to cover current public expenditure; the rest is to be reinvested in the fund. In reality the "regulation" is a political agreement between most of the political parties represented in Parliament, with the exception of the Progress Party, which claims that the rule is too stringent and that there is room for spending more of the returns. Interestingly, the government responded to the financial crisis by spending substantially more than justified by the four per cent rule; however, "overspending" will be reclaimed by cuts in next year's budget, demonstrating a policy of responsibility and "back-to-normality".

Internal challenges: revolutions of rising or disappointed expectations

Challenges arising from internal sources also drive changes in institutions, public policies, and political loyalties in small states. For example, countries all over the world are facing demographic changes, new family patterns, and more individualized lifestyles associated with longer life spans, lower birth rates, higher levels of education, and accelerating processes of urbanization and migration. These are developments that Norway and Slovakia are also struggling to tackle.

However, sources of internal unrest that may be specific to the two countries also exist, driving slow revolutions of rising expectations, and in some cases revolutions of disappointed expectations. Norway's oil-based wealth has enabled a succession of governments to pursue steadily expanding welfare programs without quite being able to keep up with the demands of the population. Paradoxically, the richer the state, the more impatient the voters become. In Slovakia high hopes have been placed first in the transition from communism to democracy and capitalism in the early 1990s, second in independent nationhood, and third in joining NATO and the European Union. Unavoidably, some of those expectations would turn into disappointments. Some of those are related to burgeoning corruption to which virtually none of the Slovak governments has been immune in recent years.[7] For some segments of the Slovak population, life may have become harsher than it was under communism. In both cases, much of political life as well as institutional and policy development can be seen as responses to rising or disappointed expectations.

Puzzles of governance – outline of issues to be analyzed

The following chapters will address a series of *puzzles of governance* in Norway and Slovakia. The book is organized into four sections dealing with four different aspects of governance: the pursuit of security and sovereignty, responses to financial crises, the development of political cleavages and representation, and institutional transformation. In these fields puzzles and paradoxes appear that may demonstrate typical predicaments and choices of governance in small states.

---

7   The Transparency International Corruption Perception Index ranks countries according to levels of perceived corruption on a scale from 0 to 10. A score of 10 indicates virtually no corruption. In 2010, on a worldwide ranking from "good" to "bad", Slovakia was ranked in 59th place with a score of 4.3, while Norway was ranked at 10 with a score of 8.6. http://www.transparency.org/policy_research/surveys_indices/cpi/2010/results. 21.09.11.

Security and sovereignty: territorial integrity is a basic objective of any state. Norway and Slovakia have sought to underpin their sovereignty through membership of a transatlantic military alliance, NATO, with big brother the U.S. as the ultimate guarantor. In recent years, two paradoxes have emerged in the security policies of the two countries. First, as a consequence of the transformation of NATO into an alliance with a global reach, the small states of Norway and Slovakia have found themselves involved in wars on other continents, far away from their own borders. These engagements have also prompted the need to radically increase spending on hi-tech military equipment and increase investments in military research and development programs, which, however, has turned out to be a tough challenge even for affluent small states such as Norway. Second, both countries are exploring supplementary security options through closer cooperation with their immediate neighbors in the Nordic and Visegrad countries respectively. This relates also to cooperation in military R&D programs, strategic weapons acquisitions, and connecting strategic infrastructures in the energy sector and other strategic sectors of society. What are the driving forces and limitations of these regional ventures, and why is the Nordic one the more advanced of the two initiatives? These issues are explored in Chapter 2 by Jozef Bátora and Janne Haaland Matlary.

Globalization brings increasing mobility of people, capital, and information across national borders. European integration is meant to ease and even stimulate such mobility. However, controlling national borders has also become more problematic as they are more porous and more closed at the same time. Through the Schengen agreement member countries (including Norway) are expected to exercise tighter controls on personal mobility from outside the Schengen area. Many aspects of globalization are beneficial to small countries with their export- and trade-dependent economies. However, mobility of workers, or would-be workers, may also challenge the integrative capacity of small states more than that of large states, especially if the newcomers arrive from areas that are culturally different. How do small states balance integrative and exclusionary policies of immigration? Živka Deleva and Leonid Tuzov address these issues in Chapter 3.

Responses to financial crises: the international financial crisis of 2007-09 has demonstrated that globalization accelerates not only investments and job creation but also downturns and job losses. The near standstill of the international banking system had repercussions in all of the EU and EEA countries. The situation represented a severe test of EU institutions, the outcome of which is as yet uncertain. However, the limits of policy freedom of individual countries were also tested. Were those limits set by constraining EU regulations, or by the capacity and imagination of national leaders? What were the margins of action for national governments? These issues are addressed in Chapter 4 through a case study of Slovakia authored by Andrej Wertlen.

Naturally, in many countries policy responses to the financial crisis became a divisive issue in national politics. Political parties took different stances on the issue. To what extent should a helping hand be extended to other countries that had pursued seemingly irresponsible fiscal policies (i.e. Greece, Ireland, or Portugal)? Suddenly, European integration might not seem so attractive anymore – how tempting was the option of self-sufficiency – cutting loose from monetary integration and even the liberal WTO regime to protect own industries? Could the stances of the respective Slovak parties be made sense of through the cleavage structures represented by the parties? Or did the financial crisis influence national politics more fundamentally in the sense that the pattern of disagreement could be said to represent an entirely new cleavage in Slovak politics? Dušan Leška discusses these issues in Chapter 5.

Since the development of the economy in small states depends largely on globally-driven trade cycles, is it likely that the health of the national economy will have an impact on voters' perception of the government of the day? Are voters aware of the limited capacity of national governments, inside and outside the EU, to influence growth patterns? Or are they likely to assign responsibility for the economic well-being of the country to the government no matter the state of the economy or the causes of upswings or downturns? Will they consistently reward the government of the day when the going is good, and punish it when the ride gets rougher? These issues are analyzed through a longitudinal study of Norway compared to other European countries. If smaller states are more subject to international economic dependencies, and the government has correspondingly less room for maneuver, are such connections less discernible in the small state of Norway than in larger states? These issues are addressed by Hanne Marthe Narud in Chapter 6.

Cleavages and representation: political cleavages denote the long-standing patterns of political conflict that characterize a country. Cleavages may spring from the economic interests of social groups, ethnic identities, religious or ideological persuasions, or lifestyle orientations. Political stability may depend upon the capacities of political institutions to reflect and respond to changes in cleavage structures. Cleavages are mediated for example through political parties. Polities can be categorized according to the socio-political cleavages they reflect, as in the model of party blocks developed by Stein Rokkan and Seymour Martin Lipset (1966). How well do the parties of Norway and Slovakia reflect the social and geographic divisions of the respective countries? As mentioned above parties are channels of political integration, conduits for the demands and aspirations of the population. Are segments of society unrepresented through the existing party systems and therefore not integrated into the political system? Cleavages have, furthermore, historical roots in the political development of a given country, for example church-state conflicts, class struggles, or urban-rural dichotomies.

Processes of modernization may dilute these roots and traditional cleavages may start fading away, for example class-based conflicts. Modernization also throws up new political issues and conflicts that may not fit into long-standing cleavage structures. How far has *dealignment*, i.e. processes of disconnection between socio-geographic divisions and the party system, proceeded in the two countries? Chapter 7 authored by Oddbjørn Knutsen addresses these and other issues related to the social roots of party politics in Norway and Slovakia.

In several European countries, the political parties of an entrenched cleavage structure are challenged from time to time by the rise of populist parties. These parties are often seen as ephemeral phenomena, dependent upon a charismatic leader able to capitalize on fleeting popular discontent. In recent years in some of the larger European countries, e.g. France or Italy, populist parties have become 'normal' parts of the political scene. Populist parties often thrive on the fear of 'the other' or resentment to the political center. Why have populist parties enjoyed sustained electoral success also in the small, socially homogeneous countries of Norway and Slovakia with fairly accessible centers? Does the rise of the populist parties indicate a decline in a traditional cleavage structure (Norway), or a weakly formed cleavage structure (Slovakia)? Or are populist parties simply one of several possible expressions of post-modern politics, i.e. politics disconnected from any stable underlying cleavage system? Anders Ravik Jupskås and Olga Gyárfášová address these issues in Chapter 8.

Political elites play a crucial role in shaping agendas and policy responses to pressing issues of the day. Consequently, understanding processes of elite selection and composition is a key to understanding the governance of a particular country. Political elites at the head of political parties and at the apex of the institutions of government may represent the embodiment of an underlying cleavage system, or may owe their rise to power to more personal qualities. In states with a stable cleavage structure the elites of the respective parties could be expected to share the typical socio-economic features of their respective electorates. In weakly structured cleavage systems, personal qualities as well as elements of chance may count for more, and elites therefore become less representative of their supporters. If Norway is in the former category and Slovakia in the latter, the composition of Slovakia's elite could be expected to deviate sharply from the Norwegian one. The representation of women among the elite is a test case in this respect. In Norway, women have over the last decades become well represented at the apex of politics. Does the selection of elites in Slovakia to a larger extent reflect the famous 'glass ceiling' that is often said to hamper the rise of women to the top of companies as well as political institutions? Or will the inclusionary nature of politics in small states even out the odds against female representation also in Slovakia? These issues are analyzed by Elisabeth Bakke in Chapter 9.

Institutional transformation: national responses to new policy challenges often require institutional transformation. To be effectively implemented, new policies may require new institutions or at least the modification of existing ones. It has also been observed that to some extent institutional changes may represent adaptations to organizational fashions of the day rather than reflections of deep policy changes (Meyer and Rowan 1977). Indeed, institutions also mediate processes of change and adaptation may be gradual, ambiguous, and inefficient (March and Olsen 1975, March 2010). Be that as it may, if and when an elite puts institutional transformation on the agenda, the extent of transformation may be one of the indicators of the governing capacity of that elite.

There are few fields that test the governing capacity of national elites more severely than the transformation of territorial governance, which requires attention to policy effectiveness as well as democratic ideals. In practical terms the modernization of territorial governance in European states in recent years has meant decentralization of powers to regions (regionalization), as well as the enhancement of local democracy at the municipal level (Baldersheim and Rose 2010, Loughlin et al. 2010). Norway and Slovakia have both launched schemes of institutional transformation in these regards. But why should small countries feel the need to regionalize their systems of governance in the first place? Their total populations are hardly greater than that of some of the larger regions of Spain or Italy. Could not efficient district agencies of the national government do the job? And why is enhancement of local democracy put on the agenda of a country such as Norway with a long historical tradition of vigorous local government? Are there pressing internal needs driving these reforms, or do reformers follow trajectories scripted by outside forces? These issues and other aspects of regional and local governance are addressed by Harald Baldersheim and Ľudmila Malíková in Chapter 10, and by Lawrence Rose in Chapter 11.

References

Anckar, Dag (2009): Small Polities: Tyrannized by Majorities? *The Open Political Science Journal*, 2: 35-46.

Bakke, Elisabeth (2002): Slovakia: Den kronglete vegen til demokratiet, Chapter 8 in Elisabeth Bakke (ed.): *Sentral-Europa og Baltikum etter 1989*. Oslo: Samlaget.

Baldersheim, Harald/ Ståhlberg Krister (eds.) (1994): *Towards the Self-Regulating Municipality: Free Communes and Administrative Modernization in Scandinavia*. Aldershot: Dartmouth.

Baldersheim, Harald/ Rose Lawrence E, eds. (2010): *Territorial Choice. The Politics of Boundaries and Borders*. Basingstoke, Hampshire: Palgrave Macmillan

Bátora, Jozef (2008): *"Foreign Ministries and the Information Revolution: Going Virtual?"* Leiden: Brill

Bouckaert, Geert/ Pollitt Christopher (2004): *Public Management Reform: A Comparative Analysis*. Oxford: Oxford University Press.

Bucar, Bojko/ Stein Kuhnle (eds.) (1994): *Small States Compared: The Politics of Norway and Slovenia*. Bergen: Alma Mater.

Diamond, Larry/ Tsalik Svetlana (1999): Size and Democracy The Case for Decentralization, in Larry Diamond (ed.): *Developing Democracy Toward Consolidation*. Baltimore: Johns Hopkins, pp.117-160.

Easterly, William/ Kraay Aart (1999): *Small States, Small Problems? Income, Growth, and Volatility in Small States*. World Bank, Policy Research Working Paper Series no. 2139.

Egeberg, Morten/ Olsen Johan P./Sætren Harald (1978): Organisasjonssamfunnet og den segmenterte stat. In: H. Hernes, ed.*: Forhandlingsøkonomi og blandingsadministrasjon*. Oslo: Universitetsforlaget.

Egeland, Jan(1988): *Impotent Superpower, Potent Small State: Potentials and Limitations of Human Rights Objectives in the Foreign Policies of the United States and Norway*. Oslo: Norwegian University Press

Financial Times (2010): "US experts close in on Google hackers", February 21, 2010 (available at http://www.ft.com/intl/cms/s/0/a6f5621c-1f21-11df-9584-00144feab49a.html#axzz1Rza5s3Fk

Gerring, John/ Zarecki Dominic (2011) Size and Democracy, Revisited. http://www.bu.edu/polisci/files/2011/04/SizeandDemocracyRevisited.pdf . 20.09.2011.

Graubard, Stephen R. (ed.) (1986): *Norden – the Passion for Equality*. Oslo: Norwegian University Press.

Gylfason, Thorvaldur/ Holmström Bengt/ Korkman Sixten/ Söderström Hans Tson/Vihriälä Vesa (2010): *Nordics in Global Crisis.Vulnerability and Resilience*. Helsinki: The Research Institute of the Finnish Economy (ETLA).
Heidar, Knut (2004): State and Nation-Building in the Nordic Area, Chapter 1 in Knut Heidar (ed.*): Nordic Politics. Comparative Perspectives*. Oslo: Norwegian University Press.
Hiscox, Michael J./ David A. Lake (2002): *Democracy, Federalism, and the Size of States*. Social Science Research Network. Working Papers Series. http://papers.ssrn.com/sol3/papers.cfm?abstract_id=1002686. (2011-13-09)
Hofstede Geert H. (1984): *Culture Consequences: International Differences in Work-Related Values*, abridged edn. Thousands Oaks CA: Sage Publication Inc. McGraw Hill.
Hofstede, Geert H./ Hofstede Gert Jan/ Minkov Michael (2010): *Cultures and Organizations: Software of the Mind*. Revised and expanded 3rd Edition. New York: McGraw-Hill USA, 2010.
Katzenstein, Peter J. (1985). *Small States in World Markets: Industrial Policy in Europe*. Ithaca: Cornell University Press.
Katzenstein, Peter J. (2003): Small States and Small States Revisited, *New Political Economy*, . 8:9-30.
Krahmann, Elke (2010): *States, Citizens and the Privatization of Security*. Cambridge: Cambridge University Press
Lipset, Seymour Martin/ Rokkan, Stein (1967): Cleavage Structure, Party Systems, and Voter Alignments: An introduction. In: Seymour Martin Lipset/ Rokkan, Stein (eds.): *Party Systems and Voter Alignments*. New York: The Free Press, pp. 1-64.
Lijphart, Arend 1999: *Patterns of democracy: government forms and performance in thirty-six countries*. New Haven: Yale University Press.
Loughlin, John/ Hendriks Frank/ Lidström Anders, eds. (2010): *The Oxford Handbook of Local and Regional Democracy in Europe*. Oxford: Oxford University Press.
March, James G. (2010): *The Ambiguities of Experience*. Ithaca: Cornell University Press
March, James G./ Olsen, Johan P. (1975): "The Uncertainty of the Past: Organizational Learning under Ambiguity" in *European Journal of Political Research*, 3: 147-171.
March, James G./ Olsen Johan P. (1989): *Rediscovering Institutions. The Organizational Basis of Politics*. New York: Free Press.
Meyer, John W./ Rowan, Brian (1977): Institutionalized organizations. Formal structure as myth and Ceremony, *American Journal of Sociology* 83:364-385.
Neumann, Iver B./ Sending, Ole J. (2010): *Governing the Global Polity*.

Practice, Mentality, Rationality. Ann Arbor, MI: University of Michigan Press.
Ott, Dana (2000): *Small is Democratic: An Examination of State Size and Democratic Development*. New York: Garland.
Panke, Diana (2010): *Small States in the European Union. Coping With Structural Disadvantages*. Farnham: Ashgate.
Romer, Paul M. (1986): Increasing Returns and Long-Run Growth. *Journal of Political Economy*, 94: 1002-37.
Rose, Andrew K. (2006):. Size Really Doesn't Matter: In Search of a National Scale Effect, *Journal of Japanese and International Economies* 20, 482-507.
Scharpf, Fritz W. (1988): The joint-decision trap: lessons from German federalism and European integration, *Public Administration*, 66: 239 – 278.
Smith, Nicola/ Pace Michelle/ Lee Donna (2005): Size Matters: Small States and International Studies. *International Studies Perspectives*, 6(3), 395-7.
Steinmetz, Robert/ Wivel Anders (2010): *Introduction*, chapter 1 in Robert Steinmetz/ Anders Wivel (eds.): *Small States in Europe: Challenges and Opportunities*. Farnham: Ashgate
Thorhallsson, Baldur (2006): The size of states in the European Union: Theoretical and conceptual perspectives, *European Integration*, 28: 7-31.
Tranøy, Bernt Sofus/Østerud Øyvind (eds.) (2001): *Den fragmenterte staten. Reformer, makt og styring*. Oslo: Gyldendal Akademisk.
Valasek, Tomas (2011): *Surviving Austerity: The Case for a New Approach to EU Military Collaboration*. London: Centre for European Reform

Chapter 2
Regional Security Integration: Nordic and Visegrad Approaches

Jozef Bátora and Janne Haaland Matlary

Introduction

For both Norway and Slovakia, NATO has been a key element in ensuring national security. Yet due to intensification of turbulences in the global security environment, and on global financial markets in recent years, the structural underpinnings of the transatlantic security community (cf Deutsch 1957) have been under strain, with NATO seeking to redefine its *raison d'être*. Ambiguities concerning the role of the Alliance, have become vividly clear in various conflicts involving NATO member states in recent decades. These include the bombing of Yugoslavia and the ensuing campaign to stop ethnic cleansing in Kosovo in 1999, the war in Afghanistan since 2001 and most recently, the Libyan conflict of 2011.

NATO as an arena of coalitions got involved in non-existential article IV and article V operations. Uncertainties regarding the role of NATO have also come to the surface in conflicts where the Alliance and its members did not get directly involved. This means the case of Iraq, 2003, the war in Georgia, 2008, and/or indeed situations involving non-military threats to member states such as the cyber-attacks on Estonia in 2007. The 2010 strategic concept underlines the hybrid character of threat assessments, but article V remains the key issue overall. The Georgian war seriously underlined the importance of Russia and article V to member states. Small and medium size states in NATO like Norway and Slovakia therefore, face both old and new risks and threats at a time when great disagreement among member states about strategic vision continues. In addition, cost factors imply that budgetary expenditures increase when alliance-wide cuts in overall spending occur (Valasek 2011a). Such a key member as the UK had to slash its defense budget by 8% in 2011.

There are two tendencies operating in this context. First, while NATO does not share a strategic vision and has developed into an arena for shifting coalitions of states, the members do have to cut budgets and therefore are in need of new and often regional forms of defense integration strategy (Matlary, 2009; Jones 2009). Second, NATO as an arena for coalitions – the Libyan one being a good case in point – is so 'pluralist' in terms of threat assessment that member states must take on more national responsibility for their own security. They must deal with the so-called "delta" themselves – the gap between something they must manage nationally and article V – instead of the cost of maintaining full-spectrum military power, which increases spending. This implies a necessity for regional military integration between states. To assess the nature of such regional integrative processes, this chapter focuses on the Nordic region (Denmark, Iceland, Norway, Sweden and Finland) and the Visegrad region (Poland, Czech Republic, Slovakia and Hungary), which are representative of the possibilities and the limits of regional security integration efforts in Europe.

The first section of the chapter focuses on the threefold dynamics of institutional crisis of NATO, which revolves around uncertainty of *rules*, uncertainty of *resources* and uncertainty of *identity*. In the second part, the chapter focuses on responses to the crisis by regional groupings of small states in the Nordic region and the Visegrad-region. The two regional settings differ in terms of the member countries' attachment to NATO and the EU. The Nordic region is characterized by asymmetric membership – only Denmark is member of both NATO and the EU, while the rest of the Nordic countries are members of either NATO (Iceland, Norway) or the EU (Sweden, Finland). The Visegrad region is characterized by symmetric membership – all four Visegrad countries are members of NATO and of the EU. Yet contrary to expectations related to this factor, Nordic cooperation has been more advanced than Visegrad cooperation.

Nordic security integration builds on decades of close and often informal ties among governments in the region, but a renewed impetus to cooperation was given in the 2009 Stoltenberg Report. It outlined certain key measures and steps to be taken in intensifying regional integration of security architectures for the five Nordic countries. This includes sharing capacities and other forms of cooperation in peace-building, airspace – and sea surveillance, arctic issues, societal security (including cyber-defense), diplomacy and military affairs. Visegrad security integration only has been operating on the level of initial political debate, which focuses on issues of energy security, cooperation in military procurement and modernization, mutual support of nominees in international organizations, logistical cooperation and co-location of embassies, and co-operation in training military personnel. The concluding part of the report discusses systemic implications of regional security integration for NATO, as a key security policy framework in Europe.

NATO as an institutionalized organization in crisis

NATO was founded in 1949. As with any organization that has endured for so long, it has necessarily become 'infused with value' in Selznick's (1957) sense, which means that its formal structures, goals and processes are complemented by a plethora of informal structures, goals and processes. The existence and operation of NATO may have taken on a life of its own. This leads to activities that are just as much about using the organizational and institutional infrastructure in place for reaching strategic goals, as it is about simple maintenance and survival of the organizational and institutional infrastructure of the Alliance as such. While there were numerous problems during the recent two decades in which NATO could qualify as being a solution, NATO may just as often have been seeking problems it could apply itself to.[8] Depending on one's point of view, both interpretations of NATO's role could be valid, for instance with Kosovo in 1999, Afghanistan since 2001, and Libya in 2011.

NATO is an institutionalized organization. Organizations can be institutionalized by acquiring a meaning beyond their specific purpose and thus maintaining a specific constellation of rules, resources and identities. Organizations of this kind usually interpret changes in the organizational environment in ways conforming with their identity, which leads to path-dependent adaptation and only gradual change (March and Olsen 1984, 1989). Yet when changes in the environment are radical and inconsistent regarding identity of an institutionalized organization, an institutional crisis may emerge leading to rapid and radical change. Faced with a rapidly changing environment, institutionalized organizations look for new ways of defining their purpose and identity (ibid.). The current situation of NATO is characterized by triple crisis: crisis of rules; crisis of resources, and crisis of identity.

Crisis of rules in NATO

A key rule underpinning NATO has been its collective defense clause (Article V). This states that NATO countries will respond in a collective manner with defensive measures to any form of physical attack on any of the member states' territories. This rule was a key element enabling collective deterrence of the Soviets during the Cold War. Obviously, its usage would have implied a global nuclear war, and the article's implication was hence never really used during the years of the bipolar confrontation. However, following the

---

8   For a conceptualization of institutionalized processes including various (re-) combinations of problems, interests, solutions, and decision-making situations, see the 'garbage can' model by Cohen, March and Olsen (1972).

end of the Cold War, the nature of the global security environment changed whereby NATO members were facing a number of security threats, while there was no longer a major threat of all-out nuclear confrontation with a competing global power. In these circumstances, the application of Article V and ensuing collective defense measures became less risky and hence more likely, but also more ambiguous.

This ambiguity became clear in at least two situations – the war in Afghanistan initiated by the US and its allies in response to the terrorist attacks on US soil on September 11, 2001, and the cyber-attacks on Estonia in 2007. In the case of the former, the terrorist attacks in New York and Washington were classified by NATO as a situation justifying collective response by the Alliance quoting Article V. Although the US administration appreciated this expression of solidarity, it was not entirely sure that collective response in the framework of NATO would be the appropriate and most effective solution for leading the Afghanistan operation. It opted, instead, for forming a coalition of the willing encompassing selected NATO member states and non-NATO allies such as Australia and Qatar. NATO eventually got involved in Afghanistan at later stages, to provide security and support reconstruction, which remains the main task of the ISAF-mission.[9]

In this situation, NATO acted as institutionalized organizations usually do. It classified and interpreted a non-standard situation (i.e. a major terrorist attack on September 11, 2001) according to its own rules, and sought to act accordingly.[10] Yet this effort was undermined by the leading member in the Alliance, who practically refused this classification of the situation and hence also the application of the Alliance rules.

In case of Estonia, 2007, the situation involved concentrated cyber-attacks on virtually all ministries of the Estonian government and on major banks. These attacks were only on virtual infrastructure (e.g. denial of service of web-sites and servers, which took days to repair) and did not involve direct physical effects. However, given the attacks targeted one of the most wired countries in the world, their effect could have been much worse (e.g. causing opening of water dams or derailment of trains), and could have had direct physical effects on the territory and inhabitants of a NATO member state. The question was thus raised by the Estonian and other NATO member state

---

9   The International Security Assistance Force (ISAF), where most troops are provided by NATO member states, was approved by the UN on December 20, 2001. Its original mandate implied providing security and support reconstruction work in Kabul and surrounding areas. It was extended to cover the whole territory of Afghanistan by another UN resolution (UNSCR 1510) in 2003.

10 This was similar when oil rigs were being introduced in Norway in the late 1960s. Lacking experience with these kinds of installations and facing the need to introduce safety regulations onboard, the Norwegian authorities have interpreted oil rigs as somewhat peculiar naval vessels, and applied safety regulations usually applied on those of shipping (Sangolt 1984, cf March and Olsen 1989:36).

governments regarding the possibility of classifying such cyber attacks as falling under Article V. This caused some debate in NATO, but there are no clear answers so far.[11]

Cyber-attacks represent a new type of threat, which are not easy to interpret under NATO rules for various reasons. It is not always easy to determine who the perpetrators are, where the attacks come from (their sources often "flow" among networks of infiltrated computers or 'botnets' world-wide) and, indeed, they do not involve physical aggression or physical entering of a territory of a member state by enemy forces. These new security threats represent a crisis for NATO, whose rules were crafted in the pre-cyber age.

This ambiguity of rules has caused some serious concern and uncertainty among some member state decision-makers about continued effectiveness and/or usefulness of NATO as a collective defense framework. This was demonstrated, for instance, in the efforts of the Czech and Polish governments to establish bilateral defense agreements with the US in support of the US Anti-Missile Defense system in Europe (Valasek 2009:13), as well as in the open letter of leading Central European intellectuals and former policy makers to the Obama administration in 2009.[12] In the Nordic countries, the responses have been less dramatic, but the 2009 Stoltenberg report includes suggestions to establish common Nordic defense systems against cyber-attacks and a number of other suggestions for strengthening regional defense cooperation in the Nordic region (see more about this in the next section of the chapter).

Crisis of resources in NATO

As has become clear in recent years, with the exception of the US and a few affluent countries such as Norway, NATO member states have been struggling with decreasing defense budgets. The reasons are complex, but the global financial crisis has been among the major factors. Some member states – notably Greece, Hungary, Iceland, Latvia, and Romania – were hit so hard their governments had to seek support from the International Monetary Fund (IMF) and/or the EU member states in order to save themselves from default. The faith of the financial sectors of Portugal and Spain were still highly un-

---

11 The diversity of views of representatives in NATO member state governments, have become clear during the Globsec conference in Bratislava in 2009, when the issue of whether cyber-attacks qualify as article V situations was debated. As a senior diplomat from a founding member state of NATO stated during a panel discussion: "It would always be a matter of political considerations".

12 See *An open letter to the Obama administration from Central and Eastern Europe* (available at http://wyborcza.pl/1,76842,6825987,An_Open_Letter_to_the_Obama_Administration_from_Central.html).

certain at the time of writing, and there were serious doubts whether the former could actually do without applying for help from the European Stability Mechanism and the IMF. Other member state governments, which have been doing somewhat better in tackling the financial crisis, have had to restructure public spending cutting resources in most sectors including defense – in some cases by as much as 30% year on year (Valasek 2009:33, Valasek 2011a).

Most new member states have not been meeting the targets of annual defense spending levels at 1.5 % of GDP, which they committed to upon their entry into NATO. Slovakia, for instance, spent only 1 % of GDP on defense in 2010, and there were no plans of increasing the budget due to an overall restrictive budgetary policy of the new conservative-liberal government that governed the country since mid-2010. Hence, as much as 70-80% of the equipment of the Slovak military was two or more decades old in 2011.[13] This is by no means sufficient to guarantee any sort of credible defense, not even speaking of credible commitments to expeditionary operations under NATO- and/or the EU umbrella.[14] Moreover, common resources of the Alliance to which member states contribute based on their size and wealth, were also being radically downsized under pressure of the financial crisis. This involved for instance heavy cutting of resources for upgrades in defense infrastructure available through the so called 'security investment program' of NATO (Valasek 2009:35). Partly, this is paralleled by continued inefficient spending on a number of fairly ineffective commands located in various parts of Europe, which may be of lower strategic importance following the end of the Cold War and the enlargement of NATO (ibid.).

Given the increasing gap in defense spending putting the US far ahead of the rest of NATO, there is also an increasing technological gap in research and development and the capabilities used by forces in the field. This leads to dangerous levels of incompatibility with NATO forces, which in some cases disables US troops trying to cooperate with soldiers from other NATO countries in operations in Afghanistan and elsewhere.

Finally, there are high levels of parallelism in the development of the NATO Rapid Reaction Force agreed to in the Prague Capabilities Commitment of 2002, and development of capacities in the framework of European Security and Defense Policy (ESDP), notably the planned EU-Battlegroups. Twenty one member states of NATO are also EU members and these countries face parallel demands for committing troops and equipment to rapid reaction forces being established in the framework of the two organizations.

---

13 Based on information from the Slovak Ministry of Defense acquired in March 2011.
14 This was one of the main reasons why Slovakia decided to support the NATO-operation in Libya only in declaratory manner, and refused to send any military forces and/or equipment. The minister of defense stated clearly that the country had no real capacity to contribute with current capabilities.

In light of the radically decreasing defense budgets, this is clearly problematic.

Overall, the resources of NATO have been diminishing as a consequence of the financial crisis and decreasing defense budgets in most member states. As an institutionalized organization, NATO is expected to carry out practices and transactions with the environment based on established patterns and structures of direction and resources. Yet when the latter are evaporating, it seriously hampers the ability of the organization to live up to its own expectations and performance aspirations.

Crisis of identity of NATO

In addition to the factors discussed in the previous paragraphs, there is a more general challenge for NATO in finding its renewed purpose in the post-Cold War environment. A number of key conflicts in recent years (e.g. Iraq) have included member states of NATO, but not the Alliance as such. Uncertainties about the involvement of NATO were related to most of the leading conflicts in the recent decade being outside North America and Europe. Since it was the latter, which NATO was designed to defend, it is not clear to what extent NATO should be getting involved in non-European (or 'out of area') operations. The situation following the escalation of the civil war in Libya in March 2011, when it took weeks for NATO member states to agree that the Alliance should actually be taking over command of the operation, was a good illustration of the level of ambiguity. While some see this lack of unity as a source of continuing problems for NATO even after the operation in Libya (Volker 2011), others see it as an emerging mode of how NATO operations will be conducted in the future, i.e. by intra-NATO coalitions of the willing (see Valasek 2011b).

In addition to uncertainty of the geographic scope of its operations, NATO remains quite uncertain as to how to relate to a resurgent Russia. Since the early 1990s, NATO has been trying to decrease tensions by stopping contingency planning aimed at Russia. Moreover, the Alliance has been engaging Russia in various forms of institutional cooperation, ranging from consultation bodies such as the NATO-Russia Council, via logistics cooperation in deliveries of supplies to NATO troops in Afghanistan through the Russian territory, to cooperation in peacekeeping (e.g. in Kosovo) and even in military operations (e.g. joint special forces operations in Afghanistan aimed at drug-producers in 2010)[15]. Moreover, the US administration under the leadership of President Obama, has been arguing for a re-set of relations with Russia overall. But following the Russia – Georgia war in 2008, some

---

15 See Simon Schuster: "Russia Returns to Afghanistan for a Drug Raid". *Time*, Oct 30, 2010 (available at http://www.time.com/time/world/article/0,8599,2028329,00.html).

member states – notably the Baltic states – have been calling for renewal of contingency planning in case of a conflict with Russia (see Valasek 2009). Similarly, in the Arctic, NATO member states Canada, Norway, Denmark, Iceland, and the US, have been dealing with increasing pressure from Russia, demonstrating its presence in an area rich in natural resources and increasingly strategically important, not least due to new sea-routes.[16]

Overall, the identity of the Alliance is less certain following the end of the Cold War. For any institutionalized organization, such a state is a source of problems as it renders it less capable to identify what appropriate steps to take in specific situations.

Regional responses to the crisis of NATO: Nordic and Visegrad approaches

For smaller NATO member states, the triple institutional crisis sketched out in the previous section, is a serious challenge. It leaves them highly exposed to a changing security environment in Europe and beyond with uncertain expectations regarding possibilities of collective action capacity within NATO. One of the emerging patterns in responding to this complex challenge is development of regional security frameworks in cooperation with and complimentary to NATO. Both the Nordic region and the Visegrad region have introduced steps towards such co-operation. There are similarities in these approaches, but the two regions also show important differences in the extent of cooperation and the drivers affecting security integration.

Regional security integration: The Nordic region

Regional security integration in the North of Europe has its roots in the early years of the Cold War. Karl Deutsch used the Nordic region as an advanced example of his notion of a 'security community' in the late 1950s (Deutsch 1957). As Forsberg (2010:128) points out, the institutional carrier of integration was the Nordic Council founded in 1955. In the framework of the Nordic

---

16 See the contributions to "The Arctic is Hot" – special issue of *International Journal* (65,4: 2010), edited by John Erik Fossum and Stéphane Roussel.

Council, the member countries (Denmark, Iceland, Norway, Sweden and Finland) introduced a passport union, common labor market and coordination of environmental policies.[17]

Besides the formal framework of the Nordic Council, most cooperation has been based on close contacts at various levels, frequent meetings and informal norms. Yet, military cooperation was canceled from the Nordic framework after negotiations on a Nordic defense union failed in 1948/49, and Denmark and Norway joined NATO. It was only after the end of the Cold War, various forms of deepening and broadening of defense cooperation among the Nordic countries started to take shape. 1994 saw the launch of Nordic Armaments Cooperation (NORDAC), aimed at improving information exchange in the defense sector and increased trade of defense goods among Nordic countries. NORDACS supported joint projects in development and upgrade of weapons systems.

A further framework of cooperation included Nordic Coordinated Arrangements for Military Peace Support (NORDCAPS), founded in 1998. It provided a platform for joint training of military personnel, planning of crisis management missions and not least, building of the Nordic Battlegroup for deployment in missions within the framework of EU Security and Defense Policy. Further developments included Nordic Supportive Defense Structures (NORDSUP) – a trilateral Norwegian-Swedish-Finnish initiative launched in 2008 to enable closer cooperation among the defense forces. This was supported by the Nordic ministers of defense in 2009 and a new cooperation structure, now encompassing also Denmark and Iceland, was launched. It is referred to as Nordic Defense Cooperation (NORDEFCO) and integrates all previous cooperation structures including NORDAC, NORDCAPS and NORDSUP.

In addition to the development of institutional structures, changes in the international security environment have also prompted strategic re-thinking of possibilities of further tightening of defense cooperation in the Nordic region. A decisive factor here is decreasing defense budgets due to the financial crisis and increasing costs of leading military technologies, leaving individual countries with only limited possibilities for keeping their military capabilities effective in the current defense environment. As the 2009 Stoltenberg Report argues,

---

17 The description of the institutional developments of Nordic defense cooperation provided in this paragraph summarize points discussed by Forsberg (2010: 128-131). See also Lundmark (2004).

the alternative to [regional] cooperation could be a situation where small and medium-sized countries lose their ability to maintain a credible defence. The result could be a Europe where only countries like France, Russia, the UK and Germany have their own modern defence forces. Looking 15 to 20 years down the road, none of the Nordic countries will be able to maintain their armed forces at their current size and quality without closer Nordic cooperation" (Stoltenberg Report, p. 28).[18]

Hence, the 2009 Stoltenberg Report, which was welcomed by the Nordic foreign ministers in a joint article published simultaneously in a number of Nordic papers in March 2010[19], has suggested a number of specific steps to enhance defense cooperation in the Nordic region.

First, the Report proposes *to enhance peace-building capacities* of the Nordic countries by establishing 'Nordic Stabilization Task Force' deployable in countries facing major internal unrest and/or other situations requiring international assistance. The task force is to have four components: military, human, state-building (including police units, judges, election observers etc.), and development assistance. Second, Nordic countries are to cooperate in *improving joint capacities for air-surveillance, in particular over Iceland.* This is in line with established patterns of cooperation between NATO and non-member countries that have joined the Partnership for Peace (PfP) program. This includes, for instance, Sweden and Finland entering into agreements on data exchange with NATO's air defense system.

Third, the report proposes *establishment of a Nordic maritime monitoring system.* The system should have a civilian nature and should enable monitoring of sea traffic in the Baltic Sea as well as in the Barents Sea. Fourth, the ability to act effectively in joint operations, tackling threats emanating from the maritime environment should be addressed by the *establishment of a Maritime response force.* This should involve, for instance, establishment of a joint Nordic center for coordination of search and rescue operations of coast-guards, as well as development of joint icebreaker capacities to support such operations in both the Barents and the Baltic Sea. Fifth, the previous two steps should be supported by the *establishment of a Satellite system for surveillance and communications.* The purpose is to have effective access to real-time satellite imagery supporting crisis management operations and maritime monitoring. The current solutions based on commercial purchase of satellite imagery by the Nordic governments from the European Space

---

18 Thorvald Stoltenberg: *Nordic Cooperation on Foreign and Security Policy.* Proposals presented to the extraordinary meeting of Nordic defense ministers in Oslo on 9 February 2009 (available at http://www.mfa.is/media/Frettatilkynning/Nordic_report.pdf).

19 Lene Espersen, Alexander Stubb, Össur Skarpheddinsson, Jonas Gahr Støre, Carl Bildt: "Stärk relationerna mellan Norden och Baltikum" [Strengthening relations among the Nordic and Baltic countries] in *Sydsvenskan,* March 11, 2010 (available at http://www.sydsvenskan.se/opinion/aktuellafragor/article636798/Stark-relationerna-mellan-Norden-och-Baltikum.html).

Agency and other commercial providers are unsatisfactory, as these satellites do not provide proper coverage north of 71°N. Yet it is in the latter geographic area that sea traffic is increasing due to the melting of ice.

Sixth, the report proposes *intensification of cooperation on Arctic issues* among the Nordic countries. This should be done in particular within the framework of the Arctic Council, and should focus on practical matters such as environmental protection, safety of sea traffic, capacities for search and rescue operations etc. Seventh, to address challenges related to cyberspace, *a Nordic resource network to protect against cyber attacks should be established*. This includes sharing of information and best practices, and establishment of joint bodies aimed at preventing hostile cyber actions against vital infrastructure throughout Nordic societies. Eighth, the report proposes to *set up a joint Disaster response unit* aimed at crisis response involving a combination of public and private resources available in the Nordic countries.

Ninth, *a war crimes investigation unit should be established* with the aim of investigating genocide and crimes against humanity committed in crisis spots around the world, and/or by residents of Nordic countries. Tenth, *cooperation among Nordic foreign services should intensify*. This is to involve establishment of joint diplomatic missions wherever appropriate and possible (following the model of the Nordic embassy compound in Berlin) with the aim of cutting costs, extending presence and sharing information. Eleventh, *military cooperation on transport, medical services, education, materiel and exercise ranges should be strengthened*. The primary drivers here are increasing costs of military technologies and the inability of individual small states to sustain credible defense without closer cooperation with partner governments in the region. Deeper regional cooperation would also increase the leverage and bargaining power of Nordic governments when they operate as purchasers on the civilian market, acquiring equipment and services for crisis operations. The argument on cost-efficiency relates also to joint procurement of weapons and military technologies, as well as to operation of firing ranges.

Twelfth, a *joint amphibious unit should be established* based on current cooperation of the Swedish and Finnish navies. This unit should be an important capability fitting defense purposes of the Nordic countries, as well as helping them to meet demands of international partners in crisis operations around the globe. Thirteenth, the report suggests *a need for a Nordic declaration of defense solidarity*. The logic here is that over time, enhanced cooperation among Nordic countries may lead to specialization in various aspects of defense and, through that, to relative decreases in defense capabilities in individual countries. Formal declarations of defense solidarity should help to diminish these effects.

There are at least three kinds of drivers of defense integration in the Nordic region – ongoing changes in the security environment in Europe; diversity of political leanings of governmental coalitions in the region; and not least, deepening of European integration. Regarding changes in the security environment in Europe, Forsberg (2010:133) lists the following three factors as influencing the Nordic region towards tighter integration: a) decreasing presence of the US military in Europe (e.g. the US forces leaving the air force base at Keflavik in Iceland in 2006), b) resurgence of Russia as a military power capable and willing to use its forces beyond its borders, and c) both NATO and the EU have been promoting regional cooperation and integration frameworks, as processes complimentary to these overarching frameworks of European security.

The second driver of security integration in the region has been, somewhat paradoxically, diversity of political leanings in governmental coalitions in the Nordic countries. For instance, the social democrats (Arbeiderpartiet) in Norway are more open to Nordic security integration than the Conservatives (Høyre), while this is precisely the opposite in Sweden. Hence, a situation in which Norway has a government led by the social democrats and Sweden a government led by the Conservatives, is favorable to promoting tighter security integration in the region.[20] The third driver of Nordic security integration – broadening and deepening processes of European integration – has led to a situation in which traditionally close coordination of policies in the realm of low politics among the Nordic countries has been gradually replaced by interconnectedness and coordination of policy-making within the EU-framework (see for instance Olsen and Sverdrup 1997). As Stoltenberg (2009:14) argues, this change dynamic freed capacities of Nordic governments, and opened up closer intergovernmental cooperation in defense – a sector where processes of EU-integration have not been too deep.

The impact of the defense integration suggested in the Stoltenberg report will need to be assessed. In a key recent study of reception of proposals featuring numerous interviews with relevant actors, Håkon Lunde Saxi concluded demand for Nordic integration is wholly led by economic concerns, and does not extend to political integration or need for a common security and defense policy (Saxi, 2011).

---

20 This point was stressed in the panel debate "Regional Security Integration: Nordic and Visegrad Approaches" during Globsec conference in Bratislava on September 13, 2010. The panelists included Espen Barth Eide, Björn Lyrvall, István Gyarmati, Robert Ondrejcsák and Jozef Bátora as panel convener.

Regional security integration: The Visegrad region

While Visegrad cooperation has been quite intensive in the period before the Czech Republic, Slovakia, Hungary and Poland joined NATO and the EU, the purpose of the regional framework has been somewhat questioned in the post-accession period. The mainstay of Visegrad cooperation are activities in the sphere of cultural- and/or educational exchange, organized primarily within the framework and funding schemes set up by the International Visegrad Fund (established in 2000). Occasionally, cooperation among the V4 countries has involved practical policy-coordination within the EU, such as cooperation among the four ministries of interior in joining the Schengen zone (Tencerová 2010). But in a number of other policy spheres, no regional cooperation was achieved partly due to lack of capability and partly due to lack of political will and interest to opt for coordinated regional solutions.[21]

Yet in the realm of foreign policy, notable progress has been made in terms of joint V4 engagement in efforts such as the EU's Eastern Partnership Initiative launched in 2009, and in terms of coordination of energy security policies. Moreover, in 2010, the V4 foreign ministries launched an initiative seeking to establish joint diplomatic presence where this may bring about cost cutting improving levels of representation. This was also done in response to formation of the European External Action Service and severe cost-cutting in some foreign services (notably Czech and Slovak foreign services).

The first 'Visegrad-house' housing diplomatic offices of the V4 governments, were opened in Cape Town in 2010. Joint external representation and external identity projection were also supported by emergence of new narratives concerning historical origins of Visegrad cooperation. One of the increasingly prominent narratives helping to "re-invent" a common identity for the imagined Visegrad regional community, is based on stories recounting meetings of kings of Hungary, Bohemia, and Poland, at Visegrad in 1335.[22]

A number of further steps toward closer regional security cooperation were suggested in a policy paper commissioned by the Slovak Atlantic Commission in 2010 (see Naď et al. 2010). The suggestions feature a number of specific political and organizational measures, including: *a) creation of specialized V4 units at the ministries of foreign affairs and ministries of defense* to facilitate security policy coordination; *b) mutual support for personnel nominations* to higher level positions in international organizations; *c) a*

---

21 As a result, V4 countries ended up with individual policy solutions, i.e. Slovakia is the only country in the group that joined the Euro-zone, while Poland remains the only country in the group without visa-free travel to the US for its citizens.
22 See Rácz, G.: "The Congress of Visegrád" in *Visegrád 1335*. Bratislava, 2009 (available on the official site of the Visegrad Group at http://www.visegradgroup.eu/main.php?folderID=1132).

mutual defense solidarity clause complimenting and not replacing existing commitments within NATO and the EU; *d) defense industry cooperation* fostering joint procurement programs and cooperation in defense related research and development projects; *e) an annual V4 defense and security conference* on a rotating basis to support development of the security policy community consisting of governmental and non-governmental institutions from the V4; f) *establishing a defense and security policy magazine* to foster security policy thinking in the region; *g) creation of common V4 military education* to foster joint procedures and development of military expertise; h) joint capabilities and training of armed forces to share resources and training grounds around the region; *i) creation of a V4 Battle group* in 2016; *j) coordination of energy security policy* along the lines indicated in the following paragraph; *k) setting up an expert group to fight against extremism and organized crime* – areas often interlinked with the issue area of illegal immigration; and finally *l) setting up a contact list of experts in defense and security* to support effective inter-linkages among the expert communities in the four countries.

This was indeed a wish-list at the time of writing, and was unclear to what extent such ambitions could be fulfilled. Challenges to effective cooperation related primarily to the viability and appropriateness of the V4 as a forum for development of security policy for countries of the region. Regional defense integration in the V4 context may be fostered by joint defense initiatives by a core group consisting of Slovakia and the Czech Republic – countries with deep historical ties conducting their strategic defense reviews at time of this writing. An important political step towards closer cooperation of V4 militaries was taken during the Slovak presidency of the Visegrad group in May 2011, when defense ministers of the V4 met in Levoča, Slovakia and announced plans to form a joint V4 Battlegroup by the first half of 2016.[23]

Some observers (e.g. Friedman 2011) see this development signalling geopolitical shifts in Europe, towards a regionally fragmented continent. Yet such readings may be overstated given the limited number of troops pledged for each individual EU battlegroup, the notorious capabilities-expectations gaps that characterize the setting up of EU Battlegroups in general, and the structural constraints on the use of EU Battlegroups given by the consensual nature of EU foreign policy decision-making in the Council of the EU.

There were at least three types of momentum for closer regional defense cooperation among V4 countries – strategic change dynamics in the security

---

23 See "*Krajiny Vyšehradskej skupiny vytvoria spoločnú bojovú skupinu pre potreby EÚ*" [The Visegrad Countries will form a joint EU battlegroup], News service of the Ministry of Defense of the Slovak Republic, May 13, 2011 (available at
http://www.mosr.sk/21431/krajiny-vysehradskej-skupiny-vytvoria-spolocnu-bojovu-skupinu-pre-potreby-eu.php?pg=1).

environment in Europe; similarity of political leanings of V4 governments following elections in 2009 and 2010; and efforts to increase security of strategic energy supplies. Regarding the first form of momentum above, there are at least three developments which lead to NATO's decreasing importance. These include the

> US inclination to go [it] alone in the War on terror, as well as the sudden German emancipation and their veto [on] the Art.4 consultations in Turkey in 2003. [Moreover, there is also] the revival of neo-imperialism and growth in strength of Putin's Russia (Naď et al (2010:2).

The second driver or form of momentum is intensified regional defense cooperation, and coming to power of governmental coalitions with similar political leanings in capitals during elections in 2009 and 2010.

All V4 governments were at the time of writing conservative/liberal with various informal links between their political leaders. This applies in particular to Czech and Slovak governments, which since 2010, were formed by centre-right coalitions with a number of former anti-communist dissidents and post-communist reformist leaders at key posts in respective administrations. This provided for like-mindedness among foreign policy elites in the V4, which now have a common normative foundation related to 'Atlanticist' views and democracy promotion (Mikulová 2011).

Finally, the third driving force or form of momentum regarding security cooperation in the V4, is the effort to ensure security of energy supplies. The imminent importance of this issue was brought home by the fact the single most serious threat to national security for Slovakia after 1989. was the cut-off of energy supplies from Russia in the early months of 2009, with Slovakia only days away from complete black-out. Hence, V4 governments agreed in 2010 to interlink their energy infrastructures and coordinate approaches to increase their leverage in energy negotiations with partners outside the region, notably Russia (Nosko et al. 2010).

Table 2.1: Regional responses to the crisis of NATO

	Nordic countries	Visegrad Countries
Crisis of rules	• pragmatic rules of cooperation; • informal networks on all levels; • informal defense solidarity principle (formalization suggested)	• formal structures and some informal ties (SK and CZ - Štiřín) • Slovak plan to launch V4 training for commanding officers (socialization)
Crisis of resources	• sharing of costs in upgrading equipment • sharing of costs in mil. R&D • sharing of costs and resources in protecting territorial waters and airspace	• plans for joint equipment acquisitions (SK and CZ) • plans to connect energy infrastructures (possibility of joint approaches in gas-price negotiations with Russia) • V4 diplomatic posts
Crisis of identity	• Reasserting the "Norden" identity (helpedby asymmetric attachment to NATO and EU) • Normative-power identity (war-crimes investigation capabilities)	• Incentives for a regional approach in EU negotiations • V4 diplomatic presence abroad • new narratives relating V4 to 14th Century alliances

Conslusion: Regionalization as an element in the transformation of NATO?

This chapter argued that NATO has been going through a triple institutional crisis – a crisis of rules, crisis of resources, and crisis of identity. In response to this, groupings of member states have been exploring possibilities of enhancing regional security cooperation to complement existing arrangements in NATO. The approach in the Nordic region has been building on decades of close ties and cooperation in various realms of low politics, and a shared sense of a regional 'security community' development since the 1950s. Somewhat paradoxically, asymmetry in terms of attachment to the key integrative frameworks in Europe – NATO and the EU – have been among the key drivers of regional security integration.

Also, asymmetry in terms of political leanings of governments, contributes positively to defense integration as tighter Nordic links in defense are preferred by different kinds of parties in each of the Nordic countries. Europeanization has also been a key factor in defense integration in the Nordic region. This is related to the fact that cooperation in the traditional realm of low politics among Nordic countries has increasingly shifted towards EU-oriented frameworks. Defense remains one of the few areas in which EU integration plays a limited role, and hence is one of the few areas left for reasserting close and special ties among the Nordic countries.

Regional security integration in the Visegrad countries has followed somewhat different patterns. There is symmetry in terms of membership in both NATO and the EU, which puts all countries on an equal footing in terms of available security guarantees and frameworks. This, however, also makes the concept of value added by an extra layer of regional defense cooperation, less clear. Contrary to the experience of the Nordic region, it is symmetry in political leanings of governments that seems to set the right conditions for enhanced defense cooperation in the region. Center-right governmental coalitions seem likely to favor closer links in the defense sector among Visegrad countries.

While there may be different sets of factors leading to closer regional defense cooperation in the two regions explored in this chapter, the question arises as to what extent these processes are representative of a broader pattern of regionalization within NATO. The Alliance itself seems to be opening up more in favor of this as one of the elements in its strategic transformation process. Further research needs to focus, first, on whether these forms of regionalization make NATO more or less effective as a defense framework, e.g. whether these kinds of processes enhance or undermine political decision-making capacities and unity of command within the Alliance. Second, we need to know more about the nature of defense identity-formation in regional clusters of member states, and the extent to which these new defense identities enhance or undermine the transatlantic security community. Third, there is a need to explore the links and relations between regionalized areas of defense cooperation addressed in the current chapter, and the EU-wide regionalization process of defense cooperation developed within the framework of the European Defence Agency (Bátora 2009). Fourth, the role of asymmetry and/or variation in attachment to European integration frameworks should be explored in a more systematic manner with the aim of assessing its potential as a driver of regional integration. Finally, and related to the latter point, further research needs to be devoted to exploring the role of regional defense integration involving non-member countries of NATO and the EU, as a way of bringing about their quasi-enlargements.

References

Bátora, Jozef. (2009): "European Defence Agency: A Flashpoint of Institutional Logics" in *West European Politics*, 32(6): 1075-1098

Cohen, Michael D./ March, James.G./ Olsen, Johan. (1972): "A Garbage Can Model of Organizational Choice" in *Administrative Science Quarterly*, 17(1): 1-25

Deutsch, Karl W. (1957): *Political Community and the North Atlantic Area: International Organization in the Light of Historical Experience.* Princeton: Princeton UniversityPress

Edstrøm, Hakan/Matlary, Janne/ Petersson, Magnus (2011): *NATO: The Power of Partnerships*, Palgrave Macmillan, UK

Forsberg, Tuomas (2010): "Det nordiska försvarssamarbetet: en kort historia men en lång framtid?" *Finsk Tidskrift*, 3(2010): 127-136

Friedman, George (2011): *Visegrad: A New European Military Force.* STRATFOR, May 17, 2011
http://www.stratfor.com/weekly/20110516-visegrad-new-european-military-force

Jones, Seth (2007): *The Rise of European Security Cooperation*, Cambridge Univ.Press, Cambridge, UK

Lundmark, Martin (2004): "Nordic Defence Materiel Cooperation" in *Strategic Yearbook 2004*. Stockholm: Swedish National Defence College, pp. 207-230

March, James G./ Olsen, Johan P. (1984): "The New Institutionalism: Organizational Factors in Political Life" in *American Political Science Review*, 78: 734-749

March, James G./ Olsen, Johan P. (1989): *Rediscovering Institutions. The Organizational Basis of Politics*. New York: Free Press

Matlary, Janne Haaland (2009): *European Union Security Dynamics: In the New National Interest* Basingstoke: Palgrave

Mikulová, Kristína (2011): "The Missionary Zeal of Recent Converts: Norm Enterpreneurs and Atlanticism in Central and Eastern Europe" IESIR Working Paper 3/2011. Bratislava: IESIR

Naď, Jozef/ Gyarmati, Istvan/Szatkowski, Tomasz/Frank, Libor (2010): *Trans-Atlantic Security*. Policy Paper – Visegrad Security Cooperation Initiative, Bratislava: Slovak Atlantic Commission

Nosko, Andrej/ Orbán, Anita/ Paczynski, Wojciech/ Černoch, Filip/ Jaroš, Jakub (2010): *Energy security*. Policy Paper – Visegrad Security Cooperation Initiative, Bratislava: Slovak Atlantic Commission

Olsen, Johan P/ Sverdrup, Bjorn.Otto. (1997): *Samarbeid og integrasjon – i Norden og i Europa*, ARENA working paper No. 20, Oslo
Rácz, Gábor: "The Congress of Visegrád" in *Visegrád 1335*. Bratislava, 2009 http://www.visegradgroup.eu/main.php?folderID=1132
Saxi, Hakon Lunde (2011): "Nordic defence cooperation after the Cold War", March 2011, Oslo: Institutt for Forsvarsstudier
Selznick, Philip (1957): *Leadership in Administration*. New York: Harper and Row
Simon Schuster: "Russia Returns to Afghanistan for a Drug Raid". *Time*, Oct 30, 2010
http://www.time.com/time/world/article/0,8599,2028329,00.html
Stoltenberg, Thorvald (2009): *Nordic Cooperation on Foreign and Security Policy*. Proposals presented to the extraordinary meeting of Nordic foreign ministers. Oslo, February 9, 2009
Tencerová, Veronika (2010): *Why Preservation of the Visegrad Group in the European Union Matters*. IESIR working paper 2/2010, Bratislava: IESIR, Comenius University
http://www.fses.uniba.sk/fileadmin/user_upload/editors/UESMV/WP_Tencerova.pdf
Valasek, Tomas (2009): *NATO, Russia and European Security*. Working Paper, November 2009, London: Centre for European Reform
Valasek, Tomas (2011a): *Surviving Austerity: The Case for a New Approach to EU Military Collaboration*. London: Centre for European Reform. April 2011
Valasek, Tomas (2011b): *What Libya says about the Future of the Transatlantic Alliance*. CER Essay, London: Centre for European Reform, August 2011
Volker, Kurt (2011): "Don't Call It a Comeback: Four Reasons Why Libya Doesn't Equal Success for NATO" in *Foreign Policy*, August 23, 2011

Chapter 3
Strangers at the gate: national policies on migration in Norway and Slovakia

Živka Deleva and Leonid Tuzov

Introduction

In times of test and trial regarding global well-being, small states may carry the heaviest burden with their economies exposed to higher level of risk, because of limited territory, small population, and restricted capacity for negotiating with larger states (Venner 2009).

To contribute to a better understanding of the phenomena of a small state in turbulent times, we focus on the issue of migration and employ comparative approaches to present a broader analytical overview of migratory regulation in Norway and Slovakia. This is based on the most recent data available mainly from MIPEX[24] III. The data sets utilized yield numerous rewarding insights into the political dichotomy of an advanced European state and a post-communist EU nation.

Norway and Slovakia are countries with nearly same size populations and quite different socio-economic and political systems. They both seek better regulation of new challenges international migration brings in time of instability and uncertainty. Both countries are alluring destinations for thousands of immigrants, while size and constitution of migrant communities as well as migratory flow management is significantly different. Our analysis highlights how integration policies seek to regulate labor market mobility, family reunion, education, political participation, long-term residence, and equal access for third country nationals.

The selection of common variables for this chapter was informed by evident similarities in legislative systems and liberal aspirations both countries share. Elaboration on each of the indicators is presented in the respective

---

24 MIPEX is a study conducted by the Migration Policy Group in cooperation with the British Council, thirty-seven national-level organizations, including think-tanks, non-governmental organizations, foundations, universities, research institutes, and equality bodies located in thirty one countries. These countries are in Europe, Canada, and the USA. It is a tool that provides the most comprehensive data on integration policies including 148 policy indicators, which could substantially be used by all concerned with these issues, either as an indicator per se, or as a reference guide for improvement.

sections of this research. In conclusion to the chapter, the scoring of both countries is reviewed in each of the policy areas, scrutinizing closely reasons that might have influenced visible change in previous years. At the same time, an all-embracing comparative chart between Norway and Slovakia is presented with generalizations made about ongoing institutionalization of the migration sector of both countries. The chapter also overviews migration in the two countries, which over time and in different time periods, experienced a shift in migratory patterns. This shift from emigration to immigration is carefully noted in both cases of comparison. Some major insights into legislative policies are also offered in the section called "Legal regulations".

Given certain limitations, the present comparative overview may still well serve as a comprehensive study of the phenomena of migration evolving in both countries. When considering concluding observations, it also supports the hypothesis that small states are more restrictive on immigration than larger states. It is also true that more economically and socially settled European countries, with a larger direct experience of migration (e.g. Norway), overall outperforms new post-communist EU member-states (e.g. Slovakia), in terms of managing migratory flows in turbulent times. Implications for further research may include using Norway-Slovakia comparative perspectives as a model for both "small state-small state" and "large state-small state" studies.

The shift from emigration to immigration countries: Slovakia and Norway

A series of migratory movements on the territory of the modern Slovak Republic took place during the last three centuries (Divinský 2004a). The earliest trends mainly followed specific emigration patterns, as Slovaks struggling to earn their living at home went abroad in quest of a better life. Since the beginning of the 18th century, emigration reached a point where thousands of inhabitants of the present Slovak Republic started to colonise regions of the Hungarian Lower Country after expulsion of the Turks (Tibenský et al. 1978).

The second major wave of emigration started in the 1850s, when in the course of nearly seven decades, some 850,000 people left Slovak lands, mainly for the United States (Bašovský / Divinský 1991). Also, during the interwar period of 1918-1939, tens of thousands of Slovaks headed towards the US, France, Belgium, Germany, Austria, Canada, and South America, to work in agriculture and industry. Pre-World War II emigration waves are, for the most part, largely viewed as devastating for the current Slovak nation. Hundreds of thousands of men and women of productive age abandoned their motherland, resulting in change of population structure and demography, and weakening of the nation-building process overall (Scheib 2011).

The immediate post-war period was marked by deportation of at least 170,000 ethnic Germans (Barnovský et al. 1988) along with Slovak re-emigration to Czechoslovakia[25]. Following the post-war period, the era of communism 1948 to 1989 was plagued by tight state controls and strict regulation of travel abroad. Emigration during those years was fragmentized and hectic, as free movement, specifically with Western countries, virtually did not exist. There was one small exception, which was a short period following the Prague Spring in 1968, when a large wave of emigration hit Slovak areas of Czechoslovakia[26]. Major recipient countries throughout all waves of Slovak immigration were Germany, neighboring Austria, France, the United Kingdom, USA, Canada, and Australia. An important migratory flow also existed between Slovak and Czech lands, as an average of three to four thousand Slovaks were moving mainly to the cities of Prague and Ostrava, as well as to the Czech borderland every year during the communist era.

Since 1993, the independent Slovak Republic started to experience a migratory net gain due to hundreds of re-emigrants. Simultaneously, the number of irregular migrants and asylum seekers from less developed Asian countries and post-Soviet states, started to grow as well. In the years preceding Slovakia's accession to the EU (2004), and further on in the Schengen Area (2008), we also saw the numbers of third country nationals greatly increase in the larger context of these overall patterns.

Norway's rich immigration history, on the other hand, traces the proto-migratory flows back to the Viking era. Between the reigns of the first Norwegian king, Harald Finehair (872-930 AD) and Håkon Håkonsson (1217-1263), eight out of ten known queens were princesses from neighboring countries (Imsen 1991) and from 1500 onwards, many immigrants were coming to Norway to work as miners and civil servants (Kjeldstadli 2003). However, a visible shift in migratory flows was recorded only on the verge of the Industrial revolution, when about 850,000 people emigrated from the country between 1825 and 1945, putting Norway second after Ireland in terms of emigrants as a percentage of the population. Most emigration was economic in nature, going to the United States, from where as many as 150,000 people

---

25 Along these same lines, another significant shift in population structure took place when nearly 90,000 ethnic Hungarians were expelled to Hungary, in a sort of informal exchange for some 70,000 ethnic Slovaks. In 1947 about 12,000 people of Ruthenian origin left Slovak Eastern provinces for the USSR, while 5,000 Slovaks re-emigrated from Ukraine (Gajdoš 2002; cf. Barnovský et al. 1988). In this same overall context, Slovakia significantly contributed to resettlement of the Czech borderland, as up to 110,000 Slovaks transferred to Czech lands, staying there for good (Vaňo 2001). Overall, during the period 1945-1950, Slovakia may well have experienced a net loss of over 300,000 people.

26 The exact number totalled 300,000 people for both modern-day Czech Republic and Slovakia, with 70,000 people fleeing immediately after the Prague Spring (Čulík 2008).

eventually returned to Norway (Cooper 2005) at some point during their lives.

After WWII, Norway established the Norwegian Refugee Council to assist refugees, gaining a solid reputation for humanitarian assistance. At the same time, Norway remained a country with very few immigrants, with few or none leaving for other Nordic nations. Importantly during the 1950s, the common labor market and common passport-control areas, allowed citizens of Sweden, Denmark, Norway, Finland, and later, Iceland, to freely travel between their countries. Equally important, the region's homogeneity made immigration among Scandinavians virtually a non-issue, as between 1966-1970 net migration totaled merely 853 people (Cooper 2005).

Things changed however, during the late 1960s, when due to discovery of oil and natural gas deposits in the North Sea, a booming economy and slower population growth, Norway adopted favorable migratory policies towards labor migrants coming from Turkey, Pakistan, and the former Yugoslavia. Invited as temporary guest workers, such persons from less developed countries eventually remained in Norway and were followed later by family members wishing for reunification. Eventually, a so-called "immigration stop" was imposed in 1975, as a response to growing concerns about a sudden increase of foreign laborers entering Norway's stable economy[27]. Restrictive measures, however, only streamlined migrant applications to other channels, as from 1970s onwards Norway saw a steady increase in applications for family reunion and asylum (Cooper 2005).

When we look at the 1980s, despite an atmosphere of widespread popular discontent with illegal immigration throughout Norway and growing electoral support for anti-immigration parties, the Norwegian government was determined to regulate these migratory flows in a rightful and lawful manner. The Immigration Act was adopted in 1988 and provided permission of entry, border control mechanisms, an internal monitoring service, and penalties for anyone that willfully or negligently would contravene the present Act. The exercise of authority under the Act was given to the Storting, responsible for the approval of the main principles for the regulation of immigration upon their issuance from the King. The provisions themselves were implemented by the King, the Ministry, the Directorate of Immigration, the police and other public authorities (Art. 5, Immigration Act 1988). According to the new law, the third country nationals (TCN) are required to obtain work permits and visas to enter Norway, with only certain categories of workers and professionals allowed to bypass the "immigration stop" threshold. There were several exemptions made for former Norwegian nationals and those married to Norwegian nationals. These concerned obtaining permanent residence

---

27 This behavior towards immigration is dutifully noted as an overall reaction by European countries, resulting from the global oil crises of 1973. This event caused restrictive policies on immigration to be implemented (Massey et.al 1998, Castles/Miller 2009).

permits on easier grounds. The rest were legally obliged to live three continuous years on the territory of Norway, to obtain permanent residence permits, with seven more years to apply for citizenship. During the last few decades, a large number of legislative initiatives were introduced to eliminate discrimination, secure protection of minors' rights, and to enhance the visa and residence permit application process.

Today, Norway, a safe and prosperous country with one of the highest standards of living in the world[28], tends to be the destination for many economic migrants and refugees from war-torn nations and regions. These include Iraq, Somalia, and Afghanistan, India and China, Middle East countries and, to a lesser extent, post-Soviet states. East Europeans from the "new" EU member-states of Poland, Czech Republic, Slovakia, Estonia, Lithuania, and Latvia, also constitute a significant amount of immigrants in Norway, which has been a member of the Schengen Area since 1996.

Legal regulations

Currently, immigration to Norway is legally regulated by the Immigration Act proposed in 2004, effective since 2010, and decided upon by Norwegian political authorities. These authorities are the Directorate of Immigration, established under the Norwegian Ministry of Justice and Police, which, along with the Immigration Act, the Anti-Discrimination Act and Citizenship Act heavily influence management of migration in Norway altogether.

The Directorate of Immigration is responsible for amending regulations and monitoring migratory trends. At the same time, it is responsible for harmonization and coordination of national acts in accordance with international law and European standards. Further legislative development at the EU level will influence Norway through both Schengen and Dublin cooperation, i.e. in regulating free movement throughout the EU as well as asylum policy. According to the Norwegian Ministry of Justice and Police, the Directorate of Immigration is the first hurdle in the decision-making process concerning application for citizenship, asylum, and most other applications pursuant to the Immigration Act. In the event applications are rejected, the Immigration Appeals Board is the appropriate body of appeal.

---

28 According to the Human Development Report prepared by the United Nations Development Program, Norway, during the last ten years scored highest, apart from 2005 and 2006 when Iceland took over the leading position, moving Norway into second position of countries with very high human development.

The Immigration Act of 2010 was amended so that it could respond to a number of migrants living on the territory of Norway. These amendments came as a reaction to general international obligations and included changes in particular areas, such as labor market mobility, family reunion, education, and anti-discrimination. In terms of regulating labor market mobility, the New Immigration Act penalizes migrant workers for trying to manipulate social assistance, which then becomes an obstacle in the process of residence permit renewal. At the same time, the act provides Norway with one of the least favorable conditions for stable family reunion in Europe, with the introduction of new requirements regarding employment, education, and housing. According to the new act, unaccompanied minors over sixteen years of age, have reduced access to secondary and higher education, which is in opposition of proposed amendments in 2007 on education, calling for 'equal education in practice'.

The body in charge of immigration for the Slovak Republic is the Department of Migration, under the Ministry of Interior. The department is the first instance regarding the decision-making process for awarding asylum and provision of additional protection for foreigners. This also includes as well, the process of awarding residence permits and long-term residence to immigrants. The legal framework that regulates the status of immigrants is the content of the law concerning residence of foreigners, which was adopted in 2002, and amended respectively in 2008 and 2009.

Further analysis of Slovak policy reveals the following. Specific guidelines, rules, and laws regarding issues of nationality and citizenship acquisition are to be found in the Citizenship Act, Anti-Discrimination Act, and Language Act. Namely the Citizenship Act, with its 2007 amendments, discourages the process of integration by making the naturalization process less favorable. The same act as amended in 2010, states that having Slovak citizenship cannot benefit those attempting to have dual citizenship overall. The Anti-Discrimination Act thus represents a huge step forward in the harmonization of Slovak legislation relative to EU law, by introducing new definitions and enhancing enforcement of anti-discriminatory initiatives. At the same time, the Language Act on the other hand, was highly criticized since it was amended in 2009, for discouraging use of minority languages in specific areas through imposition of financial penalties.

Internationally harmonized migration statistics

According to the most recent statistics Norway in 2010 experienced an immigration peak. Subsequently 73 852 immigrations and 31 506 emigrations were registered amounting to 42 350 net migration (Statistics Norway 2010). Respectively the Slovak statistical office reports that on 31.12. 2009 the inflow of international immigrants in the territory of the SR throughout the whole year was 15 643, while there were 4 753 emigrations registered. Thus this amounted in the positive status of the net migration ratio at 10 890 (Statistical Office of the SR, 2010). As regards Norway, although the highest proportion of the immigration comes from European countries, namely Polish, Lithuanian and Swedish immigrants to Norway, a significant part is constituted by immigration from Eritrea and Somalia from the African continent and Philippines, Thailand and Afghanistan from Asia. Moreover US citizens constitute the greatest contribution to Norwegian immigration from the Americas (Statistics Norway 2010). Third country nationals legally residing in Slovakia amount to 38 per cent of the total foreign population. 61 per cent of immigrants come from the EU 27 countries. The biggest donors among the non-EU countries are Ukraine, Serbia, Vietnam, Russia, China, Korea, the USA, Macedonia, Croatia and Norway, respectively with the highest proportion belonging to the 5 907 Ukrainian citizens. Third country nationals constitute 0.44 per cent of the total population in Slovakia (24 165 in 2009) (Statistical Office of the SR, 2010), while Norwegian statistics report that on 1st January 2010, 17 per cent of the total population had immigrant background (Statistics Norway, 2010).

Migration integration policies

Integration policies help us measure the ability of a country to welcome, host, and accommodate immigrants into society. These policies allow the newly arriving migrants to develop each aspect of their lives respectively, trying to avoid possible discrimination that might occur between host and immigrant populations. Migration integration policies measure e.g. labor market mobility, possibility of family reunion, study programs offered to immi-grants, exercise of the right to vote and form political parties, or be representatives in one or the other. These areas represent the long-term way to long-term residence permits, and eventual opening of society to admit and grant nationality and citizenship.

As mentioned earlier, through elaboration of these policies, one prevents recurring discrimination. As the OECD (2009) reports, future prospects for economic advances in OECD countries lie in active recruitment of international migrants thus surpassing the shortage of not enough newly-born, and addressing the heavy burden arising from large numbers of retirees. In times of economic crisis like the last one, the labor market in Slovakia was hit by increases in unemployment rates and decreases in employment offers for immigrants. In times of economic downturn, immigrants are prone to experience racism from the native born in any home country, but at the same time however, it has been shown they are keen on rotating and helping keep the market moving due to their great willingness for flexibility (Castles/Miller, 2009a). Labor market mobility as outlined below, represents one of the main components of government regulation objectives, particularly during financial cutbacks amid an economic downturn. The OECD (2009) states the following:

> Governments need to be vigilant, to ensure that deteriorating immigrant labor market outcomes do not mortgage the possibility of further migration when growth resumes. Integration programs need to be maintained, anti-discrimination measures reinforced and immigrants profit equally from active labor market policies for the unemployed (OECD, 2009).

According to the last publication of MIPEX III, Slovakia ranked 29th of 31 countries examined in this regard, while Norway ranked 7th on these overall scores. These scores included seven policy areas[29] having impact on immigration. Norway is joined by its neighboring countries near the top of the rankings, with Sweden being number one and Finland being fourth. Slovakia on the other hand, is on the very bottom followed only by Cyprus (30th) and Latvia (31st) (Huddleston et al.2011: 11). In brief, these key findings place Nordic countries among those that manage migration the best, while countries belonging to central and Eastern Europe have all scored below EU averages. This makes them either slightly unfavorable (Slovakia at number 21), opposite the highly favorable Norway scoring at 66.

---

29 Labor market mobility, family reunion, education, political participation, long-term residence, access to nationality and anti-discrimination.

Figure 3.1: Overall score for 2010 on the MIPEX rank

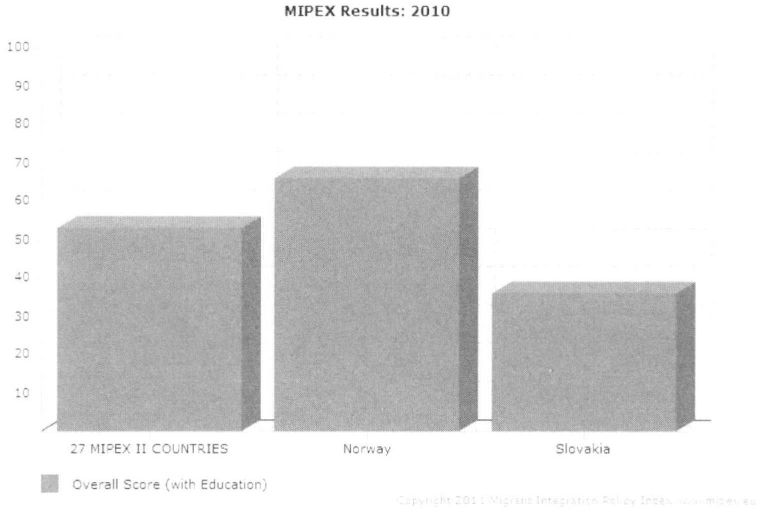

MIPEX Results: 2010

[Bar chart showing: 27 MIPEX II COUNTRIES ~50, Norway ~70, Slovakia ~35; Overall Score (with Education)]

Source: www.mipex.eu

Labor market mobility

Labor market mobility indicates the possibility of a migrant to live and work in a country and have the same opportunities as local populations in the labor market (Huddleston et al. 2011: 12). It implies that all migrants, once employed, are granted the same rights as working nationals of the host country, including recognition of qualifications acquired outside the European Union. This includes, as well the right to improvement of their skill levels by undergoing language and professional training provided by the new host country itself. At the same time, it presupposes the possibility for an immigrant to take active part in the public sector, and eligibility to work under the same conditions as local employees. With these achievements, such immigrants must be included in the social security system as well (Huddleston et al. 2011: 12).

According to the MIPEX III report, Slovakia scored worst of all selected countries, getting 21 points (out of 100), lagging behind even Bulgaria and Romania, who entered the EU after Slovakia. On the other hand, Norway earned 73 points scoring well above the EU average of 57, meaning its policies overall encourage non-EU families, long-term residents, and some migrant working people to improve their career skills (Huddleston et al.

2011:148). Thus the ratio of TCN employment for 2009 is 58.9%, from the total TCN population registered in Norway, with a total 76.4% national employment rate (Eurostat 2011).

At the same time and to the contrary, the migrant working force in Slovakia suffers from unfavorable migration policies and lack of coordination and regulation of the labor market. The process of recognition of qualification is not standardized and very complicated, usually allowing for vague reasons in issuing denials of recognition. This allows for further exclusion of several professions and full economic integration as well. In this respect, in both countries due to poorly developed qualification recognition mechanisms, the TCN are often subdued to accepting lower employment positions inadequate to their larger skill sets. The TCN are largely excluded from the public sector in Slovakia as well, while in Norway they still have opportunity for integration in this area, as well as the possibility of receiving public grants, training support, and larger study possibilities in order to improve their skills overall.

In a recent report the OECD (2010), discussing the issue of employment possibilities for immigrants, i.e. labor market integration in Norway, presented policy recommendations thus acknowledging the inadequacy of policy regulations currently existing. These recommendations emphasized the need to:

a) Enhance the effectiveness of language training and of the introduction program;
b) Make better use of migrant skill sets;
c) Establish official footholds in the labor market for migrant populations;
d) Give more official attention to children of these immigrants;
e) Improve the framework for anti-discrimination policies to be effective.

Figure 3.2: Labor market mobility in Norway and Slovakia for 2007 and 2010

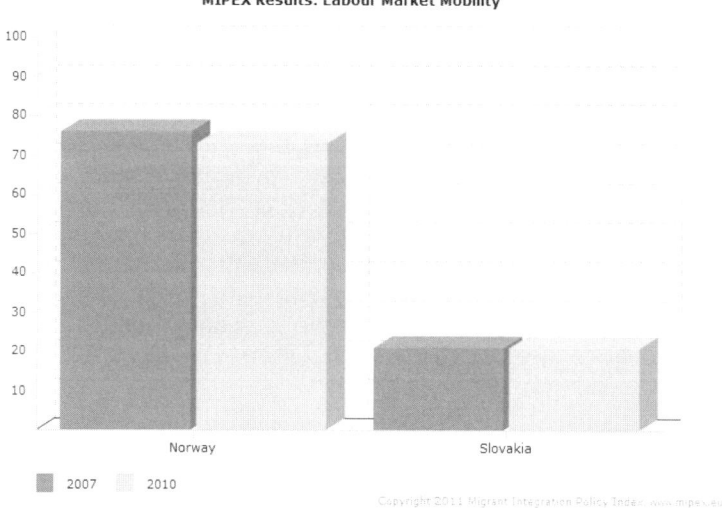

Source: www.mipex.eu

Family reunion

Now we turn to the powerful issue of family reunion, strongly affecting the ability of migrants to integrate into a new community. This means the newest arriving family members joining and supporting his/her earlier members in the host country. Countries with less stringent definitions of family and already established as immigration nations, do have more favorable approaches to the institution of family reunion overall. This is much better than those that have no such policies or initiatives. Very importantly, those who apply to have their families reunited with them, need to prove they have *stable and sufficient* income, which at times could be *more* than what nationals actually need to live on. This surprising reality could well be decribed as one of the most burdensome conditions imposed upon those family members sponsoring the reunion of their other family members still in their poorer home countries (Huddleston et al. 2011: 14).

In this regard, Norway and Slovakia stand close to each other in securing similar conditions for family reunion of third-country nationals in terms of eligibility, conditions for acquisition, and security of status. One major disparity, however, may be found in the area of rights associated with family reunion. Slovakia scores thirty three points on this, while Norway ninety-two. In both countries, the family is heavily dependent on the sponsor, while only in Slovakia, the reunited family does not have full rights to participate in society yet. As opposed to Slovakia, Norway manages to provide the reunited family with basic support and knowledge they will need to succeed in that nation. Overall, Slovakia discourages the autonomous status of the family, placing it in sole dependence of the sponsor, while Norway secures better conditions overall for them, and reserves the right for a certain degree of independence of the family from the sponsor as well.

Figure 3.3: Family reunion for third-country nationals in Norway and Slovakia for 2007 and 2010

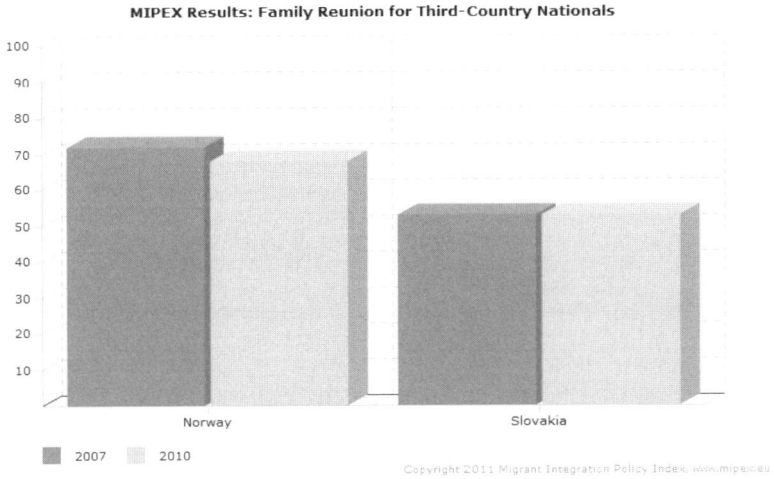

Source: www.mipex.eu

Education

In its report from MIPEX in 2010, education was included as a new strand in the integration process. This supports the possibility of each child to attend kindergarten and compulsory education, along with assessment at the professional level to which the child has been educated abroad. However, many of the European states show weakness in the level of overall execution regarding education integrative policy (Huddleston et al. 2011: 16). Apart from the normal and everyday obstacles national students meet during their school life, students of migrants and migrant students have to acquire a new language of communication, and try to integrate into the education system at the fullest level.

As a primary obstacle, which for some is impossible to overcome due to irregular use of the language, there is strong need for countries with significant numbers of migrants, as well as migrants coming from diverse backgrounds, to recognize the need for establishment of new opportunities for students. This includes diversification of the teaching staff as well as adoption of the curriculum. From another perspective, the country in question must manage to recognize the fact that the environment has turned into a multicultural space for the presentation of different languages and cultures. Therefore, every attempt should be made to organize courses for the migrants so they stay in touch with their cultures and languages as well as prepare and educate the national population in general regarding manners and character traits of the immigrant population.

In Europe, the areas of integration on the MIPEX III scale showed least success among certain countries. It is to be noted that Norway, along with its neighbor countries are again rated among the first five, winning sixty-three points, while Slovakia scored twenty-four, again falling behind most others. Thus, this big gap among these two nations can be observed in Figure 3.4. According to the New Act, as stated previously, unaccompanied minors over sixteen have reduced access to secondary and higher education. This is in opposition of proposed amendments in 2007 on education, which called for 'Equal education in practice'. On the other hand, Norwegian society indicates it is aware of the target group issues. It has successfully met many of their needs by offering them lectures in Norwegian language at all school levels while allowing migrants to develop their mother tongue as well.

Slovakia, on the other hand, by slowly acknowledging the presence of migrant populations on its territory, has managed to move backwards instead of forwards in targeting the needs of migrant groups as pupils and students. This consequently creates less and less new opportunities in development. Unlike the Slovak stagnation process regarding education, the Norwegian system has even established a national body of multicultural education (NAFO), which calls for diverse and well-trained teachers overall. Both countries though, have shown significant development in the sphere of intercultural education. As mentioned earlier in the case of Norway, with the development of NAFO, amid indications it may even include undocumented migrants into its education system, in Slovakia, the government does plan to introduce intercultural education priorities, which will teach all students how to better live in a diverse society (Huddleston et al. 2011:149).

Nevertheless, such discussions overall remain ineffective since the reality is that Slovakia offers support for Slovak language courses only to those in the asylum system. Other migrants however, are forced to pay for themselves an entire course costing 3750 Euros if the migrant is interested in proceeding to one of the Slovak universities, and 3650 Euros if the migrant needs proof of obtaining Slovak language skills for the purpose of receiving a residence permit. Furthermore, there is only one institution in the country authorized to issue this diploma, the Comenius University – the oldest and largest university in Slovakia.

Figure 3.4: Education

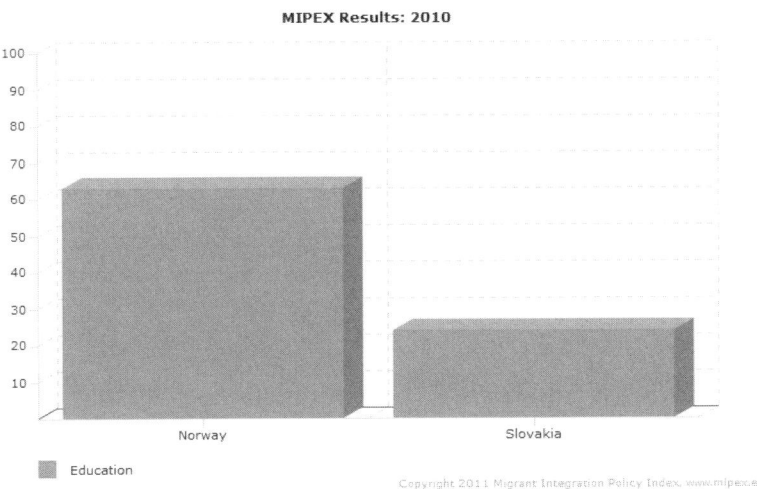

Source: www.mipex.eu

Political participation

Ultimately, when a nation grants political and civil rights to immigrants, this is a sign the country has accepted immigration issues overall with poise and maturity. For most countries in Europe though, this does not come until the migrant is granted national citizenship with which s/he becomes a full member of society, thus exercising full political, economic, and civil rights.

Regarding full political participation in any nation, we understand that possibilities exist for immigrants to take part in the policy creation process, whether on national, regional, or local levels. MIPEX indicates that immigrant political opportunities are not improving significantly overall, but that changes in trends are a reaction to implementation of EU law, as well as Council of Europe Convention directives, n. 144. Also, though not solely as a reaction to the aforementioned, but because the issue of voting rights might be hard to obtain as well, they are even harder to revoke. This means countries that have already started this process are left with having to continue developing this overall policy sphere, regarding migrant political participation and access.

Even though both countries in this study are relatively new countries for the serious study of immigration, they do in fact manifest the highest degree of divergence regarding indicators of political participation for immigrants overall. Norway on the one hand, scores first among thirty-one countries[30] with maximum scoring in granting electoral rights and political liberties to immigrants, allowing them to organize and improve policies by supporting them in formation of consultative deliberative bodies and implementation of those policies agreed upon. This is so in particular through the National Contact Committee for Immigrants and the Authorities (KIM). The structure of KIM includes immigrants nominated regionally, and is lead by experienced leaders as respective chairpersons for that body. Since 1984, the law requires migrant groups to propose their own issue priorities and to act upon specific requests for consultation, as well as facilitate dialogue on matters affecting immigrants with government, researchers, political parties, and other stakeholders.[31] On the local level, cities like Oslo and Drammen, that are strongly affected by immigration, have formed independent consultative bodies to consult with immigrants directly (Huddleston et al. 2011: 150).

When assessing Slovakia on the other hand, it is ranked twenty-sixth among the thirty-one nations studied, making it one of the worst performing countries in granting and appreciating immigrant civic political participation. It has only managed thus far to partially grant electoral rights to those immigrants with permanent residence, which places it only about halfway in terms of what Norway has achieved regarding this important issue. In Slovakia as well, there are neither consultative nor implementation policies that offer to discuss and facilitate dialogue between authorities and immigrants on these issues. Immigrants in Slovakia also cannot be members of political parties, and are not licensed to broadcast TV/radio programs, and are neither consulted to share their experiences for purposes of achieving comprehensive and thorough integration policy (Huddleston et al. 2011: 173). Thus, the European Integration Fund remains the only tool by which ministries involved can take certain steps in creation of a concept, policy, or directive favorable to the migrant community.

---

30   EU 27, Norway, Switzerland, Canada and the USA.
31   More information on KIM could be found on www.kim.no.

Figure 3.5: Political participation among immigrants in Norway and Slovakia for 2007 and 2010

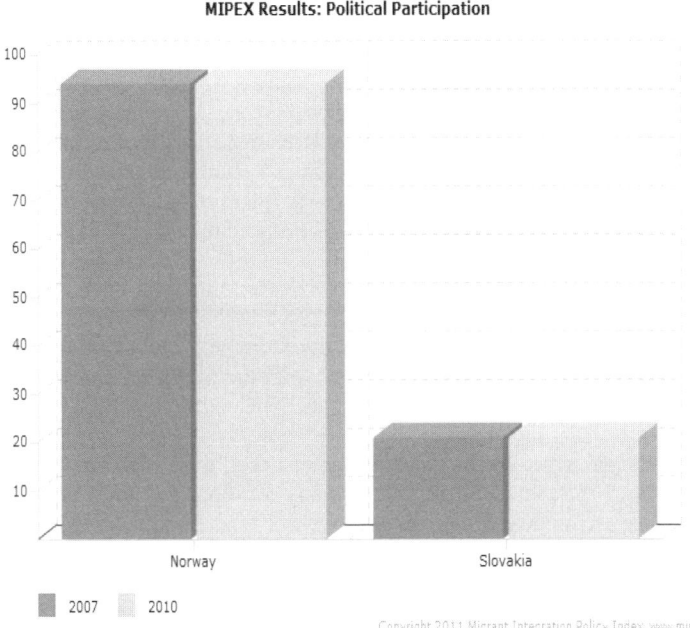

Source: www.mipex.eu

Long-term residence

Under long-term residence rulings, it is understood there must exist a possibility for an immigrant to work, study, retire, and live just like the larger national community. According to the EU, the member states must recognize long-term resident status after five years of continuous legal residence. Absences from the member state for periods of less then six consecutive months (and not exceeding ten months in total within the five-year period), or specific reasons provided for by national law (e.g. military service, secondment for work purposes, serious illness, maternity, research or studies) will be regarded as not interrupting the period of residence (Directive 2003/109/EC). Slovakia, as a member state of the EU, is bound by this Directive and in its

Law on foreigners, includes the process of granting two types of residence permits, the first being temporary and the second one, permanent.

Permanent residence is issued in different circumstances, but the regulation of five years of continuous legal residence is not explicit for all such immigrants in applying for permanent residence overall. On the other hand, they are eligible for gaining equal access to employment and social benefits. Also, having a temporary permit issued consecutively for more then five years is not grounds on which one could apply for permanent residence. Furthermore, all visits to the foreign police remain difficult for immigrants, as applicants are never fully prepared to answer all questions asked as well as deal with conditions established for moving forward in the larger process. These difficulties make the situation of immigrants more volatile then in most other European countries.

Norway, on the other hand, manifests not so much an easy process regarding procedures overall, but instead a more favorable route for those immigrants already having long-term residence, moving quickly into full participation in Norwegian society. In this setting, the preservation of the status quo is not under the discretion of authorities, but instead a part of the regulations set forth in the Immigration act.

At the same time, security considerations regarding acquisition of long-term residence status is achieved in many European countries with implementation of language courses and testing (CZ, DE, DK, UK, FR and NE). This establishes required regulations and, at the same time, improves the integrated environment overall and standardized conditions. These tests and language courses have been successfully implemented in the Czech Republic, which could be a better example for Slovakia as well, requiring slight but not severe change in future Slovak direction. This includes Norway's language courses being implemented as a form of the Introduction Act, which regulates Norwegian language training for newly arrived immigrants from 2005.

The Introduction Act is designated for such persons who need to obtain basic qualifications in general. In the case of Norway, the introduction program aims to 1) provide basic Norwegian language skills; 2) provide basic insight into Norwegian social conditions; and 3) prepare such persons for participation in working life. Investment into various provisions such as the Introduction Act, would definitely allow migrants in Slovakia to feel more secure regarding the keeping of their long-term (permanent) residence status, without fear they would lose these under suspicious circumstances.

Figure 3.6: Long-term residence in Norway and Slovakia for 2007 and 2010

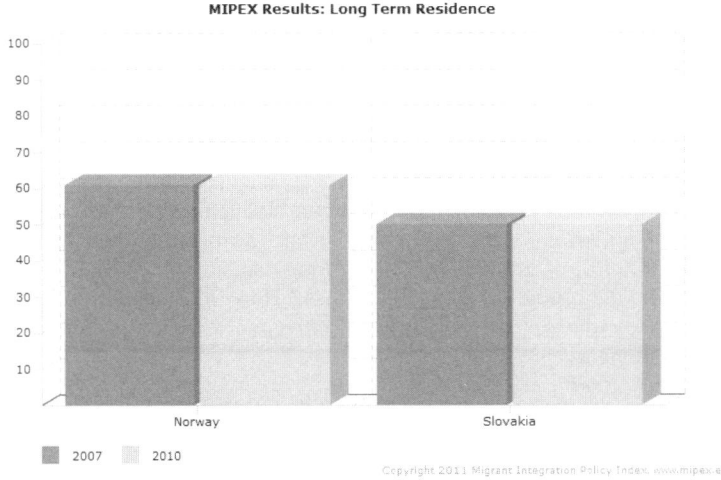

Source: www.mipex.eu

Access to nationality

As the standards of MIPEX imply, the "best case" of access to nationality would mean that all settled residents willing to stay in a country, get full governmental support to become citizens, thus able to equally participate in public life. Ideally, citizens should be allowed to carry a dual nationality, with the *jus soli* principle being applied. Requirements to pass language tests or undergo professional courses should be highly standardized and not excessively complicated.

Norway occupies fifteenth position on the MIPEX Access to Nationality scale, with forty-one points total, while Slovakia stands significantly lower with twenty-seven total points. Both countries have mediocre rankings among MIPEX-selected countries in terms of eligibility for nationality, while Norway offers better conditions for acquisition of citizenship as well as enhanced security of status. Obtaining either a Norwegian or Slovak passport is a challenging task for even well-settled TCNs; however, unlike Slovakia and the vast majority of EU countries, Norway offers a broader range of political opportunities for the foreign-born. Also, Norway encourages integrating migrants more than Slovakia does, with an official introduction program and qualifying period for minor crimes.

In Slovakia, the Citizenship Act amended in 2007, transformed the country's immigration policy into one of the strictest in Europe. The longer wait and subjective conditions introduced by the Interior ministry on the brink of the country's accession to the Schengen Area in 2008 were aimed at curbing "the growing danger of organized crime and international terrorism". In reality however, it was intended to put more obstacles into the path of integration in general (MIPEX, 2011). Currently, immigration procedures are unnecessarily complicated, and application fees disproportionally high for those of Central Europe, and standards (e.g., for the Slovak language test) remain largely unspecified. Security issues regarding citizenship status also raise concerns as to whether in certain cases (e.g. fraud or crime) migrants may be deemed never naturalized, without regard to how long they have been Slovak citizens or whether they might become stateless. However, according to 2010 amendments to the Act itself, naturalized citizens were allowed to retain their original nationality.

Figure 3.7: Access to nationality in Norway and Slovakia for 2007 and 2010

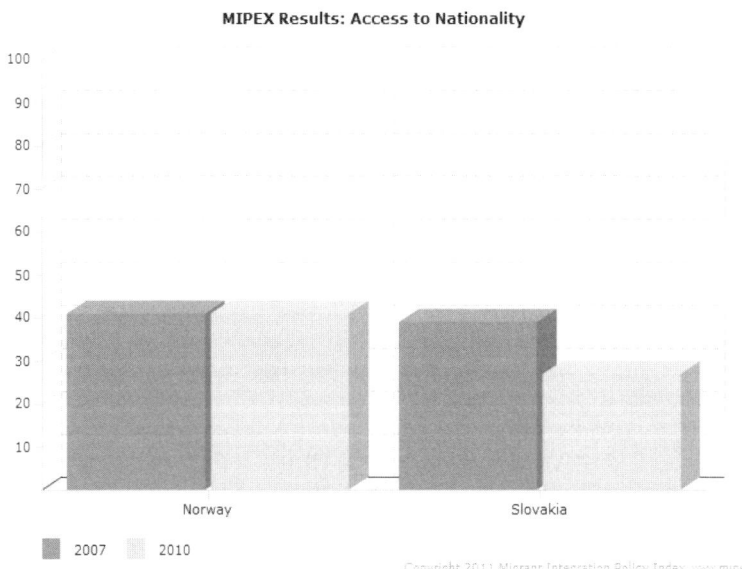

Source: www.mipex.eu

Anti-discrimination

The issue of anti-discrimination criteria rests upon the notion that in a well-performing country all residents, whatever their background and nationality, can fight discrimination and benefit from equal opportunities. Any sort of discrimination, from racial profiling to incitements to hatred, are outlawed in all areas of public life, while victims are well-informed and empowered to seek justice. The role of the state is to introduce actions and duties aimed to encourage openness of its institutions, and to facilitate effective information, communication, and ethical and successful passing of legislative, laws carefully reflecting the full realities of that state.

According to MIPEX estimations, anti-discrimination is the only category under which Norway and Slovakia share sixteenth place with fifty-nine (59) points out of a hundred, including a "halfway favorable" ranking. Both countries are praised for their anti-discrimination concepts as well as for clearly defined methods regarding the application process. Slovakia is slightly more persistent in elaborating anti-discrimination enforcement mechanisms, while Norway's equality policies are considered to be more effective.

Slovakia, within the last several years, improved its score across all related dimensions required by introducing legal protection for victims and setting up an independent Center for Human Rights. New discrimination definitions and broader access to justice, significantly improved Slovak integration policy. The 2008 amendments regarding anti-discrimination and advertised *actio popularis,* have allowed for effective protection of victims' rights as well. However, a set of issues, including equal treatment of national minorities and TCNs, remain acute, needing serious attention, much like in neighboring Central European states.

Norway, in its turn, steadily maintains a positive image of a nation fighting discrimination, by outlawing nationality inequities and strengthening its enforcement mechanisms, including greater sanctions and legal aid. Overall, MIPEX sees Norwegian government commitments to equality as among the strongest in Europe and North America, pointing out, however, that

> the Equality and Discrimination Ombudsman has slightly favorable powers to help victims, except representing them in court (MIPEX, 2011).

Figure 3.8: Anti-discrimination law in Norway and Slovakia for 2007 and 2010

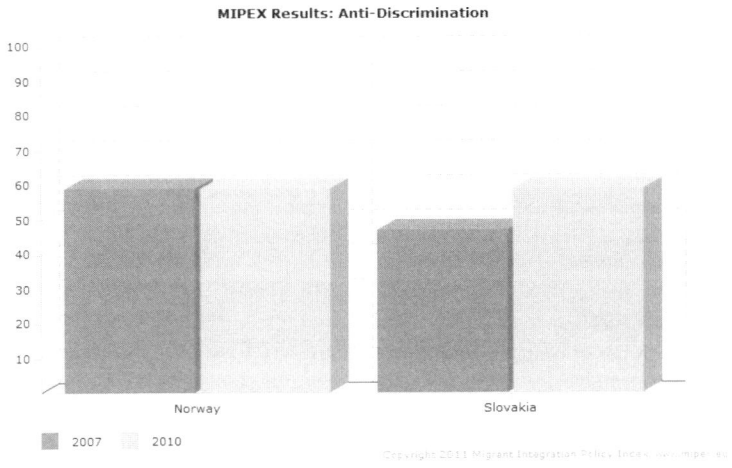

Source: www.mipex.eu

Conclusion

Finally, in each policy area investigated, Norway has indicated higher levels of readiness to manage such issues, thus affording better integration opportunities to immigrants. Slovakia, in the meantime, has managed to stay at the bottom of most testing on such policies, apart from anti-discrimination policy. Surprisingly, it actually has equality with Norway's performance overall on such issues, which could be because of its implementation of the 2008 amended anti-discrimination law, as elaborated previously. At the same time, owing to membership in the European Union, Slovakia has tried to follow European trends on regulating migration (e.g. trends concerning a more liberal approach towards family reunion for third-country nationals). However, apart from the anti-discrimination laws, the Slovak Republic currently lacks organization and teamwork needed to conduct the amount of work related to international migration. Norway, on the other hand, by becoming part of the Schengen agreement has approached European Union realities to such an extent, its regulation of migration trends already certainly draws upon the overall European Union experience.

Figure 3.9: Overall comparison between Norway and Slovakia for 2010

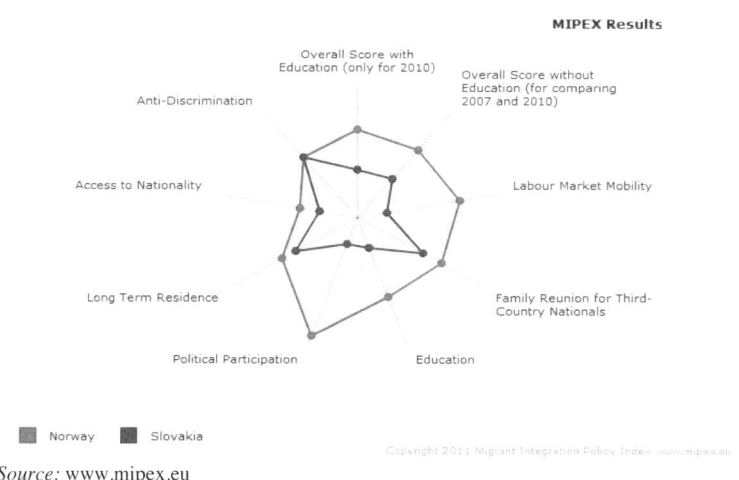

Source: www.mipex.eu

Crucially, as can be observed in Figure 3.9, overall Norwegian scoring is higher, while Slovakia scores in the mid-range or below. The most obvious difference between Norway and Slovakia concerns participation of immigrants in the decision-making processes: while Norway offers a great deal of freedom, Slovakia excludes immigrants from the processes per se.

Norway, just like Slovakia, turned from being a country of emigration to a nation of immigration. Both countries have relatively small percentages of foreign born population or immigrants, but the amount suffices to induce talks on integration opportunities for immigrants. Citizenship acquisition, however, considered to be the ultimate form of integration into all areas of society in both countries, remains a difficult act to follow. Access to their potentially new nationality for the immigrant, remains a common point of difficulty for immigrants, whether in Norway or Slovakia, and is one of the reasons the immigrant population remains vulnerable to vague and heavy regulation regarding citizenship acquisition.

Unlike Norwegian responses and adaptation of their policies regulating the status and well-being of arriving immigrants, Slovak political representatives do not seem to be prepared to invest in realization and creation of a comprehensive migration policy. If they did, this would encompass not only legal status regulations but also emphasize in clear-cut and appropriate measures, what an immigrant needs to undertake upon arrival in the Slovak nation.

In the absence of political will and overt communication concerning issues regarding migration most Slovak policies remain deliberately vague[32].

References

Barnovský, Michal/ Cambel, Samuel/ Čierny, J/ Kamenec, Ivan/ Ďastný, Jiri/ Vrablic, Emil (1988): *Dejiny Slovenska VI.* Bratislava: Veda.
Bašovský, Oliver/ Divinský, Boris, (1991): The development of modern urbanisation in Slovakia and its present problems. In: *Revue Belge de Géographie*, 115, #1-2-3, pp. 265-277.
Castles, Stephen/ Miller, Mark J. (2009): *The Age of Migration: International Population Movements in the Modern World*, 4th ed., New York: Palgrave Macmillan
Castles, Stephen/ Miller, Mark J. (2009a): *The Age of Migration: Migration and the Global Financial Crisis* – A Virtual Symposium Available at: http://www.age-of-migration.com/uk/financialcrisis/update1.html
Cooper, Betsy (2005): Norway: Migrant Quality, Not Quantity. Migration Policy Institute. Available at:
http://www.migrationinformation.org/Feature/display.cfm?ID=307
Čulík, Jan (2008):Den, kdy tanky zlikvidovaly české sny Pražského jara. *Britské Listy*.
http://www.britskelisty.cz/9808/19980821h.html (2008-23-01)
Directive (2003): Council Directive 2003/109/EC concerning the status of third-country nationals who are long-term residents. *Official journal of the European Union*
http://eurlex.europa.eu/LexUriServ/LexUriServ.do?uri=OJ:L:2004:016:0 044:0053:en:pdf
Divinský, Boris (2004): An Acceleration of Challenges for Society Volume V – Slovakia International Organization for Migration
Divinský, Boris (2004a): Zahraničná migrácia Slovensko 2004 *Súhrnná správa o stave spoločnosti rozšírená a prepracovaná verzia*
Eurostat (2011): Eurostat statistics.
http://epp.eurostat.ec.europa.eu/portal/page/portal/statistics/search_datab ase

---

[32] As reported by an official representative of the Ministry of Labor and Social Affairs of the Slovak Republic in April 2011.

Gajdoš, Marián. Ed. (2002): Čo dala – vzala našim rodákom optácia, Zborník z medzinárodnej ved. konferencie k 55. výročiu optácie a presídlenia, SvÚ SAV et Koordinačný výbor reoptantov, Košice et Prešov.

Huddleston, Thomas/ Niessen, Jan/ Chaomh, Eadaoin Ni/ White, Emilie (2011): Migrant Integration Policy Index III Brussels: British Council and Migration Policy Group

Imsen, Steinar (1991): *Våre dronninger*. Oslo: Grøndahl og Dreyer

Kjeldstadli, Knut (2003): *Norsk innvandringshistorie*. Oslo: Pax ISBN 82-530-2541-6

Massey, Douglas/ Arango, Joaquin/ Graeme Hugo/ Kouaouci, Ali/ Pellegrino, Adela/ Taylor, J. Edward (1998): *Worlds in Motion: Understanding International Migration at the End of the Millennium*.Oxford: Oxford University Press.

Ministry of Justice and the police (1988): Act concerning the entry of foreign nationals into the Kingdom of Norway and their presence in the realm (Immigration Act): http://www.ub.uio.no/ujur/ulovdata/lov-19880624-064-eng.pdf

MIPEX (2011): Maps and Figures. http://www.mipex.eu/play/map.php?countries=&objects=&periods=&group_by=

OECD (2009): International migration outlook: SOPEMI 2009 Paris: OECD

OECD SOPEMI (2010): International migration outlook: SOPEMI 2010 Paris: OECD

Scheib, Ariel (2011): *The Virtual Jewish History Tour: Slovakia Jewish Virtual Library*: A Division of the American-Israeli Cooperative Enterprise http://www.jewishvirtuallibrary.org/jsource/vjw/slovakia.html

Statistics Norway (2010): *Focus on immigration: Immigrants and Immigration*. Oslo: Statistics Norway

Statistical Office of the SR (2010): Zahraničná migrácia Bratislava: Štatistický úrad SR

Tibenský, Ján/ Bárta, Juraj/ Točík, Anton/ Paulík, Jozef/ Beňadik, Blažej/ Kolník, Títus/ Dekan, Ján/ Chropovský, Bohuš/ Marsina, Richard/ Mésároš, Július/ Michalec Ján (1978) *Slovensko – Dejiny*. Bratislava: Obzor.

UNDP (2010) Human Development Report http://hdr.undp.org/en/statistics/

Vaňo, Boris Ed. (2001): *Obyvateľstvo Slovenska 1945-2000*. Bratislava: INFOSTAT

Venner, K. Dwight (2009): Small States Face Big Challenges. *Development Outreach*, Dec. 09, pp. 25-28. World Bank Institute. http://wbi.worldbank.org/wbi/devoutreach/article/261/small-states-respond-global-economic-crisis

Zolberg, Aristide in Douglas Messey/ Joaquin, Arango/Graeme, Hugo/ Kouaouci, Ali/ Pellegrino, Adella/ Taylor, J. Edward (1998): *Worlds in Motion: Understanding International Migration at the End of the Millennium*. Oxford: Oxford University Press.

Chapter 4
Economic Crisis Management: national vs. supranational responses in Slovakia

Andrej Wertlen

Introduction

This chapter aims to highlight the constraints and opportunities of economic governance for small states during turbulent times[33]. In terms of economic governance, there are times when small states can execute effective economic policies, and some cases when they are sidelined as simple "implementers" of supra-national or international decisions. Economic openness, an advantage of small states in normal times, becomes a vulnerability in turbulent times.

One of the issues that needs to be addressed is the overall margin of national decision-making. Since small states are almost always members of international and supra-national organisations, the obligations and limitations stemming from their membership limit the overall margin for national decisions. However, there are always ways to make the best of this limited margin, depending on the activity of national governments.

In turbulent times, much attention is paid to the concept of competitiveness, with competitive policies of small states required to pass two tests. First, they must be structural and second, they must be feasible from the perspective of interdependence. This chapter focuses on the example of Slovakia and draws from experience during the current economic downturn (2008-11), but looks beyond it as well. It specifically addresses long-term competitiveness that is often missing from expert and public debates.

The stages and effects of the Global Crisis

In order to understand the crisis measures described later in this chapter, this section briefly presents the evolution of the crisis, the mechanisms of contagion, and impact on the economy of small states.

---

33 I would like to thank Dr. Helmut Krämer-Eis from the European Investment Fund for his valuable remarks that helped me improve the quality of this chapter.

Stage 1: financial crisis

In a globalized financial world, there are factors that increase the vulnerability of a single country's financial system, understood as the notion of systemic risk. Aglietta defines systemic risk as:

> the eventuality that certain situations might occur in which the decisions of actors, vis-a-vis the risks they face, instead of creating a better repartition of risks, increase the level of general insecurity. (Aglietta 1991).

This means the decisions of individual actors can undermine the general stability of the global financial system that is now intertwined across institutional and national borders. A financial crisis can hit a country through three main channels: exposure to equity markets, exposure of the banking system, currency exposure and exposure to foreign exchange loans.

Exposure to equity markets
In the case of an equity markets collapse, investors lose money: if the investors are banks this limits their lending ability and thus causes credit contraction; if the investors are households – they lose their savings and will consume less in the future. However, a collapse of asset prices in capital markets does not infringe losses solely upon investors, because in reality the whole of the economy is concerned.

A bank's health depends on the value of asset prices – if their value decreases the quality of the bank's balance sheets deteriorates (the assets become inferior to liabilities and the bank's own capital gets consumed by the losses). As a result, banks aim to improve their balance sheets by restricting lending and thereby ease pressure on their own capital. The reduced lending can lead to a credit crunch, which happened after the collapse of Lehman Brothers, due to the illiquidity of interbank markets (the source of refinancing for banks) following a confidence crisis in the banking sector.

In Slovakia, exposure to equity markets is low, as the financial system is dominated by retail banks, representing almost 90 per cent of total financing of retail sector assets. This places a greater burden of responsibility for stable financing of the economy on the country's banks (National Bank of Slovakia. 2010).

Exposure of the banking system
If a country's banking sector relies on the financial markets for their refinancing operations, a collapse of equity markets affects directly that country's banking system as well. In Slovakia, the banking sector has a conservative attitude, which means it focuses mostly on domestic lending and is financed mainly by domestic deposits. The loan-to-deposit ratio in Slovakia has been low, and thus its banking system was not directly hit by the financial crisis as

hard. On the other hand, more than 90per cent of banking sector assets in Slovakia are foreign owned (Wertlen 2010).

This increases cross-border systemic risk and may compromise the liquidity position and functioning of Slovak banks in case of trouble with foreign parent banks. This is because the group's prudential and other policies are determined on the parent banking level. It is worth noting the most important business and source of income for Slovak banks is interest income from retail loans. The bulk of the loans are residential mortgage loans to households, which are relevant to understanding the house pricing bubble described in part two.

Currency exposure and exposure to foreign exchange loans
During a financial crisis, a country's currency can come under attack from speculators who bet on the fall of the currency, but there can also be other forms of attack as well. The country can respond using its reserves, but these can be depleted and the country may be forced to carry out devaluation. During the current economic downturn, the countries of Central Europe have been subject of a confidence crisis with considerable pressures against their currencies, resulting for example in the Czech Republic's currency being hit hard in 2009 (Wertlen 2010).

Another form of exposure is denomination of loans in foreign currencies. The idea is to take on a loan in a strong currency because these have lower interest rates. The problem is when the domestic currency loses value. For example in Hungary, borrowers were offered mortgage loans in foreign currencies (mostly the Swiss Frank), and since as a result of the crisis t heir currencies lost value their debt has grown immensely. Slovakia was shielded from this problem, since only a negligible proportion of household and business loans were denominated in foreign currency (less than 1per cent for households and less than two per cent for businesses) (National Bank of Slovakia 2010).

Since 2009, Slovakia is part of the Eurozone and thus Slovakia's monetary situation depends on the policies of the European Central Bank. Being part of a monetary union has both its pros and cons. The greatest advantage of the Euro for Slovakia is elimination of transaction costs and foreign exchange risk, which should further stimulate integration with the Common Market. The Euro as the world's number two currency, is less volatile and should protect the country from short-term fluctuations. The value of the Euro has not yet been seriously affected by the overall debt crisis of some of its members. The disadvantages of the Euro stem from the fact the Eurozone is not an economically homogeneous area, nor an optimal currency area according to economic theory. Thus, interest rates and value of the Euro, which are decided externally, may not be optimally set for the needs of the Slovak economy.

On the national level, measures to mitigate the impact of the financial crisis on Slovakia can be undertaken, but final regulatory solutions must be found at the EU and ultimately at the global level.

Stage 2: economic crisis

In present day economies, the real economy non-financial corporations as opposed to banks and financial institution, depends on financing by the banking system and/or capital markets. If this financing is cut, either by credit crunch in the case of banks or market illiquidity for capital markets, corporations face financial problems compromising their solvency and future production. Corporations as a result decrease investment and anticipate lower future demand, which triggers lay-offs of the workforce leading to unemployment. This in turn lowers income and thus consumption of households, and in the end the whole economy faces problems. In the globalized economy, even countries with sound financial systems suffer from economic crises when their partner export-destination economies suffer, thus lowering their imports (Wertlen 2010).

The present crisis has brought forward a weakness of small states previously thought to be an advantage- their high degree of economic openness. Such openness is observable through high levels of exports and imports, high cross-border capital flows, and foreign direct investment. For small states this often implies that economic performance depends more on performance of their export sector than on internal demand. They thus indirectly rely on performance of their export-destination economies. While exporting may be very profitable in good times, an export-dependent country will face an economic downturn in bad times. It also has limited political tools to influence the situation, since the demand for its goods depends on the economic situation in other countries. Slovakia, mostly untouched by the financial crisis, has been hit by the economic crisis due to the fall in external demand (Artus, Betbèze, Boissieu, Capelle-Blancard, 2010).

In an export-oriented economy like Slovakia's, the cause of the economic crisis stems from the slump in external demand, and there is little the national government can do in such situations. The government's role should be to minimize short-term effects of the crisis on both the population and business. The long-term solution is the enhancement of domestic demand and diversification of industry and trade partners, as well as development of small and medium enterprises, the SME sector, due to its local base, innovation, and employment potential.

Stage 3: the sovereign debt crisis

The latest stage of the global crisis is related to the problem of sovereign debt. The origins of the situation stem from the fact that governments nowadays spend more than they generate in tax and social security income. The crisis has exacerbated the situation, mainly through astronomical spending on banking bail-outs such as in Ireland, and fall in overall tax revenue. To cover the deficit, governments finance themselves through bond issues in international financial markets. The problem starts when this credit line becomes either too expensive or frozen. This happens when investors fear the country may default on its debt, which is currently the case of Greece. Slovakia, fortunately, is not in imminent danger of default, but general government debt levels have risen as a result of the crisis from 29,6 per cent of GDP in 2007, to 43 per cent of GDP in 2010 (National Bank of Slovakia 2011).

Slovakia's experience with the present crisis has highlighted yet another danger of highly open economies, which is insufficient diversification. As with an investment portfolio, a country's vulnerability to external demand collapse is lowered by sufficient cross-industry diversification. During the crisis the Slovak export sector suffered from a decrease in foreign demand. That lead to a decrease in government revenue, which, accompanied by increased government spending necessary during a crisis, lead to an increase in the overall level of indebtedness. The solution for government finances lies in finding the right balance between fiscal discipline, and spending. Slovak governments will need to find structural solutions to the social and health security system, and address issues regarding insufficient government income from taxation as well insufficient diversification of the economy.

Limited scope of action for national governments

A shift of regulation from national to European levels is resulting from the crisis as the European Commission (EC) proposed the following set of measures in order to ensure future financial stability:

Establishment of new regulatory institutions

The most important institutional change was the establishment of the European Financial Regulation Framework that came into force in January 2011. It consists of the European Systemic Risk Board (ESRB) and three European Supervisory Authorities (ESAs) for the financial services sector: the European Banking Authority (EBA) based in London; the European Insurance and Occupational Pensions Authority (EIOPA) based in Frankfurt, and a European Securities and Markets Authority (ESMA) based in Paris. The EC describes the framework as a *"control tower"* (ERSB) and *"radar screens"* (ESAs), to detect risks which can accumulate across the financial system (Europa Press Release 2010).

Elaboration of new legislation

Banking regulation – A set of measures named Basel III has been developed by the Basel Committee on Banking Supervision, and will be transposed into EU law by the Capital Requirements Directive IV. The most substantial elements are the increase in regulatory Tier-1 capital from two per cent to seven per cent and a countercyclical buffer. Its full implementation is planned to be effective by December 2019 (McNelis 2010).

Insurance regulation – The EC elaborated the Solvency II Directive based on three pillars like Basel II, introducing measures such as risk-weighting (setting aside capital according to the riskiness of a financial asset), public disclosure of information, and possibility of the regulator to withdraw authorization. It should come into effect in January 2013 (European Commission 2011).

Alternative investments regulation – The EC placed the previously unregulated hedge funds and private equity funds under regulation of the Alternative Investment Fund Managers Directive AIFMD). Its transposition into national law of EU member states is scheduled for 2013 (Europa Press Release 2011).

Establishment of the European Stability Mechanisms

In the wake of the sovereign crises in the Eurozone, in May 2010, Eurozone member states decided to create a temporary mechanism called the European Financial Stability Facility, that could provide financial assistance to member states having difficulties raising funds via the international bond markets. The mechanism operates by issuing debt instruments that are highly rated and thus cheaper because of the Eurozone member guarantees of up to 440 billion Euros (European Financial Stability Facility 2011). In March 2011, the Eurozone member states decided that a permanent mechanism – The European Stability Mechanism will replace the EFSF in 2013. The capital structure of the ESM will total 700 billion Euros that will enable up to 500 billion Euros of total loans. An important feature of the mechanism is *"private sector involvement"*, consistent with IMF practice, which implies a possibility of direct losses for private bondholders in case of debt restructuring (European Council 2011).

The limitations on national responses to the crisis

The membership of small states in international or supranational organizations always comes at the expense of limited sovereignty. Slovakia, as a member of the Eurozone, has a legally limited margin for economic policy management. Most importantly, it has to respect the Pact on Growth and Stability criteria (Maastricht criteria) on budget deficit and government debt. The two greatest limitations for Slovakia are the loss of exchange rate flexibility and fiscal limitations, as devaluation and debt inflation are not possible under ECB rules. The three per cent budget deficit is a political criterion, with the exact level not determined by economic fundamentals. Cutting government spending can become a problem in times when falling government revenues coexist with the necessity for excessive spending, for example during a crisis along with a cap on the budget deficit. This may lead to a deflationary spiral as Paul Krugman often warns (Krugman 2009).

On the other hand, membership of small states in international organizations can also be a source of additional funding. For Slovakia, the most important sources of external funding are the EU structural funds. Unfortunately, Slovakia has a very poor record on EU funds exploitation out of the total allocation of 14,4 billion Euros for the 2007-2013 period, only 3,9 billion Euros (27 per cent) have been contracted and merely 0,7 billion Euros have been paid down. In Central and Eastern Europe (CEE) the ratio of contracted funds varies from 44per cent in Estonia to 16per cent in Romania, but Slovakia's absorption ratio is 3rd worst after Bulgaria and Romania (KPMG 2010).

EU funds exploitation is subject to two factors:

1/ the efficiency of administration (since the funds are allocated for a limited time period);

2/ the ability to raise one's own funds (since projects are never 100 per cent EU financed).

However, EU funds are not the only means of supranational funding for Slovakia. During the crisis, the European Investment Bank (EIB) played an important role by substantially increasing its lending. The EIB's role is to provide long-term financing in support of investment projects in line with EU objectives. Since cohesion is one of the EU's top objectives, Slovakia is most eligible for EIB funding. This requires a pro-active approach from both the public and private sphere, which is currently not always the case.

Why is it advantageous to borrow from the EIB?

The EIB can borrow cheaply in international markets thanks to its triple A credit rating and strong support from shareholders – the 27 EU member states. As it is not profit-driven, the EIB offers loans at unrivalled interest rates. Moreover, EIB loans can be used to complement EU structural funds, as EU funds do not fully cover costs of a project, meaning the EIB can finance up to 50per cent of a project. The problem with EIB loans is that despite being advantageous and cheap, they do count as government deficit under ESA-95 rules governing the Eurozone Convergence and Stability Pact (Eurostat 2010). However, there exists a solution for this problem as in some cases EIB loans that are part of Public Private Partnerships (PPP), are not counted as government debt. (See Annex no. 2) (EIB, European PPP Expertise Centre 2011). Moreover, there exists the potential of attracting private investors into financing long-term investment projects, such as infrastructure. At the moment the EC and EIB are working on infrastructure *"Europe 2020 project bonds"*, that aims to attract private investors (European Commission 2011).

What is the margin for national action?

Taking into account the effects of the crisis, in general there are three issues to tackle:

1/ Better regulation of the global financial system – cannot be done on a national scale;

2/ Mitigating the effects of economic crisis upon a country – must be done on the national scale;

3/ Finding harmony between saving and spending and operating within supra-national and international constraints – can be done on a national scale within supranational limits.

Taking into account the described limitations, the national responses of small states may concentrate on the following three areas of action:

1/ Government spending within externally set constraints;

2/ Non-financial reforms (improving the business and legal environment, eliminating corruption);

3/ Enhancing competitiveness (promoting SMEs, innovation and improving education).

Long-term challenges for Slovakia

The crisis hit Slovakia in the second half of 2009 prompting the Fico government to respond by proposing a set of measures to mitigate its impact. After change of government in June 2010, the newly installed Radicova government proposed its own measures labelled *"Short-term structural measures*". (The different approaches of political parties to the crisis in Slovakia are described further in chapter 5).

For Slovakia however, the turbulent times did not end by reprise of the GDP growth in 2010 (in 2009 the GDP plummeted -4.8 per cent against a rise of 4 per cent in 2010) (National Bank of Slovakia 2011). Slovakia suffers from income and regional disparities, a narrow economic base, and underdeveloped infrastructure. There exists a consensus on the challenges Slovakia is facing. For example, the international rating agency Moody's perceives three challenges for Slovakia: ensuring fiscal stability without hampering the economic recovery; a competitiveness challenge due to export concentration; labour market rigidities, and finally an ageing population. (Moody's 2011). Another rating agency, Standard & Poors (S&P), outlines two threats to long-term economic growth: an economy heavily dependent on cyclical sectors, which was proved during the crisis, and high structural unemployment (Standard & Poors 2010). *Also*, both agencies regard Slovak government debt levels as a credit strength, despite the recent surge in debt. The following three key problems cover most of these challenges.

Unemployment – eliminating the structural causes

In regard to the effects of the Global Crisis on Slovakia, the most negative impact so far has been growth in unemployment (from 9,6 per cent in 2008 to 12,1 per cent in 2009, and 14,4 per cent in 2010) (National Bank of Slovakia 2011). There are fears a large proportion of unemployment is structural, which means it cannot be easily solved by short-term measures. Disappointingly, since 1993, unemployment descended below 10per cent only once in 2008, reaching 9,6 per cent.

The structural unemployment is due to a large extent to the underdeveloped infrastructure (the unemployment is regionally concentrated in the central and eastern part of the country that lack good quality infrastructure) and to the failure to integrate the Roma minority. Tackling unemployment should therefore be at the heart of the political agenda in Slovakia.

Unemployment can be theoretically solved by attracting new foreign investments and promoting domestic employment creation by SMEs simultaneously.

Low tax revenues vs. social dumping – re-thinking taxation

The other short-to-medium term challenge facing Slovakia is insufficiency of government revenue. Moreover, current taxation further constrains already weak domestic demand. First, it is worth mentioning two important facts on taxation in Slovakia:

1/ Slovakia had by far the highest rate of tax cuts in the EU for the 1995-2008 period (-11.2 per cent measured as proportion of total taxes to GDP). These tax cuts mean lower government revenue.

2/ Slovakia has the 2nd lowest share of direct taxation as part of total taxation (22.1 per cent), with the lowest share being in Bulgaria. It has a much larger share of indirect taxation (36.9 per cent) and VAT (23.6per cent). This means people are taxed much more on consumption rather than income (figures for 2008, European Commission 2010).

In the EU, there is a clear division between old and new member states in respect to the balance of direct and indirect taxes. The new member states have a lower proportion of direct taxes than older member states, which have a longer tradition of solidarity on such issues (European Commission 2010). The reason why indirect taxes are so popular is because they are hidden, as the consumer pays them during every consumption purchase. However, in comparison, when filling out an income tax return, the consumer is painfully aware of what he is giving away to the taxman. The new member states lack certain comparative advantages of old member states, such as the know how, expertise, trade-mark and copyright, etc.,, so instead they compete by lower direct taxation and/or lower social contributions. The latter is not the case for Slovakia, which has high but capped social contributions.

Unfortunately for the majority of the population in these countries this is translated into lower government revenue. The ultimate losers are the middle and lower classes of these countries since they suffer from a decaying public sector (health-care and education) and do not have the means to take benefit of the new private institutions (private hospitals, schools). Moreover, these countries also suffer from endemic tax-evasion that further damages public finances. In Slovakia the wealth structure of the population is evolving towards a society with a populous lower class, disappearing middle-class and a quick-bred *"upper-class"* that controls the majority of the wealth and is running the country.

The taxation topic has not yet been expertly addressed in Slovakia, since major tax reform was conducted in 2003. The current Radicova government produced a set of measures shifting the tax burden yet further to consumption and lower income persons, including an increase of the VAT from 19 per cent to 20 per cent. The same current government also increased the threshold for non-taxable income while increasing social contributions of the self-employed and sole-traders. This results in higher taxation of labour that negatively affects employment and in higher taxation of consumption as well. Slovakia does not apply a reduced VAT on food like many EU countries do, as for example Germany, whose basic foodstuffs are taxed at 7 per cent compared to 20 per cent in Slovakia. (European Commission 2011) The Slovak government relies heavily on VAT income for the 2011 budget, while tax income from physical persons is estimated to be about 110 millions Euros.

The VAT income is about 4,6 billion Euros. (Národná Rada Slovenskej Republiky 2010)

It is important to state that because of tax competition in the CEE region and international mobility, a country cannot unilaterally increase taxation in a major way. A single country's rise in taxation should be accompanied by a reduced administrative burden and improved public services to maintain the business attractiveness of the country. Taxes are not the main attractor of high value added businesses and should not serve as a base of a country's competitiveness. A qualified workforce, good quality infrastructure, stable political environment and cooperative public administration are deemed equally important by businesses. Slovakia has much catching up to do in these areas.

In Slovakia, a re-balancing of taxation for labour, consumption, and capital would seem necessary. One of the solutions would be to introduce progressive taxation. In this case the thresholds of marginal tax rates should be carefully adjusted to prevent a fiscal squeeze of the middle-class, allowing for lower social contributions, especially for sole-traders and small businesses to encourage an increase in employment. The taxation of dividends (complete or partial) should be re-introduced with an exemption for lower amounts to exclude and protect small investors.

Finally, it seems necessary to adopt a tougher approach to tax evasion, together with tougher regulation of existing situations in both politics and business, as a number of leading politicians and businessmen have difficulties explaining the origin of their wealth. A study into the feasibility of a large scale regularization (a sort of a tax-amnesty) operation should be launched with an ex-post standard taxation of wealth of non-fraudulent origin and criminal inquiry in other cases (in line with the OECD standards on money laundering which cover among others tax crimes, fraud, bribery and corruption) (OECD 2009).

Negative demographics- reversing the trend

The biggest long-term problem Slovakia must face is negative demographic evolution. Like the rest of Europe, Slovakia's population is ageing at a fast pace. This, together with prolonged life expectancy will have repercussions on present and future generations. The rating agency Standard & Poors has published a series of reports on demographic risk and is not optimistic in assessing future demographic evolution in Slovakia. It expects the population of Slovakia to shrink from 5.4 million currently to 4.9 million in 2050. The working-age population would then fall from 73 per cent to 57 per cent. Without structural reforms, the current rate of age-related spending would increase Slovakia's net debt to an alarming 330 per cent of GDP (Standard &

Poors 2010). This would mean the fiscal burden would dramatically increase for the working-age population. The year 2050 is only two generations away, so if this situation is to be avoided, something must be done to reverse the negative population growth well before 2050. Inspiration could be drawn from the example of Norway, where pro-active child-care and family support policies have succeeded in bringing the birth-rate in Norway well above the European average.

Economic reasons are to a large extent, behind this negative evolution. Young families cannot afford decent housing and additional expenses linked to having children. In Slovakia, the purchase of real estate by non-residents, but especially bank lending that artificially boosted purchasing power of households (before 2009, mortgages with a loan-to-value ratio of 100per cent were common), inflated the housing market. The effects were most dramatic in Bratislava, due to the high concentration of economic activity in the capital.

One solution for the problem is regulation of housing prices by the market. The EC is working on harmonization of residential mortgage regulation and proposed a Directive on credit agreements relating to residential property. The directive obliges the creditors (banks) to execute an obligatory *"Creditworthiness assessment"* and refuse to grant credit to non-compliant borrowers. The criteria, for example limiting the loan-to-value or loan-to-income ratios, are to be determined by member states themselves (European Commission 2011). Such limitations would cause a fall in house prices because if the average worker cannot afford a house with a 40 years mortgage, either there is a problem with his wage or the price of the house. If the artificial means of boosting households purchasing power are cut-off, new houses will not be sold for the current astronomical prices and will start to fall. This will negatively affect the prices of the older houses as well, but may cause a few systemic financial problems.

The other solution is increasing supply by the construction of public housing. Such a scheme could be co-financed by the EIB, and would simultaneously provide employment and put downward pressure on house prices. However, government deficit limitations could prove to be a problem in this case, since government spending would have to increase to carry out such programs.

Conclusion

The first part of this chapter explains causes and effects of the crisis, which is necessary to evaluate adequate responses to the economic downturn. The chapter further outlines the scope for supranational and national action in response to the crisis. Slovakia faces a limited scope for national action, but does have the opportunity to exploit advantages offered by its membership in the EU, such as the structural funds and EIB loans, to address some or many of its current problems. The second part of this chapter analyzed three problems regarding the long-term competitiveness of Slovakia. The two solutions presented, improving infrastructure and supporting SMEs, can help tackle Slovakia's problem with unemployment and regional disparities, and falling government revenues as well. The demographic situation is more difficult to solve, but sorting out the housing problem is a crucial part of the solution. There are opportunities offered by the EIB and EIF, but they must be exploited rationally and responsibly. This will require a pro-active approach from the Slovak government, the public sector, and the private sector as well, banks, SMEs, and all such related actors.

Despite much deserved criticism, positive steps have been taken and in some areas, improvement is actually under way in Slovakia. The EC has highlighted the public procurement virtual portal in Slovakia as an example of good practice in SME policy making (European Commission 2008). The launch of the working-phase of the JEREMIE programe and creation of the first business angel network in March 2011, are also very positive occurrences in this regard (Klub podnikateľských anjelov Slovenska 2011).

In the end, Slovakia is facing and will face growing challenges in the future. The EU funding for the next six year period under the "*EU 2020*" agenda will focus on innovation (European Commission 2011). Slovakia will need to adapt to this situation, but currently spends only 0.47 per cent of its GDP on R&D, which is the second worst result in the EU (Eurostat 2008). Slovakia will need to invest more into R&D and education to promote the knowledge economy which are crucial factors for its future economic development. Most importantly, it is essential to identify challenges correctly, and to have well qualified and honest people to decide and implement the right strategies at all levels.

References

Aglietta, Michel (1991): *Le risque de système*. Revue d'economie financière n.18
Artus, Patric. Betbèze, Jean-Paul. Boissieu, Christian. Capelle-Blancard, documentation Gunter (2010): *De la crise des subprimes à la crise mondiale*. La Française
European Commission (2011): *Solvency II – Basic architecture*
http://ec.europa.eu/internal_market/insurance/solvency/architecture_en.htm (2011-03-30)

European Commission (2010): *Taxation trends in the EU 2010*
http://ec.europa.eu/taxation_customs/resources/documents/taxation/gen_info/economic_analysis/tax_structures/2010/2010_main_results_en.pdf (2011-03-30)

European Commission (2010): *VAT rates applied in the Member States of the European Union*
http://ec.europa.eu/taxation_customs/resources/documents/taxation/vat/how_vat_works/rates/vat_rates_en.pdf (2011-03-30)

European Commission (2011): *Proposal for a DIRECTIVE OF THE EUROPEAN PARLIAMENT AND OF THE COUNCIL on credit agreements relating to residential property*
http://ec.europa.eu/internal_market/finservices-retail/docs/credit/mortgage/com_2011_142_en.pdf (2011-03-30)

European Commission (2011): *Stakeholder consultation paper, Commission Staff Working paper on the Europe 2020 Project Bond Initiative*
http://ec.europa.eu/economy_finance/consultation/pdf/bonds_consultation_en.pdf (2011-03-30)

European Commission (2011): *Europe 2020*
http://ec.europa.eu/europe2020/index_en.htm (2011-03-30)

European Council (2011): 24/25 March Conclusions.
http://www.consilium.europa.eu/uedocs/cms_data/docs/pressdata/en/ec/120296.pdf (2011-03-30)

European Council (2011): 24/25 March Conclusions.
http://www.consilium.europa.eu/uedocs/cms_data/docs/pressdata/en/ec/120296.pdf (2011-03-30)

European Investment Bank (2009) *EIB Statute*
http://www.eib.org/attachments/general/statute/eib_statute_2009_en.pdf (2011-03-30)

European Financial Stability Facility (2011): *About EFSF*
http://www.efsf.europa.eu/about/index.htm (2011-03-30)

European Investment Bank (2011) *Data available on website*
http://www.eib.org

Eurostat (2010): *Manual on Government Deficit and Debt 2010*
http://epp.eurostat.ec.europa.eu/cache/ITY_OFFPUB/KS-RA-09-017/EN/KS-RA-09-017-EN.PDF (2011-03-30)

European Investment Bank, European PPP Expertise Centre (2011): *A Guide to Guidance- Sourcebook for PPPs*

Europa Press Release (2010): *Financial Supervision Package – Frequently Asked Questions*
http://europa.eu/rapid/pressReleasesAction.do?reference=MEMO/10/434&format=PDF&aged=0&language=EN&guiLanguage=en (2010-12-06

Europa Press Release (2011): European Commission statement at the occasion of the European Parliament vote on the directive on hedge funds and private equity
http://europa.eu/rapid/pressReleasesAction.do?reference=MEMO/10/573
&format=HTML&aged=0&language=EN&guiLanguage=en
(2011-03-30)
Klub podnikateľských anjelov Slovenska (2011),
http://www.podnikajte.sk/klub-podnikatelskych-anjelov-slovenska.xhtml
(2011-04-10)
Krugman, Paul (2008): *Road to Depression Economics*. Penguin Books
KPMG (2010): *EU funds in Central and Easter Europe. Progress Report 2007-2009*
http://www.kpmg.ee/dbfetch/52616e646f6d49569ec6ca687de886a93198
08ff3ecaba5b891f423df6bdc6a7/eu_funds_in_the_cee_2010_kpmg.pdf
(2010-12-06)
McNelis, Sean (2010): *An Overview of Basel III: An evolving framework for banks*. HSBC Bank
www.euromoneyconferences.com (2010-12-06)
Moody's (2011): Credit Opinion on Slovakia 2011
http://www.moodys.com/
Národná rada Slovenskej Republiky (2010): *Vládny návrh zákona o štátnom rozpočte na rok 2011*
http://www.nrsr.sk/Default.aspx?sid=zakony/zakon&ZakZborID=13&Ci
sObdobia=5&CPT=81 (2010-11-26)
National Bank of Slovakia (2010): *Analysis of the Slovak Financial Sector for the first half of 2010.*
http://www.nbs.sk/_img/Documents/_Dohlad/ORM/Analyzy/2010-
1a.pdf (2010-12-06)
National Bank of Slovakia (2011): *Selected Economic and Monetary Indicators of the Slovak Republic*
http://www.nbs.sk/_img/Documents/_Publikacie/OstatnePublik/ukazovat
ele.pdf (2011-03-30)
Organization for Economic Co-operation and Development (2009): *The Impact of the Global Crisis on SME and Entrepreneurship Financing and Policy Responses*
http://www.oecd.org/dataoecd/40/34/43183090.pdf (2011-03-30)
Organization for Economic Co-operation and Development (2009): *Money Laundering Awareness Handbook for Tax Examiners and Tax Auditors*
http://www.oecd.org/dataoecd/61/17/43841099.pdf (2010-11-26)
Standard & Poors (2010): Global Ageing 2010- Slovakia
http://www.standardandpoors.com/home/en/eu (2011-03-30)
Standard & Poors (2010): *Sovereign Rating Slovakia 2010*
http://www.standardandpoors.com/home/en/eu (2010-12-06)

Wertlen, Andrej (2010): *The Financial Impact of the Global Crisis on the Slovak Republic and Czech Republic*. Master thesis. Bratislava. Institute of European Studies and International relations, FSES, Comenius University

Chapter 5
Responses to the financial crisis through party programs in Slovakia: national or europeanized?

Dušan Leška

Introduction

The aim of this chapter is to explore the development in the positions of Slovak political parties in their response to the financial crisis and related euro crisis. The chapter will analyze and compare the electoral programs of the main Slovak political parties during the 2009 European Parliament election, and the 2010 election for the National Council of the Slovak Republic. Regarding the former, we compare the electoral programs of European political parties, mainly those of the European People's Party (EPP) and the Party of the European Socialists (PES), and the influence of these programs on those of the relevant Slovak political parties. These parties are SMER-SD, the Slovak Democratic and Christian Union – Democratic Party (SDKÚ-DS), the Christian Democratic Movement (KDH), and the Party of Hungarian Coalition (SMK).

During the 2010 Slovak parliamentary election, the the parties that entered the election were the right-wing coalition of the Slovak Democratic and Christian Union – Democratic Party (SDKÚ-DS), Christian Democratic Movement (KDH), and two new parties: Freedom and Solidarity (SaS), and Bridge (Most-Híd). Their main agenda was to find a way out of the crisis. Before the election, the parties had been affected by events in the EU – the debt crisis which spread to Greece, Ireland, Portugal, and threatened other EU countries, and the threat to the very existence of the euro. We will analyze the attitudes of the electoral programs and the specific policies of Slovak parties, as well as policies that found the EU adopting the European Financial Stabilization Facility (EFSF), the European Stabilization Mechanism (ESM), and measures to strengthen economic cooperation in fiscal and political union.

Impact of the economic crisis on Slovakia

The government coalition led by SMER-SD entered office when economic prosperity in Europe was at a peak, and the positive effects of reforms by the previous administration were still visible. Slovakia's GDP growth rates reached record levels of 8.5 per cent in 2006 and 2007, and even reached 10.4 per cent at one point. Unemployment, a long-term problem in the Slovak economy, fell from 12 per cent in 2005 to 7.6 per cent in 2008. In this period, however, financial and economic problems had already emerged in the USA and were gradually spreading to Europe. The Slovak government at first believed the crisis would either not manifest itself in Slovakia, or would have no significant impact.

> Prime Minister Robert Fico argued higher domestic consumption would help Slovakia get through the crisis and perhaps reverse disturbing trends in employment (Slovakia: Fastest-Growing E.U. Economy. 2008).

However, in 2008, the GDP growth rate had already decreased compared to previous years, but nonetheless did reach a growth rate of 6.4 per cent. The economic crisis manifested itself more forcefully in Slovakia in 2009, with Slovakia registering a GDP decrease to 4.6 per cent compared to 2008: unemployment jumped to 12 per cent (Kárász 2009:8). The government sought solutions and measures to diminish the impact of the crisis on the Slovak economy: it also declared it would not allow the impact of the crisis to affect working people, and it would try to eliminate negative social impacts.

The Slovak economy is relatively small and open, with exports constituting approximately 87.5 per cent of GDP creation (Proexportná politika Slovenskej republiky na roky 2007 – 2013). Slovakia thus largely depends on nearby countries, mainly Germany and France, which are Slovakia's target export countries. Therefore, the possibilities for Slovakia to halt the crisis and ensure economic recovery were largely limited and dependent on developments in nearby countries. The impact of the crisis on the Slovak economy also affected the automobile industry which accounts for a significant share of the country's exports.[34] Less demand for vehicles led to less production, lay-offs and a decrease in exports. Economic recovery largely depended on the recovery of the automobile industry.

The government established emergency work-teams which regularly evaluated situations and adopted a number of reforms aimed at reducing the impact of the economic crisis. These teams were established in accordance

---

34   In Slovakia, there are affiliated branches of Volkswagen, PSA Peugeot Citroen, and the Kia automobile companies.

with recommendations by the European Commission. There were also two rounds of money for scrapping cars: automobile owners could be awarded a favorable state grant to buy a new vehicle if they scrapped their old one.

Financial incentives for business activities were also provided, mainly for sole traders.[35] This led to the better exploitation of European funds and offered financial incentives for the creation of new opportunities, and/or the preservation of the current state of employment, and the establishment of "social enterprises" for groups of people who had difficulty finding employment. The government also paid great attention to highway building with the participation of public and private capital. In addition, the government adopted a social concept focusing on easing the conditions of unemployment benefit to alleviate the negative impact on the social conditions of the population at large.

The right-wing opposition parties criticized the implementation of these measures, claiming they would not benefit Slovakia but host countries where automobile companies' headquarters were located. After the outbreak of the crisis, they proposed decreasing unitary tax from 19 per cent to 16 per cent, which they believed would stimulate entrepreneurial activities. The government opposed such measures, claiming they would decrease revenues to the state budget even more. In the final stage of the crisis, there was a proposal to extend the terms of unemployment benefit payments from six months to twelve months: this was rejected as economic recovery had already started. It was also feared that such an extension might make the unemployed less motivated to seek work. Moreover, such a step would excessively increase state budget expenses.

Since unemployment was growing significantly, expenditures on unemployment and other social benefits also grew, leading to an increase in the deficit. The opposition criticized the government for not being prepared for the crisis, claiming that measures were adopted too late and would therefore not help stabilize the economy. Later, the opposition focused mainly on criticizing the growing state budget deficit and overall economic debt, which culminated after the debt crisis broke out with Greece requesting a major loan from the EU.

---

35 If someone had been unemployed for at least three months, and had proven his/her interest in owning a business and drew up a business plan, he/she was given a state grant from 3,000 up to 5,000 EURO. This depended on the economic indices of the county where the person wanted to create a business.

The 2009 European Parliament elections

It was within this context that the electoral campaign prior to the European parliamentary elections took place, forcing political parties to show their policies for solving the crisis. In terms of political power and the solution of domestic problems, European parliamentary elections are often considered less important: they are not as representative, and most power lies within the party system. However, they may signal trends in the profiles of individual parties, and play a significant role in forming the attitudes of political parties to European issues. It is also important for parties to be able to promote and explain such topics to the electorate, and interconnect the issues of domestic development with the development of the European Union. Based on analyses of electoral programs, one can identify the attitudes of political parties toward the continuation of European integration.

All the relevant parliamentary political parties have long-lasting cooperation with European parties, so electoral preparations and the campaigns were run in close collaboration with their partner Euro-parties. The main cleavage was between the European right and left, i.e. between the Party of European Socialists (PES), and the European People's Party (EPP). While Smer-SD is a member of the PES, all the other right-wing parties in the Slovak opposition – SDKÚ-DS, KDH, and SMK – are associated with the EPP.

European and Slovak political parties made great efforts to interconnect both European and national ideas regarding solving current social problems. Accordingly, the Slovak political parties' programs were more elaborate than in previous EP elections, as they emerged from a common European concept, leading to perspectives of development for Slovakia as well. A survey of the electoral programs of SDKÚ-DS and SMER shows that more than seventy per cent of their programmatic ideas were in line with the programs of their European partner parties (Bátora 2009:48-49).

The European Socialist Party drew up a rather detailed anti-crisis plan with the EU, drafting solutions to the crisis as well as a package of measures to prevent similar crises. The program emerged from the criticism of a "blind belief" in an uncontrolled market that would always ensure economic balance, but which in reality creates uncontrolled financial markets, causing a financial crisis that grew into an economic crisis, moving from the USA to Europe. Their plan requires stricter regulation of financial markets, with greater transparency and responsibility in terms of individual actors in the system. Moreover, it requires greater protection for the employed in labor relations, the more effective exploitation of EU funds for educating/training working people, the integration of the unemployed in the labor market, and

ECB support for economic growth and employment (PES: People first. A new direction for Europe 2009).

All these fundamental goals and measures were projected in Smer-SD's program. The party also expressed its support for effective security and green growth. Its program additionally emphasized the need to respect the national interests of Slovakia and hinder interference by EU bureaucrats and the egoism of larger countries, thereby allowing Slovakia to develop its self-confidence as an EU actor. This would create a truthful and undistorted picture of Slovakia in Brussels, according to Smer-SD, and the interests of Slovakia would be rigidly defended (Sociálna Európa – odpoved' na krízu 2009)

The other two coalition parties, mainly ĽS-HZDS, had long had difficulty affiliating with some of the European political parties. The SNS had been an associate member of the Union for Europe of the Nations since 2002, an association of nation-oriented and nationalist parties. The association stresses a need to preserve national identity and opposes those aspects of the European Union that it sees as a bureaucratic super-state. The association not only advocates limiting Brussels bureaucracy, but also proposes establishing a second chamber of the European parliament – a Chamber of Nations.

The SNS party managed to win one seat in the elections overall, and became a member of a new faction established after the EP elections – the Europe of Freedom and Democracy party, (EFD) founded by the British nationalist Nigel Farage. This replaced the group called Independency/ Democracy. In its official statement the SNS claims that in the European parliament it had become a member of a newly created Euro-realistic group the members of which, besides the SNS party, are other significant political subjects. As a result of its membership of this group the SNS may be in the process of changing its overall policy orientation.

As a parliamentary party and a member of ruling coalitions, it pragmatically supported all government policies and behaved in a pro-European fashion. As of 2011, it has shifted its policy toward a euroskeptic position, which is also demonstrated by its participation at a conference of right-wing parties in Vienna arranged by the Freedom Party of Austria (FPÖ). This was to promote closer cooperation between such parties in European matters.

Although ĽS-HZDS had had three MEPs since the 2004 elections, it had not managed to join any European political party. Only after the 2009 elections did it become a member of the European Democratic Party, as part of a representative group, and the Alliance of Liberals and Democrats for Europe (ALDE). ĽS-HZDS had a detailed electoral program, in which it vowed to balance continuation of the integration processes and reform the Lisbon treaty, while advocating the preservation of tax sovereignty and the suitable regulation of financial capital.

After the elections, ĽS-HZDS won only one seat. This was yet more evidence of its gradual decline in attractiveness to voters. However, following its failure in the 2010 parliamentary elections, it managed to anchor itself in the European political party of Liberals. This was when ĽS-HZDS did not win a single seat on the National Council of the Slovak Republic (Parliament), its "final stage" that apparently ended the Mečiar era.

The European People's Party (EPP) as a conservative party criticized socialists whose leftist measures allegedly destroy job creation and thus make Europe weaker overall. At the same time it rejected the approaches of market fundamentalists who see the market as the best kind of regulation with no state intervention. The EPP would like new financial rules to be set which would allow better control and regulation, but which would not lead to any curtailment of economic freedom in individual countries. Additionally, they want the elaboration of measures to support joint steps by EU countries against the financial crisis based on common values, but not a shift to economic nationalism and protectionism (EPP: Ten priorities for the EPP Group 2009 – 2014. 2009).

The program of the most powerful party in opposition, SDKÚ-DS, emerged from these fundamental points of view, but it also contained different views against the continuation of European integration. It opposes intervention in the tax assessment powers and policies of member states, and it supports recognizing national competencies in the area of social security, and the right of each country to preserve its own labor-market model. It wishes to preserve the tax-base in nation states, which it believes represents a strong tool for Slovakia's economic development (Za prosperujúce Slovensko v silnej Európe, 2009).

The attitudes in KDH's program seem even more restrained. It highlights the importance of fully fledged Slovak membership of the EU as a source of freedom, democracy and security, while declaring its belief that the Union can be built only on Christian conservative values and beliefs. Regarding the protection of traditional values, it argues for the absolute sovereignty of the member states and sees the Union as only an association of sovereign states. In the fight against the crisis, it demanded support for small and medium-sized enterprises, decreases in tax obligations and funding contribution levels, the elimination of barriers, and the more effective utilization of euro funds (Volebný program KDH do Európskeho parlamentu. 2009).

SMK requires member states to act in common to dampen or resolve the crisis, and the elimination of barriers and the protectionism of the common European market. It requires an increase in regional cohesion and harmonized energy policy, and wants a common EU foreign policy within transatlantic relations. But it primarily wants the protection of human rights, mainly minority rights, as a minimum value goal for the EU, and it proposes measures to improve the conditions of minorities in the EU (Naša budúcnosť v Európskom parlamente. 2009).

During the EP elections, SMER-SD won 30 per cent of votes cast and five seats in the European parliament. It became a member of a socialist faction that had been renamed the Progressive Alliance of Socialists & Democrats (S&D). This had resulted from the integration of the European Socialist Party (PES) and Italian Democratic Party MPs, who were at that time divided between PES and ALDE. Notably, a SMER MEP became deputy chairman of the socialist fraction in the EP.

SDKÚ-DS won 16.98 per cent of votes cast and thus two seats, while KDH won 10.87 per cent. SMK gained 11.33 per cent of votes cast and two seats in the European parliament. The right-wing parties associated in the EP thus won six seats overall (Výsledky volieb do Európskeho parlamentu 2009).

On the political scene before the elections a new political party appeared called Freedom and Solidarity (SaS). Although it has not yet won any EP seats, it has won seats on the National Council. It became a key factor in the establishment of the right-wing coalition, and its programmatic theses and political views play an important role in the politics of Slovakia. Its leaders are mostly businessmen, and its main goal consists of entering politics to create suitable conditions for business enterprise. Thus, it strives to implement the principles of business enterprise or company management rules to the management of society, and officially supports liberalism and freedom of trade. Its participation in the EP election was its first opportunity to promote its manifesto and address the electorate.

Its electoral program shows the party appreciates the foundation of the EU as a unique project unprecedented in European history. Simultaneously, however, it declares reservations to the Lisbon treaty, which purportedly leads to the creation of a European super-state. It believes there should be principal reform of and reduction in the Common Agricultural Policy (CAP), which is considered to be an unnecessary intervention in the proper functioning of market mechanisms. It also advocates the primacy of member states in the creation of an optimal model of economic, social, and political development. It vows to reform EU institutions as it believes too much legislative activity is in the hands of unelected bureaucrats, considered non-transparent actors (Programové priority SaS 2009). However, SaS did not gain any representation in the EP, due to winning only 4.7 per cent of votes cast. Its performance was very promising for a new party, however, and later developments have confirmed an increasing voter preference for this party. Since its establishment, SaS has cooperated at the European level with the ELDR party. SaS is an observer, and it was interested in becoming an affiliated member in record time. In 2010 the supreme body of the ELDR refused to reclassify SaS's status to that of an affiliate, reasoning that the party needed more time to realize its obligations and attitudes in practical politics. At the same time, the most influential faction in the EP became the European People's Party which won 256 seats: in second place there was the Progressive Alliance of Socialists and Democrats (S&D) with 184 seats. The Alliance of Liberals and Democrats for Europe (ALDE) won 84 seats, while the party called Europe of Freedom and Democracy (AFD), to which SNS is affiliated, has 32 seats.

Interestingly, in spite of the efforts by political parties and the state to mobilize the electorate, voter turnout was just 19.6 per cent, again the EU's lowest. However, compared to previous years it had grown by 2.6 per cent, while total voter turnout in all member states reached 43.6 per cent. The most votes in Slovakia went to SMER-SD, winning 30 per cent of votes cast and five seats.

The 2010 national elections

The 2010 parliamentary elections for the Slovak National Council represented the next opportunity for political parties to express their positions regarding solutions to the crisis. In 2010, Greece fell into a spiral of speculative capital weakening its economy, with amassing debt and potential state bankruptcy. As Greece is a member of the monetary union, bankruptcy could weaken the position of the euro as a common currency, and there were fears that the Greek problem could cause a chain reaction in other countries facing similar problems – Portugal, Ireland, Spain, and Italy. After prolonged deliberations, EU decided to provide Greece with a loan of 110 billion euros to save the currency, divided over three years and paid down by the member states, the European Commission, and the International Monetary Fund. In Slovakia, agreement to provide the loan was signed by the minister of finance for the Fico government, which was finishing its term. As a result, Slovakia bound itself to lend Greece 800 million euros. Provision of the loan and developments in Greece became part of negative and emotional electoral campaign statements, with opposition parties using such emotion to attack the coalition government.

The main focus of the criticism was that the coalition government had failed to manage the economic crisis, which meant growth in unemployment, GDP reductions, an increase in the state budget deficit and external debt for

Slovakia. Developments in Greece were used as an example of irresponsible management bringing the country to the brink of state bankruptcy. The election campaign slogan, "the Greek way", was applied to Slovakia, meaning that Slovakia could already be on the way to state bankruptcy, and only responsible government could save it.

Thus, developments in Greece became issues in the national political conflicts in Slovakia. Those who argued for refusing the loan to Greece based their argument on the view that the loan only supported irresponsible Greek management, so a principle of true solidarity could not be built on by providing support to the rich by the poor. Average wages and pensions were significantly higher in Greece than in Slovakia, and it was claimed that such a bailout was saving only German and French banks. SDKÚ-DS, for example, states that:

> In European foreign policy, the government of Róbert Fico became an obedient servant and executor of the will in Brussels, regardless of the real interests of Slovakia. Thanks to the active work of SDKÚ-DS in opposition and our foreign political activities, we managed to stop Róbert Fico´s government in ... making Slovak citizens pay compensation due to irresponsible politics by some politicians in Greece, and irresponsible activity by certain private commercial banks, as well as lax inspection-regulation activity of the EU bodies (Generálna línia SDKÚ-DS. 2010, p. 6).

SDKU's electoral program mainly emphasizes the need for responsible management, the establishing of a competitive environment, and improving enterprise areas; its main goal is to reduce the state budget deficit and national debt. Improving these macroeconomic indices is considered to be the main condition for resolving the crisis and promoting stable development. Its electoral program consists only of general statements, such as:

> In relation to the EU, we will support all measures that accelerate the establishment and liberalization of a single European market, but will oppose any increase in European regulation and bureaucracy. We are expressly for the preservation of the sovereignty of member states in the areas of economic and social policy, as long as this does not apparently and expressly contradict the needs of the common European market (Volebný program SDKÚ-DS. 2010, p.8).

The program of SaS concerning its relations to the EU or European integration is imbued with a neo-liberal orientation. It does not focus on utilizing the common market or deepening integration, but on establishing certain protective mechanisms in Slovakia to hinder such tendencies. The general attitude is formulated in the introductory section, in which it is stated:

> Adoption of the Lisbon Treaty provides the European bureaucracy with the possibility to markedly extend its power and influence. Due to the unanimous consent of the member states´ representatives, the Council of the EU will be able to

significantly change the way the EU functions. This would deprive competencies from the member state governments without offering additional compensatory power. In Slovakia, many of these changes are possible only via the amendment of the Constitution, and they require a three-fifths majority in Parliament (120 nápadov SaS. 2010, point 43).

Accordingly, Sas wants to prevent any competencies being taken over by the EU in the areas of tax or criminal law, without the necessary consent of elected Slovak representatives. Moreover, SaS proposes decreasing bureaucratic power over euro-fund management and changes in the overall purposes on which such funds are spent:

> European money should not be allocated to private companies that lobby and bribe to gain support for the project funded by EU Funds, but instead to build up generally the beneficial infrastructure in the areas of transport, education, health, an environment all citizens and companies will benefit from (120 nápadov SaS. 2010, point 46).

KDH has the most elaborate standpoints in economic policy and involvement in the European integration process (Volebný program KDH. 2010, p. 7). It argues that more attention must be paid to the effective use of euro-funds to benefit regional development, and has detailed proposal for the spending of these funds for the next period. It supports cross-border regional cooperation, close links with neighboring regions, the establishing and running of regional associations (clusters), and will promote a more active for Slovakia in the formation of new regional policies by the EU and how they are implemented.

In KDH's view, after joining the EU, the Eurozone and Schengen, today's common challenge is to responsibly realize institutional reform, and effectively react to global challenges. KDH wants to bring Slovak attitudes into greater alignment with EU decision-making. At the same time, it wants to cultivate a European awareness of Slovakia, as encapsulated by the motto "We are the EU, too". The KDH further states that Europe will be strong if its member states are strong, which in practice means emphasizing the principles of freedom, subsidiarity, solidarity, and justice. Slovakia, due to its human potential, economy, and cultural riches, strengthens Europe. The KDH will protect, enforce, and develop Slovak interests in the EU (Volebný program KDH. 2010, p.32). Exercising the principles of subsidiarity and unanimity, based on cooperation, trust, and equality between countries in the areas of direct taxation, criminal law, family policies, foreign policy, and defense, will, according to KDH, bring about true harmony at all levels of society.

Results of the 2010 national election

The results of the 2010 national elections and the creation of the coalition government surprised many. The election was won, as expected, by the SMER-SD party, with 36.8 per cent of votes cast, capturing sixty-two seats on the National Council. The surprise was that ĽS-HZDS did not win a single seat. Surprisingly, SMK did not reach the required threshold, but instead a new party called Most-Híd won 8.12 percent of votes cast and fourteen seats. Most-Híd was established by the splitting of SMK. Its main objective is to promote understanding between Slovaks and the Hungarian minority. Even more surprisingly, a new party – Freedom and Solidarity (SaS) – made the biggest gains, winning 12.14 per cent of votes cast and twenty-two seats, coming in third place overall. SDKÚ-DS, in spite of its new electoral leadership, gained less than in previous elections: it won 15.42 per cent of votes cast and twenty-eight seats. KDH won 8.52 per cent of votes cast and fifteen seats. The SNS was returned to Parliament, achieving 5.07 per cent of votes cast and winning nine seats.

The right-wing parties, SDKÚ-DS and KDH, and the new parties, SaS and Most-Híd, were thus given an opportunity to split the Smer-SD party from its potential allies by signing a preliminary coalition agreement. Based on this, they refused to enter into negotiations with Smer-SD. Accordingly, during the second round of negotiations, I. Radičová, the leader of SDKÚ-DS, was empowered with creating a new government, in which the new coalition had seventy-nine of 150 total parliamentary seats.

The coalition parties had already expressed reservations regarding continued integration with the European Union. This was mirrored in the government's opening declaration:

> ...it will use the principle of unanimity in EU decisions as a basis for cooperation based on trust and equality between countries, in the areas of direct taxation, criminal law, family policy, foreign policy, and defense. It will monitor all legislative and non-legislative drafts and proposals of the European commission, allowing the National Council of the Slovak Republic to use those rights that arose from the Lisbon Treaty (Programové vyhlásenie vlády: 2010, pp 51 – 52).

In other words the new government would, enforce the right of veto and guard its pregrogatives vis-à-vis the European Union. KDH wants, furthermore, to safeguard Christian morality in areas of family policy and respect agreements with the Vatican, while SDKÚ-DS and SaS will not allow any reference to be made to harmonization of tax policy.

After taking office, the new government had difficulty to deliver on its electoral promises. It could not reverse its official viewpoints without losing credibility in the eyes of the electorate, so Slovakia was the only EU member state to refuse the loan to Greece. After this, however, it proceeded more in a manner of European solidarity. To help alleviate the crisis, it supported the creation of the European Financial Stabilization Facility by agreeing to guarantee Slovak backing for an emergency loan to Ireland and Portugal.

As the Eurozone countries continued to be jeopardized economically by the global economic slowdown, EU decided to establish a permanent European Stability Mechanism (ESM), which will start operating in 2013. This will require the partial regulation and/or amendment of the Lisbon Treaty to enable and legalize its establishment. The credit capacity of the mechanism will be 500 billion euros. From this amount, 80 billion will be paid out in cash; the rest will consist of capital available upon request up to a total of 700 billion Euros. However, certain warning signals have been issued by some coalition parties. The presidency of the new SaS party decided in advance that the party and its MPs would not support any Slovak contributions to the European Stability Mechanism, although they would support amending the Lisbon Treaty. In addition, representatives of the Civil Conservative Party (OKS), elected to parliament on the party list of Most-Híd, declared that they would also find supporting such a proposal difficult. Currently, approval of any required contribution and amending of the Lisbon Treaty by the National Council of the Slovak Republic would be controversial.

If coalition parties maintain their positions, approval would be possible only with the support of the most powerful opposition party, Smer-SD. SaS has stated that such an emergency loan would not solve the problems of overall debt, as it would only postpone a proper solution (Radšej majme recesiu ako euroval. 2011).

As relations between the coalition and opposition are highly confrontational, it is questionable whether the government at this point (August 2011) can negotiate any solution at all that has the support of a majority of the Slovak Parliament.

Conclusion

The differences between the attitudes of individual Slovak political parties toward the European Union and European integration are most noticeable depending on whether the party concerned is in a governing coalition or in opposition. SDKÚ-DS, for example, acted as a flagship in leading the accession of Slovakia to the European Union. In certain key situations, however, it chose to disregard the Union´s collective needs, preferring instead political expediency: this led to expected gains in the domestic political sphere (as with the Lisbon Treaty vote, for example). However, as the most powerful party of the current government, it changed its approach to bailouts toward supporting the establishment of the European Financial Stabilization Facility, and the ESM, including support for the Pact for euro stabilization.

SMER-SD, an opposition party of a euroskeptic orientation (Henderson 2009: 300), changed its behavior in government and wholly supported the adoption of the euro and access to Schengen. Similarly, SNS, a nationalistic party in the governing coalition, ended up supporting a deepening of relations with the EU. These observations illustrate that Slovak opposition parties tend to succumb to populist inclinations when in opposition but behave more responsibly when in government. It remains to be seen, however, whether a common policy towards a Union plagued by a financial crisis will emerge out of the current confrontations and negotiations between the Slovak political parties.

References:

ALDE: 10 political priorities. (2009):
  http://www.alde.eu/fileadmin/webdocs/key_docs/10Priorities-booklet-EN1.pdf (2010-12-06)
Bátora, Jozef (2009): Vzniká európsky systém politickej reprezentácie? In: Mesežnikov, Grigorij, Gyarfášová, Ol'ga, Kollár, Miroslav (eds.) *Slovensko volí. Európske a prezidentské voľby 2000*. Bratislava: IVO, pp. 41-55.
EPP: Ten priorities for the EPP Group 2009 – 2014. Putting people at the heart of Europe. (2009):
  http://stream.epped.eu/Activities/docs/year2009/2009-2014group-priorities-en.pdf (2011-23-3)
Európska demokratická strana považuje snahu o zapojenie strany SaS do Európskych politických štruktúr za predčasnú. (2011):
  http://www.eds-sk.sk/article/showDetail/europska-demokraticka-strana-povazuje-snahu-o-zapojenie-strany-sas-do-europskych-politickych-struktur-za-predcasnu (2011-13-04)
Európski liberáli medzi seba mečiarovcov nezobrali. In: *Aktuálne.sk* (2008):
  http://aktualne.centrum.sk/domov/politika/clanek.phtml?id=1159525 (2011-11-03)

Euro Pact Plus. (2011):
http://www.consilium.europa.eu/uedocs/cms_data/docs/pressdata/en/ec/1
20296.pd (2011-24-03)
Generálna línia SDKÚ na roky 2010 – 2014. Sloboda a zodpovednosť, poriadok a spravodlivosť. Bratislava 2010. (2010): http://www.sdku-ds.sk/data/MediaLibrary/911/generalna-linia-2010.pdf (2011-21-04)
Henderson, Karen (2009); Evropeizace politických stran na Slovensku. In: Kárász, Pavol (2009): *Vplyv globálnej ekonomickej krízy na vývoj hospodárstva Slovenska so zreteľom na trh práce*. Bratislava: Fridrich Eber Stifftung.
http://www.euractiv.sk/fileadmin/images/Microsoft_Word_-_PK__studia2.pdf (2011-02-07)
Naša budúcnosť v Európskom parlamente. Volebný program SMK k voľbám do Európskeho parlamentu 2009. (2009):
http://www.mkp.sk/eu/volebny-program---nasa-buducnost-v-europe_61.html (2011-14-03)
Občianska zodpovednosť a spolupráca. Programové vyhlásenie vlády Slovenskej republiky na obdobie rokov 2010 – 2014. August 2010. (2010):
http://www.government.gov.sk/data/files/6257.pdf (2011-17-03)
PES: People first, A new direction for Europe. (2009):
http://www.pes.org/downloads/PES_manifesto_2009-EN.pdf
(2011-15-04)
Pre silnejšiu strednú vrstvu, pre modernejšie Slovensko. Volebný program SDKÚ-DS pre voľby 2010. (2010): http://www.sdku-ds.sk/data/MediaLibrary/629/2010-04-12_SDKU-DS_program.pdf
(2011-04-04)
Proexportná politika Slovenskej republiky. Na roky 2007 – 2013. (2007):
http://www.foreign.gov.sk/App/wcm/media.nsf/vw_ByID/ID_2CC5A44
537350E77C12576740024615A_SK/$File/proexportna_politikaSR_%20
2007_2013.pdf (2011-02-07)
Programové priority SaS (2009)
Radšej majme recesiu ako euroval, tvrdí pre HN Sulík. (2011):
http://hnonline.sk/ekonomika/c1-51636130-radsej-majme-recesiu-ako-euroval-tvrdi-sulik-pre-hn 23.4,2011 (2011-25-04)
SaS sa zaradí do rodiny európskych liberálnych demokratov. (2010):
http://www.sme.sk/c/5586855/sas-sa-zaradi-do-rodiny-europskych-liberalnych-demokratov.html#ixzz11wzjbW3c (2010-10-10)
Slovakia: Fastest-Growing E.U. Economy Slowing Down. Oxford Analytica, 12.16.08 (2008):
http://www.forbes.com/2008/12/15/slovakia-eu-economy-cx_1216oxford.html (2011-22-03)

Slovensko – stabilné srdce Európy (Program pre voľby do Európskeho parlamentu 2009). (2009): www.hzds.sk (2011-13-04)
Sme cesta pre Slovensko. Volebný program Kresťanskodemokratického hnutia 2010. (2010):
http://www.kdh.sk/data/upload/documents/KDH_volebny-program_2010.pdf (2011-24-04)
Sociálna Európa –odpoveď na krízu. Volebný program strany Smer – Sociálna demokracia pre voľby do Európskeho parlamentu 2009. (2009): www.strana-smer.sk (2011-19-04)
The European Financial Stability Facility. (2010):
http://www.efsf.europa.eu/about/index.htm (2011-27-04)
The European Stabilization Mechanism. (2010):
http://europa.eu/rapid/pressReleasesAction.do?reference=MEMO/10/173 (2011-23-03)
Volebný program KDH do Európskeho parlamentu. (2009): Dostupné na: www.kdh.sk (2011-08-04)
Výsledky volieb do európskeho parlamentu. (2009):
www.elections2009-results.eu/sk/index_sk.html (2011-07-04)
Za prosperujúce Slovensko v silnej Európe. /Skrátený program SDKÚ-DS pre voľby do Európskeho parlamentu 2009. (2009):
www.sdkuonline.sk (2011-24-05)
120 nápadov pre lepší život Slovenska. Volebný program strany Sloboda a solidarita.(2010):
http://120napadov.sk/ (2011-27-04)

Chapter 6
The impact of the economy on governments' electoral performance

Hanne Marthe Narud

Introduction

Former British Prime Minister Harold Wilson once stated that:

> All political history shows that the standing of a Government and its ability to hold the confidence of the electorate at a General Election depend on the success of its economic policy (in Dalton 2004: 126).

It is a widely recognized assumption among politicians, political commentators, and social scientists that elections are referenda on the economy.[36] The belief is that voters will reward the government when economic conditions are good, but will punish it in times of economic recession. This more or less universal "truth" has been subject to an extensive amount of empirical research, in which students have attempted to define which types of conditions are most relevant for the economic vote. Much of this research indicates that there is a relationship between the economy and the vote, but the direction and strength of this relationship are complex and less intuitive than the simple notion of economic voting would predict (see e.g. Lewis-Beck/Paldam 2000; Van der Brug et al. 2007; Duch/Stevenson 2008). Moreover, the electoral fortunes of incumbent parties are not conditioned by economic factors alone. Systematic research across countries reveals that electoral performance varies according to system-specific variables such as type of government, critical events, and changes in the political environment of political parties (Bengtsson 2004; Narud/Valen 2008). The important question is which kinds of political and economic contexts are likely to condition the economic vote.

This overall question forms the point of departure for this paper, in which I will explore the electoral rewards and punishments of incumbent parties in a

---

36 A first draft of this paper was presented at the Comparative Politics Speaker Series, Department of Political Science, UCSD, February 1 2011. In addition to those participating there, I would like to thank Emily Matthews for helpful suggestions. A second draft was presented at the Politics Seminar, Institute for Social Research, Oslo, March 4 2011, and I would like to express my thanks for the comments I was given there. I am also grateful to Ingvild Stakkevold Reymert for research assistance.

Northern European context. Three questions are analyzed. First, to what extent is the "adverse incumbency effect" in parliamentary systems conditioned by economic factors? Second, under which conditions is the economy a constraint on incumbent parties? Third, what is the overall impact of the economy compared to other types of issues, for instance factors related to social structure, policy issues, and ideology? In the subsequent empirical analysis I will analyze these questions based on data from the Norwegian political system. Norway is an interesting case because of its role as a petrostate. It also has one of the most highly developed welfare systems in the world. Hence, the political consequences of its oil fortune will be a key issue in the paper.

I shall begin by reviewing some of the previous research on the electoral performance of governments, and then discuss the possible link between the economy and the vote. A brief overview is then provided of economic development in Norway, and the electoral performance of governments in the postwar period. I then explore the possible effects of the economic development on the electoral performance of governments. In so doing, I lean on survey data from the national election studies. My main concern is to explore the magnitude and nature of economic voting in Norway. To illustrate the analytical points, I shall restrict my analysis to three selected cases (elections). I begin with the assertion that there is a degree of "wear and tear" on incumbent governments in Western democracies.

The electoral performance of governments

The theoretical assumption behind the "negative incumbency effect" hypothesis is based upon the notion that voters judge governing parties retrospectively upon their performance (Fiorina 1981). Governing parties may be held to stricter standards than opposition parties, particularly in consistency between promises and performance. In terms of vote-seeking, holding office may therefore be a disadvantage. Indeed, this assumption runs contrary to the hypothesized effect of incumbency in the U.S., where exploiting office would be a more likely outcome (Cronin 1980; Polsby/ Wildavsky 1980). Within the parliamentary context of Western Europe, however, the idea that there is "wear and tear" on parties in government has received fairly wide empirical support (e.g. Rose/Mackie 1983; Narud/Valen 2008).

In their analyses of seventeen European countries between 1945 and 1999, Narud and Valen (2008) clearly demonstrate that in all the countries studied there is an adverse incumbency effect, as indicated by Figure 6.1. Even though great variations may be observed between countries in the magnitude of the electoral losses (and gains), their analyses show that the average incumbency loss has increased monotonically over a period of fifty years.

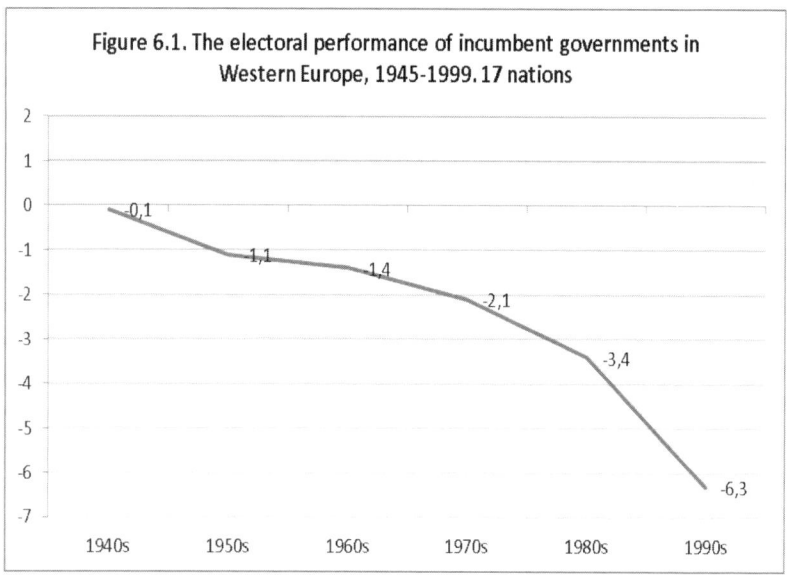

Figure 6.1. The electoral performance of incumbent governments in Western Europe, 1945-1999. 17 nations

Source: Narud and Valen, 2008:380

A number of scholars have attempted to define the institutional conditions under which voters constitute a constraint on parties in government (e.g. Strøm 1990; Powell/Whitten 1993; Narud/Irwin 1994; Müller/Strøm 1999; Anderson 2000; Bengtsson 2004; Narud/Valen 2008). The main argument has been that the performance of incumbents is conditioned by the clarity of responsibility of the parties involved. Clarity of responsibility is enhanced by party-system characteristics; such as the number of parties, the cleavage system, and consequently, the dimensionality of policy space. In addition, clarity of responsibility may be linked to the type of government, i.e. minority vs. majority, and coalition vs. single-party government. The most fundamental difference is between two-party systems and multiparty systems, since these generate different types of government. According to the logic of retrospective voting, with only two parties competing, voters can more easily assign blame and punish the government for poor performance by voting against it.

Voters in multi-party systems, however, are less likely to employ such retrospective penalties, since coalition governments are the norm rather than the exception. With a coalition government, there is no indication of which incumbent the voters should hold accountable – or to which alternative party they should turn.[37] The basic argument in the literature on democratic choice has been that coalition government obscures accountability, thereby reducing the electorate's ability to assign blame (Dahl 1966; Epstein 1967; Schattschneider 1942; Austen-Smith/Banks 1988; Laver/Shepsle 1990; Strøm 1990; Narud 1996; 1996a). To a certain extent, the same logic applies to minority governments. Since to enact legislation these governments must rely on the support of opposition parties, they can always attempt to shift the blame for policy failures on to other parties (Strøm 1990; Powell/Whitten 1993). Based on the above reasoning, Narud and Valen (2008) have tested whether weak governments (i.e. coalition government and minority cabinets), which can deflect accountability, do better at the polls than strong governments (i.e. single-party majority government). In addition, they have examined whether the electoral performance of cabinets correlates positively with party-system fragmentation, polarization, and extremism, since these attributes of the party system are likely to make alternatives to the incumbent government less likely (Narud/Valen 2008:372).

Their findings reveal that there are some very complex relationships, in which cabinet size as well as party-system characteristics play a role. For instance, voters tend to be less hard on incumbents if no feasible alternatives are apparent. Consequently, the greater the fragmentation of the bargaining environment, the better the performance of the incumbents. Furthermore, some of the strongest effects lie in the most proximate circumstances surrounding the election, in critical events, and macro-economic conditions. When linked to the literature on economic voting, these results are of great relevance. Systematic research across countries reveals that the impact of the economy varies according to system-specific variables such as the type of government, critical events, and changes in the political environment of political parties (Anderson 2000; Bengtsson 2004; Narud/Valen, 2008).

---

37 This argument is valid also in prospective terms. The proposition would then be that the effect of incumbency is related to the voters' perceptions of the parties' future achievements, and that they vote for those parties they believe would be best qualified for dealing with certain policies.

The economy

Considerable research efforts have been expended on specifying precisely the way in which the economy influences elections. A key variable in this respect has been *clarity of responsibility*, as the traditional accountability model of retrospective voting has already suggested. Voters are more likely to vote economically if political institutions clarify who is responsible for what, and if there is a viable alternative to the incumbent government (Powell/Whitten 1993). Anderson (1995), for instance, demonstrates that the effect of economic conditions on cabinet support varies with party-system change (measured in terms of the effective number of parties). The greater the effective number of parties, the more complex the coalition's bargaining environment, and consequently, the harder it is for voters to obtain the information needed to hold the government accountable for economic measures. For instance, economic voting is less likely as coalition governments become larger (oversized) and more complex, since voters find it difficult to attribute responsibility to specific incumbent parties. By the same logic, economic voting is less likely in systems dominated by minority governments, since they must rely on the support of opposition parties, thereby blurring the responsibility for economic outcomes.

On this point it should be mentioned that a methodological discussion has taken place in connection with the application of aggregate data versus survey data. The main criticism raised against macro-level studies concerns their lack of sensitivity to shifts in social and political forces (see e.g. Lewis-Beck 1986). Micro-level data, on the other hand, are more sensitive to "small-nation" problems, resulting for example from the influence of the international environment. Individual level data do, however, allow for testing the importance of retrospective versus prospective evaluations of the economy, as well as detecting whether voters have sociotropic rather than egotropic concerns (Listhaug 2005:217). Concerning the impact of the economy on the individual vote, a number of scholars have found that the effect is marginal compared to other factors of importance to the electorate (Lewis-Beck/Paldam 2000:114; Dorussen/Taylor 2002:101). Bengtsson's analysis of the elections in twenty-one Western nations between 1950 and 1997, for instance, indicates that "pure" economic conditions can explain only three per cent of the changes in the governments' popular support. The result improves markedly, however, when various types of contextual variables are included in the model (Bengtsson 2004:756-758). Contextual factors that help clarify the responsibility for economic management, such as the target size of the governing party or the availability of alternatives, contribute to the understanding of differences in economic effects across countries (Anderson 2000; Bengtsson 2004). Moreover, the effect of the economic variables is stronger when volatility is low and turnout is high, especially in political and institutional environments with clear responsibility structures and available alternatives (Bengtsson 2004:762).

Consequently, the relative importance of economic factors varies between countries and over time, and with the level of analysis. There is some very strong evidence for economic voting in the U.S., for example, whereas the empirical evidence for other parts of the developed world is much weaker. The economic effect on the vote also seems to vary with the level of welfare-state development, suggesting that the economy plays less of a role in states with high levels of spending (Pacek/Radcliff 1995; for evidence in the U.S., see Singer 2010).[38] Unemployment, real disposable income, and inflation have had the most consistent influences, whereas a country's balance of trade has generally not been significant (Harrop/Miller 1987:218). Furthermore, the various types of economic indicators seem to hit differently governments with a different policy platform. Using rates of unemployment, inflation rates, and economic growth (in terms of the annual percentage change in GDP) as the independent variables, Narud and Valen (2008) have shown that the election result varied between governments of different ideological leanings. Hence, the results consistently showed that conservative parties were much more susceptible to inflation than leftist parties were to unemployment. These findings are in line with the notion of "issue ownership" of right-wing parties on economic issues, but inconsistent with the issue ownership attached to social democrats on unemployment issues. In this context, the Swedish scholar Johan Martinson (2009) argues that electoral outcomes of governments are best understood through an "integrated model" of economic voting and issue ownership, taking into account the effects of both economic changes and the public agenda. A high level of unemployment, for instance, usually means that the issue of unemployment will be salient during the election campaign, potentially damaging support for the incumbent government. The incumbent's issue ownership of the issue, however, could cushion the

---

38 Pacek/Radcliff (1995: 46-47; 56-58) suggest at least two reasons for these variations. The first has to do with the relationship with the economy and turnout, and the role played by welfare in conditioning this relationship (in nations where welfare provisions are especially generous, poor economic conditions do not depress turnout), implying that the welfare state will indirectly affect the vote via its impact on the composition of the electorate. The second is the manner in which welfare systems affect voter sensitivity to economic conditions, suggesting that welfare provisions will directly affect the vote by altering voter decision calculi. In marginal welfare states, the lack of a social "safety net" will tend to increase citizen sensitivity to economic fluctuations, making them particularly alert to economic declines. By contrast, in true welfare states the general public seems to have created a system whereby they have removed short-term economic performance as the major electoral issue. "In this way", Pacek/Radcliff (1995: 58) argue, "the existence of the welfare state is itself a kind of standing accountability – a way of assuring material well being – which makes an American-style electoral obsession with the economy unnecessary".

negative effect of unemployment, since voters have confidence in the government's ability to deal with the problem (Martinson 2009:8).

In terms of party difference, Narud and Valen have found that the electoral result varied for parties with different governmental responsibilities. The minister of finance was affected most severely by the macro-economic variables, particularly inflation, but the ideological composition of the government was also of relevance. The combination of a rightist profile and inflation had a significant, negative impact upon the electoral result of the party of the minister of finance. This fact indicates that voters on aggregate are surprisingly discriminating in their judgments, even though the prime minister's party was less affected in this respect, as Figure 6.2 demonstrates.

Figure 6.2: The impact of the economy on different cabinet parties. Western Europe, 1945-1999

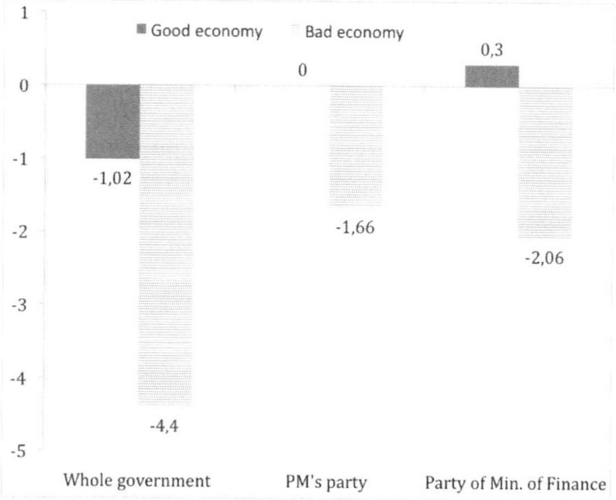

	Good economy	Bad economy
Whole government	-1,02	-4,4
PM's party	0	-1,66
Party of Min. of Finance	0,3	-2,06

Source: Narud/Valen, 2008:386

It is also evident that the government as such does not receive any extra credit (votes) for a growing economy. In fact, Figure 6.2 points to some very clear negative effects from economic recession, whereas there is little indication of any positive effects from economic improvement. This kind of "grievance asymmetry" indicates that there is a negative bias in the electorate, making voters more alert to economic troubles than to good news (see e.g. Nannestad/Paldam 1997; Dorussen/Taylor, 2002:10).

This suggests that dissatisfaction with government performance is a more important predictor of electoral behavior than satisfaction. Hence, there is a tendency for poor economic behavior (or voters' perception of such) to have a stronger relationship with voters' choice than positive performance.

The "Curse" of the Oil Purse

"Ten years from now, twenty years from now, you will see: oil will bring us ruin... Oil is the Devil's excrement". This citation is taken from former Venezuelan politician J. P. Pérez Alfonso, one of the founders of OPEC. It serves to illustrate the "resource curse thesis," which claims that there is a negative link between natural resource affluence and economic growth, as has been the case in some of the oil-producing countries (Auty, 1993). Like many other nations in Western Europe, over the last few decades Norway has experienced rapid economic and social changes. Norway's first political parties were founded when the country was one of Europe's poorest, in the late 1800s, a decade that also marked the peak of Norwegian emigration to the United States (Rokkan, 1970; Valen, 1981; Strøm/Svåsand, 2000). A hundred and plus years later, the country may be characterized as one of the most prosperous welfare states in the world, and indeed, one of the richest in terms of GNP per capita. Enjoying huge incomes from the oil industry, Norway's GNP reached an all-time high in 2009 at USD 59,300 per capita (the population of Norway is about 4.8 million). Petroleum was found in the North Sea in 1969, and in the following years a number of major discoveries were made. At present Norway ranks as the world's third largest oil exporter, and the second largest exporter of natural gas after Russia.[39] The country has an extensive social welfare system,[40] and one contributing factor is of course the wealth acquired from the oil industry. However, the bulk of the welfare arrangements are publicly financed through taxation, as all wage earners contribute a fixed percentage of their earnings in national insurance. Welfare expenditures form a considerable part of GDP, and concerns have increased that growing demand for welfare goods due to demographic and social changes will lead to the "overloading" of public expenses in the future.

No doubt, Norway's oil and gas resources have boosted considerably the country's economy. However, the Norwegian story is not a typical one and does not follow the predicted effect of the "resource curse thesis". In her book with the telling title *The Paradox of Plenty*, Terry Lynn Karl (1997) analyzes how some major petrostates have mismanaged their oil fortunes. It is not only poor countries that can mismanage income from oil, as we learn from the expression 'Dutch disease' which is used to describe the effects of the Netherlands spending its income from natural gas in the 1960s and 1970s, leading to unsustainable growth in the public sector and a decline in manu-

---

39 Available at: http://www.regjeringen.no/upload/FIN/Statens%20pensjonsfond/The_Norwegian_Petroleum_Sector_te.pdf.

40 A compulsory national insurance scheme provides citizens with benefits such as universal child benefit, one year's paid maternity leave, and pensions for the elderly, the disabled, widows and widowers, and so forth. Health insurance is mandatory for all inhabitants.

facturing industries (Larsen 2004). In contrast, Karl (1997) describes Norway's management of its oil fortunes as a success. The country is more developed than most petrostates and is not dependent on this resource alone. More importantly, Norway has developed strong state institutions to handle the financial risks of oil. A key institution is the oil fund or, to use its official name, the Government Pension Fund, which invests the income from oil abroad, and sets a rule for spending per year – four per cent. The oil fund and the procedures for spending from it have reined in many of the dysfunctionalities of a large oil income and have stabilized the economy. In this respect, the establishment of the oil fund has been a tremendous success. However, not all problems have been solved. Recently, the government has attempted to reduce excess spending – which was one of the means used to fight the financial crisis in 2008-9. An important part of its efforts has been to make the spending rate from the oil fund return to the annual four per cent level. By any standard the fund is very large, as Figure 6.3 demonstrates, and it has shown strong and continuous annual growth.

Figure 6.3: The value of the Government Pension Fund. NOK billions (August 2010)

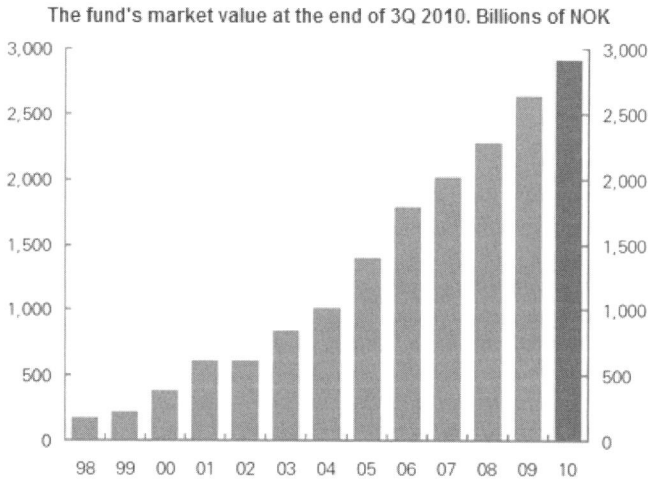

Source: http://www.nbim.no/en/Investments/Market-Value

Figure 6.4 presents the total gains and losses for the government parties in all the elections in the post-war period. The period from 1945 to the turn of the millennium is presented by decade, whereas the three most recent elections (2001, 2005 and 2009) are presented separately.

Figure 6.4 clearly demonstrates that negative incumbency effects have been on the rise in Norway, an observation that parallels the evidence we saw in Figure 6.1 concerning all Western European countries. While some variations are evident in the Norwegian case, the overall trend of negative incumbency effects are most severely pronounced in the elections of 2001 and 2005, with the governments (from different party blocks) losing 11.7 per cent on both occasions.

Figure 6.4: The costs of ruling. The electoral performance of parties in office at the time of the election (in per cent of national vote). Norway 1945-2009, total average gained/lost = - 1.8

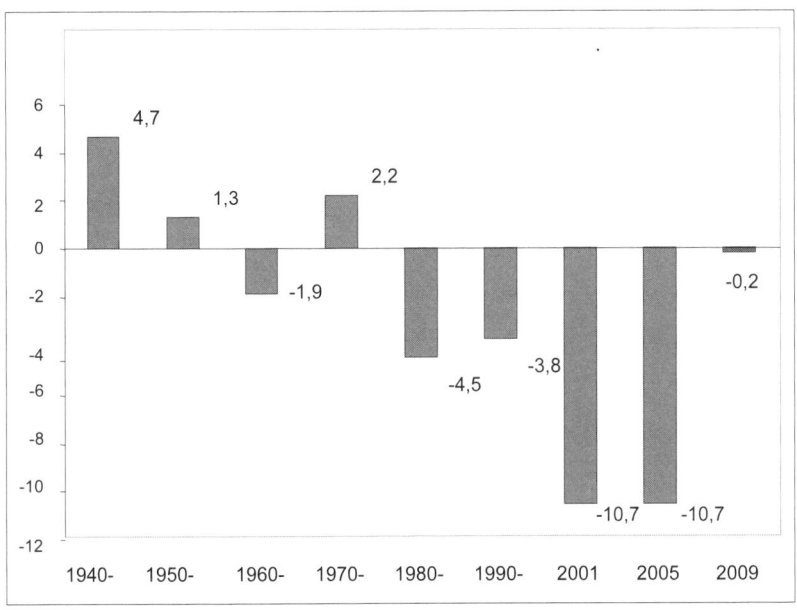

These are striking results, given the enormous economic growth in the period at hand. By contrast, we can detect virtually no incumbency effect (positive or negative) in the 2009 election, which took place in the shadow of the financial crisis. In fact, the 2009 centrist-left government was the first one to survive an election in sixteen years. Indeed, the results of these three elections run contrary to any intuitive understanding of the economy and the vote. How can we explain this paradox?

Even though a number of factors must surely have played a role in the electoral fate of the incumbent parties, I would argue that the contrasting patterns of the three elections are related to economic factors, and particularly to the size of the oil fund, but in very different ways. While most of the oil money is kept out of the domestic economy (due to the nature of the Pension Fund), it is not kept out of the minds of voters. Public opinion data from the 1997-2005 period show that citizens want to spend more of the money than actual government policies allow for (Listhaug, 2007; Narud/Valen, 2007: 277). Hence, the conflicting views between government policies and the mass public on public spending have created over the years a "frustration gap". With relevance to these issues, Listhaug (2007: 135) writes as follows: "Political parties, especially the Progress Party and the Socialist Left Party,[41] as well as important interest organizations and advocacy groups, immediately started to observe the contrast between important tasks and problems that cannot be solved within the constraints of current state budgets, and the pile of money that steadily grows under the label of the oil fund. But this pile of money cannot be accessed easily: it is likely that frustrations caused by seeing the cake and not be able to eat it, if shared by many citizens, may undermine political trust."

In the next part of this paper I attempt to substantiate the effect of the economy on the relationship between citizens and government. My emphasis is on the three most recent elections in Norway, in 2001, 2005, and 2009. I will show that these elections display very different patterns with regard to the impact of the oil wealth. In 2001 and 2005 in the form of a "curse" – in the sense that the frustration effects of oil wealth had grown over time (in line with the size of the fund), causing voters to expect more than the governments were able to deliver, particularly in terms of welfare goods. By contrast, in 2009 in the way of a "blessing" – in the sense that the economic resources available from the oil fund enabled the government to run a series of economic programs to counteract the negative effects of the financial crisis. In the 2009 election, in contrast to in 2001 and 2005, 'economic shock' from the global financial crisis may have had a moderating effect on voters' expectations vis-à-vis the government.

---

41 These are the two wing parties on the left-right scale in Norwegian politics. At present, following the parliamentary elections in September 2009, there are seven parties represented in parliament. Two are left-of-center parties (the Socialist Left and Labour), three are centrist parties (the Center Party, the Christian People's Party, and the Liberals), and two are right-of-center parties (the Conservatives and the Progress Party).

Empirical analysis

Norway has a complex multiparty system[42] with a record of single-party and coalition governments (both minority and majority) (for an overview see Narud/Strøm, 2000). In terms of links between government type and economic effects on the vote, Listhaug (2005) observes that there are only weak and irregular effects found for Norway, and that these trends may be explained by the dominance of minority governments, a weak opposition and political events that overshadowed economic concerns in the elections studied (1985-1997). The retrospective evaluation of the national economy has been the most consistent dimension of economic voting, but even this dimension was without impact in the 1997 election. Listhaug did not include any preference variables examining the effect of the oil wealth in his model, even though he has linked this aspect to declining political trust in later publications (Listhaug, 2007; see also Aardal, 2003).

The three governments to be analyzed in the present paper differ in terms of cabinet type, ideological composition, and size. The incumbent facing the electorate in 2001 was a single-party Labor government. In 2005, however, there was a center-right minority government consisting of the Christian People's Party, the Conservatives and the Liberals, which had to give way to a center-left majority coalition of Labor, the Center Party and the Socialist Left Party which met the electorate as the incumbent government in the 2009 election.

I have already noted that the revenues from the oil fund can have opposite effects than those predicted by the conventional model of economic voting. Even though the overall impact of economic factors has been modest compared to other factors, Norwegian voters seem to have been well aware of the changes that have taken place in the economy. Hence, Narud and Valen (2007:270) found that voters' retrospective evaluations of the national economy between 1985 and 2005 went hand in hand with the actual development of the macro economy. Moreover, the rapidly improving economy which formed the bases of the elections in 2001 and 2005 was clearly reflected in the eyes of voters, as Figure 6.5 confirms.[43] This is evident particularly in 2005, when very few voters said that their personal or the national economy had deteriorated (nine and eleven per cent). The great majority of them reported that the economic conditions were the same as earlier. In addi-

---

42   Cf. previous footnote.
43   Identical wording has been used in all surveys. "**Personal economy**: *We are interested in how people are doing economically nowadays. Would you say that you and your household have a better or worse economy than a year ago? Is it much better or a bit better? Is it much worse or a bit worse?* **National economy**: *Would you say that the economic situation in the country has become better in the last 12 months, almost as before or worse? Would you say much better or a bit better? Would you say much worse or a bit worse?*"

tion to the retrospective evaluations reported there, the voters' prospective perceptions of the economy as well as that of unemployment were positive (Narud/Valen, 2007; Narud/Aardal, 2007). As expected, in 2009 the number of voters with a positive perception of the national economy dropped substantially. However, the same is not the case for personal economy – in spite of the surge of the economic crisis. In addition, and more surprisingly, the number of voters stating that the economy had deteriorated did not increase in 2009 (figures not shown). Again, the majority of voters said that the economy had stayed about the same.

Figure 6.5: Voters' retrospective perceptions of their personal and the national economy, 1985-2009. Per cent stating that the economy has become "much better" or "somewhat better"

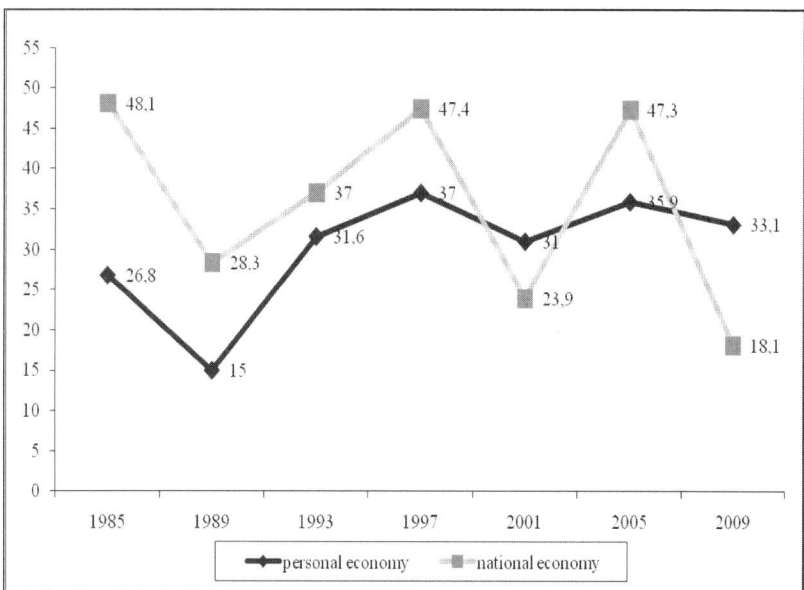

Returning to the elections of 2001 and 2005, none of the incumbent governments at the time was able to cash in on any benefits from the positive developments. Instead, the incumbent parties suffered record high losses (cf. Figure 6.4). These observations are interesting in light of the "grievance asymmetry" hypothesis and the alleged "curse of the oil purse". I have argued that a positive economic development over a longer period of time will have a tendency to create expectations among voters that are almost impossible to meet. Perhaps the policy performance of the governments were falling short of voters' expectations, simply because voters demanded the governments "deliver" more than they were in terms of welfare, education, and other types of benefits.

Indeed, analyses of the 2001 and 2005 elections indicate a clear tendency in this direction, even though the political context of the two elections varied (Narud/Valen, 2007; Narud/Aardal, 2007). In 2001 Labor faced the electorate after just eighteen months in office. In the spring session of 2000, the party had joined the rightist parties in toppling the centrist "mini-coalition" headed by Kjell Magne Bondevik, whose government was quite popular according to the opinion polls (Aalberg, 2002:377; Narud/Strøm, 2011). In 2001 the Labor government had no real challengers, however, as the opposition parties failed to form a viable alternative. By contrast, the center-right minority coalition of 2005, which had been in office for the entire four-year period, was challenged by the red-green alliance, consisting of Labor, the Center Party and the Socialist Left, which for the first time in history formed a joint majority alternative left-of-center. This fact made the question of governing alternatives a dominant issue in the election campaign. In addition, the election agendas of the 2001 and 2005 campaigns were quite different. In 2001 two issues dominated the agenda: taxes and schools. The 2005 campaign had a wider spectrum of issues in which a number of welfare questions were at the forefront (Aardal, 2003; 2007). What the two governments had in common, however, was a context of favorable developments in the macro-economy: a low level of inflation and unemployment, considerable growth in GNP, and a swelling oil purse.

Yet the economy, at least in terms of the traditional macroeconomic indicators, played a very modest role in voters' party choice in both elections. If we first look at the 2001 election, the economic indicators explained only two per cent of the support for the incumbent party (Narud/Valen, 2007:301). Voters' perceptions of their own economic situation in the future were the only indicator with a significant effect, whereas their perceptions of the national economy, which in many comparative studies as well as the national ones have emerged as the most relevant variable, had no significance. However, when taking into the equation voters' views on the use of oil money, the explained variance of the model improved considerably. Evidence showed that voters who supported a policy of increased spending of the oil revenues were much more inclined to vote against the government than those with a more restrictive view of public spending. In addition, many voters indicated that the parties to the right, the Conservatives and the Progress Party, had a better policy with regard to the oil fund than the incumbent government did. The single most important factor for voters' choice, however, was the government's performance on welfare issues, which was evaluated negatively by many voters. The overall analyses of the 2001 election showed that Labor had lost its traditional ownership of welfare issues (Aardal, 2003). Indeed, the discrepancy between voters' positive perceptions of the economy, and their negative evaluation of the government's performance, must have damaged the government considerably (Narud/Valen, 2007: 288-301).

The 2005 election had many parallel features to that of 2001, although the incumbent government was one of a different ideological "flavor". Incidentally, the electoral losses were the very same as for Labor in 2001. However, in coalition governments, the incumbent parties rarely suffer the same fate. In fact, they often vie with each other for votes, and this was the case here too. The Christian People's Party and the Conservatives suffered enormous losses, and reached their lowest ever share of votes. The third coalition partner, the Liberals, gained votes – benefiting substantially from the losses of its coalition partners (Aardal, 2007). The great victor this time was Labor, which retook many of its lost votes from four years back, and the Progress Party, which reached an all-time high in the history of the party. As was the case in 2001, the standard economic indicators played only a meager role for voters' support of the incumbent parties in 2005. Table 6.1 presents a blockwise regression of various clusters of explanatory variables identified by Narud and Aardal (2007:195) in their analysis of the election. The dependent variable is the joint electoral performance of all cabinet parties.

Of particular interest for us are the blocks showing the effects of the economic variables, even though it should be noted that three of the background variables (education, income, and age) retained significant effects after control for all other factors.[44] In other words, social and demographic background are by no means irrelevant for voters' choice, even though the various models of issue voting are the predominant explanatory tools these days. These observations suggest that economic voting should be assessed within a broader model of voting behavior.

The table shows that voters' evaluation of the national economy had a significant impact on the level of support for the government parties. The effect was quite strong and went in a positive direction, suggesting, rather unsurprisingly, that support for the government parties increased with positive evaluations of the country's economy. However, block 2 increased the explained variance only modestly. The same is true of voters' evaluations of the government's tax policy, which was one of the most important issues in the 2001 campaign – much to the benefit of the Conservatives. Voters' views of how to spend the revenues from the oil fund had a strong and negative effect on the incumbent parties' support, suggesting that the government's restricted oil policy did not fit well with voters who held a more expansive view on this question. Indeed, this result corresponds to the 2001 election with relevance to the Labor government.

---

44 References are made to the unstandardized coefficients when comparisons are made between the blocks.

Table 6.1: The impact of five sets of explanatory variables for the support of the incumbent parties in 2005 (voted for The Christian People's Party, Liberals or Conservatives). Block-wise linear regression. Standardized coefficients (beta)[45]

	Block 1 Background	Block 2 Economy	Block 3 Political issues	Block 4 Oil Money	Block 5 Ideology
Education (high)	.13**	.12**	.13**	.09**	.10**
Gender (women)	-.04	.00	.01	.01	.04
Income (high)	.16**	.14**	.13**	.11*	.07**
Age (high)	.04	.03	.04	.04	.12**
Occupation (low status)	-.09**	-.08**	-.07**	-.07**	-.03
Own economy better, retrospective		.02	.00	.00	-.02
Own economy better, prospective		-.01	-.01	-.01	-.01
Country's economy better, retrospective		.17**	.16**	.16**	.11**
Fear of unemployment		-.04	-.04	-.04	.01
Government's tax policy good			.14**	.14**	.06*
Government's tax policy bad			-.09**	-.08**	-.03
Spend more of the oil money				-.17**	-.18**
Public-private					.40**
R² (adjusted)	.07	.10	.13	.15	.29

* sig. on .05 level, ** sig. on .01 level   Source: Narud and Aardal, 2007:195

The overall importance of the oil question was not extensive, however, as the explained variance by introducing block 4 increased by only two per cent. What really mattered the most for voters' support (or failing support) for the government was their ideological leaning, i.e. their orientation along the public-private policy dimension. The substantive interpretation of this observation is that support for the incumbent government decreased with a favorable view of public enterprises. Interestingly, voters' views of the government's tax policy turned out to be insignificant after the inclusion of block 5, whereas the effect of the national economy and oil money held up in the final model specification.

---

45 Some claim that with a binary dependent variable logistic regression is a more suitable method than ordinary linear regressions. One argument is that with linear regressions we risk meaningless results, since the predicted probability may fall outside the range 0-1. Another argument (and the main one) is that the statistical tests for linear regressions are inappropriate with a binary dependent variable. Hellevik (2009) argues against these propositions claiming that the use of the two methods produces almost identical results for the two kinds of significance tests. Since results from logistic regression are difficult to understand, and in many cases may seem counterintuitive from a substantive point of view, he believes that OLS regression may well be used in these kinds of situations. Narud and Aardal (2007:195) tested both methods on the 2005 data, and the results were as good as identical.

So far we have discussed the relationship with government and the opposition as though the opposition parties were one entity. This is of course too simple given the prominent position of the Progress Party in Norwegian politics, particularly with relevance to the question of oil revenues. We have already mentioned the restrictive attitudes of Norwegian governments concerning the use of these revenues, and how all governments have advocated the rule that they would not use more than four per cent of the return of the fund to finance the state budget. This self-imposed rule has been controversial, however, and certainly not in line with the views of the majority of voters, as is clear from Figure 6.6.[46]

In all elections, save for the most recent one in 2009, voters who want to spend more of the oil income have greatly outnumbered those with a more restrictive view on this matter.

Figure 6.6: Voters' attitudes towards the governments' spending of oil revenues, 1997-2009

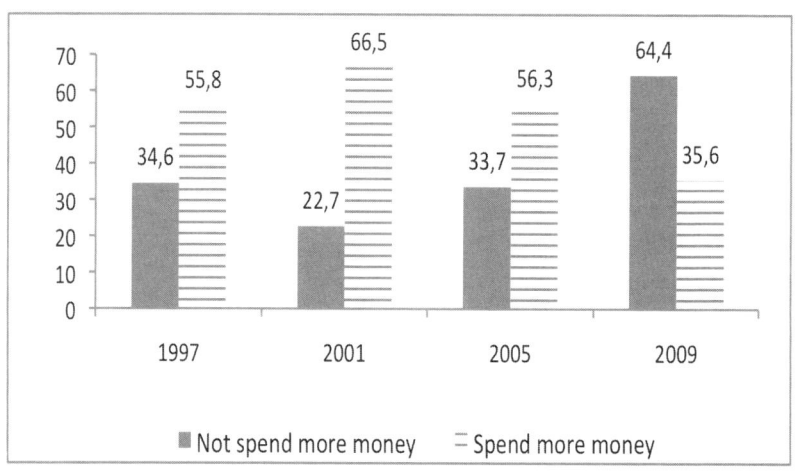

---

46   The wording of the question (which has been the same in all four surveys) is as follows: "Let's think about two people, A and B discussing a current question. We provide you with two assertions they came up with. A says: To avoid an increase in interest, and higher prices, we should not spend more of the oil income than we do at present. B says: To solve current problems in society we may spend considerably more of the oil income than we do at present. Which one of these persons would you agree more with?" In the figure we have excluded the number of voters holding a middle view (i.e. agree both with A and B, which was about ten per cent in all the surveys) and voters who responded "don't know".

The striking change that took place in voters' attitudes in connection with the 2009 election is a matter I will return to soon. The polarization between the two groups increased from 1997 to 2001, as the number of voters in the latter group decreased considerably. Voters who wanted to spend more of the income, on the other hand, increased in number. One reason for this development was surely the debate prior to the 2001 election in which the opposition parties recommended more liberal spending of the oil income. The strongest and most insistent advocate of this view was then (and still is) the Progress Party, which time and again has pointed to the marked discrepancy between private affluence and public poverty. Consequently, the party has demanded that the large surplus from oil revenues should be used to help solve domestic problems. The fact that the number of voters in favor of spending more of the oil revenues decreased somewhat in 2005 is most likely a reflection of the change of government in 2001, with the former opposition parties now in office adapting to the more "responsible" four per cent rule. With even the Socialist Left Party (not traditionally known for its fiscal conservatism) included in government, since 2005 the Progress Party has stood alone as the only "true" opposition party in Norwegian politics. The party's supporters stand out as the most ardent defenders of the increased use of the oil revenues (Aardal, 2003; Narud/Aardal, 2007). In 2005 even the majority of Socialist Left voters took a more moderate stance on the spending issue, whereas an overwhelming majority of Progress Party voters (eighty-three per cent) took the opposite position (Narud/Aardal, 2007:188).

How much is there to gain from being an advocate of increased spending of the oil money? Table 6.1 demonstrated that voters' attitudes towards the use of the oil income did not in themselves explain very much about voters' support for the government. However, when we examine the importance of this issue for the support of the Progress Party, the result is noticeable. Narud and Aardal (2007:197) leave no doubt as to the importance of the oil issue for the party's recent success. The explained variance more than doubled when attitudes towards the oil revenues were included in the model. In other words, what the Progress Party wins from its views on the oil issue is a potential loss for the incumbent parties advocating a stricter policy. As was the case with Labor in 2001, dissatisfaction with government performance on welfare policies clearly contributed to the poor result of the center-right cabinet also in 2005. Voters' evaluations were particularly negative concerning education, health policy, and care for the elderly, three of the core areas of the Conservatives and the Christian People's Party (Narud/Valen, 2007).

If we turn to the election of 2009, a rather different situation may be seen. Not only were the red-green parties able to hold on to government power, Figure 6.6 shows that the number of voters with a *restrictive* view of using more of the oil fund increased substantially from 2005 to 2009. Indeed, this group was now in the majority, while the number of voters holding a more expansive view formed the minority. A closer look at individual parties reveals that the Progress Party's voters are amazingly stable in their views. Even though some of the party's voters have moved in a more restrictive direction, a great majority of them are still in favor of spending more oil money. This means that the Progress Party is still the main recipient of frustrated voters wanting to show their discontent with the established parties. All other party voter groups have taken a more moderate stand. The importance of this latter development has to do with the frustration gap. This gap more or less closed in 2009 as a result of voter movements towards a more restrictive view of public spending.

2009: the "blessing" of the economic shock

The observed changes are most likely related to the effect of the financial crisis, and the necessity of the government to use more of the oil fund. Because of the global problems in the economy, the run-up to the 2009 election was quite different from those to the elections in 2001 and 2005. Around the world stock markets had fallen, large financial institutions had collapsed, and governments had to come up with rescue packages to counteract the effects of the financial "tsunami". Regarding the Norwegian government, the crisis started to show its effects in the second half of 2008, and from this point on the support for the government increased markedly. The effect, however, was restricted to the Labor Party and did not influence the support for the two junior partners of the coalition, the Socialist Left and the Center Party. At the same time the largest opposition party, the Progress Party, experienced a downturn in popular support, as demonstrated by Figure 6.7.

The surge for Labor was in line with similar trends for government parties in other European countries at the time. As the arrows for the banks and the stock markets pointed downwards, they pointed upwards for Gordon Brown in the UK, for Merkel in Germany, Sarkozy in France and Berlusconi in Italy. In other words, the economic crisis seemed to favor the parties in office. Some commentators related these trends to the phenomenon of "risk aversion", and people's general preference for certainty over uncertainty in times of emergency (see e.g. Colomer, 2008, for this line of argument). When subject to serious shocks, people seek refuge in the arms of the sitting government under the maxim: "you know what you've got, but not what you'll get". Indeed, the success of the Labor party in the 2009 election indicates that these kinds of psychological mechanisms may have played a role.

Figure 6.7: The popular support for Labor and the Progress Party, June 2008 – September 2009. Average per cent of all polls

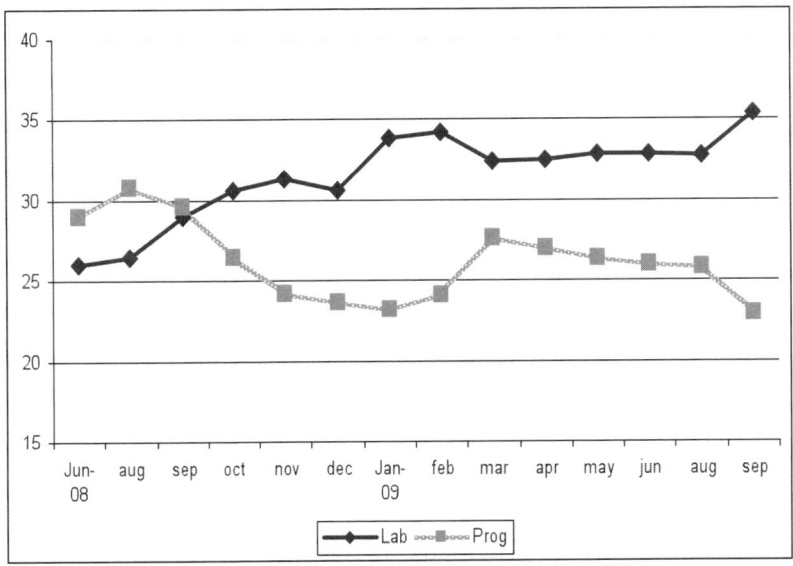

On the other hand, the lack of credible government alternatives, as well as the incumbent government's handling of the financial crisis, are among the more likely causes of its victory. During the campaign Prime Minister Jens Stoltenberg expressed the government's willingness to increase public spending in order to avoid a worsening recession. Hence, the government presented an expansive budget breaching the four per cent rule from the oil fund. Indeed, this limit had already been severely broken through various sets of stimulus packages before the election. The observed changes in voters' attitudes toward the spending of oil money between 2005 and 2009 (Figure 6.6) are probably partly a reflection of the economic measures already implemented by the government.

Figure 6.8 demonstrates that the government's strategy was a tremendous success in the eyes of voters.[47]

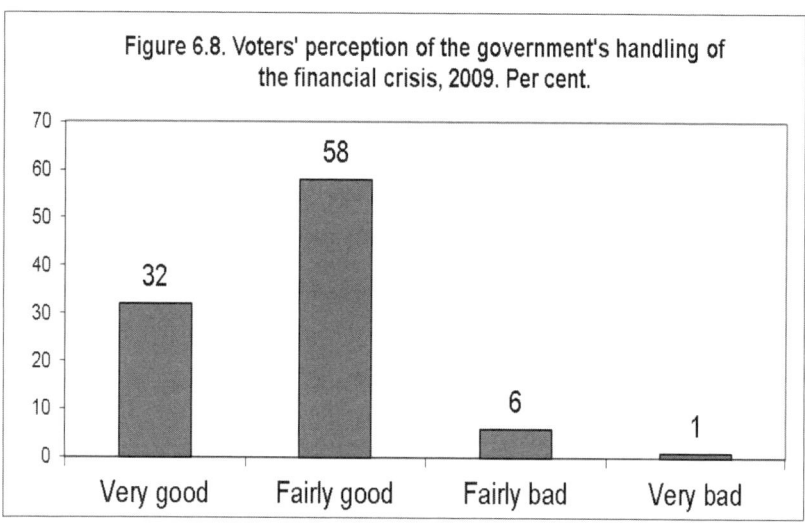

Figure 6.8. Voters' perception of the government's handling of the financial crisis, 2009. Per cent.

It is evident that a great majority of the voters were satisfied with the way the government had handled the financial crisis. Figure 6.8 shows that ninety per cent of the respondents indicated a positive view, whereas only seven per cent were critical of the government's actions.[48] These tendencies could be observed already in June 2009, in other words before the election campaign started (Listhaug/Narud, 2011). Of course, the most satisfied voters were those supporting the government coalition parties – Labor, the Center Party, and the Socialist Left. However, a majority of the Conservative Party's and the centrist parties' voters (the Liberals and the Christian People's Party) looked favorably upon the government's handling of this issue as well. The Progress Party's voters expressed the most negative opinions, but they were rather few. Only fourteen per cent believed that the red-green parties had done a poor job in handling the crisis.

The final question to be analyzed here is the overall impact of the economy on voters' support for the incumbent parties. Did economic factors play a more prominent role in the 2009 election than they have normally done in

---

47 The wording of the question is the following: *We now have a question about the financial crisis that struck Norway last year. How do you think the red-green government has handled this crisis? Do you think it has handled the crisis well, fairly well, fairly badly, or very badly?*

48 Three per cent of the respondents answered "don't know".

Norwegian elections? Again, let us lean on a multivariate regression model to shed light upon this question. I have included six blocks of variables to tap into the relative importance of the economy vis-à-vis other factors. No sign in front of the coefficient means a positive effect of the variable for government support, whereas a negative sign means that the indicator has a negative effect upon the support of the incumbent government. The results are shown in Table 6.2.

The table shows that only gender has a significant effect in the first block, confirming that female voters are more likely to support the center-left parties than men are. However, the explained variance of the first block is next to nothing. Introducing the classical economic variables in block 2 only slightly increases the explained variance. Two of the indicators are nevertheless significant: voters' retrospective perceptions of both their personal and the national economy. Hence, the probability of voting for the incumbent government increases as we move from negative to positive perceptions of the economy. Voters' views of the government's handling of the financial crisis, however, improve the explained variance considerably (block 3). This item has a strong, significant effect, suggesting that positive evaluations of this matter are strongly related to voting for the incumbent parties.

The explained variance increases by six percentage points when block 4 is introduced. Hence, a liberal view of spending more of the oil money has a significant and negative effect on voting for the incumbent parties, whereas a restrictive view of this issue has a positive effect. Of course, if voters' attitudes towards spending were to revert to a more liberal level, this may very well reopen the frustration gap. As past experience has shown, this may indeed be a liability for future governments. Dissatisfaction with government performance on school and transport policy (block 5) has a significant and negative effect upon the support for the governing parties.[49]

---

49 Analyzing voters' perceptions of government performance, Narud (2011) demonstrates that these were the two areas that caused most dissatisfaction among the respondents.

Table 6.2: The impact of six sets of explanatory variables for the support for the incumbent parties in 2009 (voted for the Socialist Left, Labor or the Center Party). Block-wise linear regression. Standardized coefficients (beta)

	Block 1 Background	Block 2 Economy	Block 3 Financial crisis	Block 4 Oil money	Block 5 Government performance	Block 6 Ideology
Education (high)	.00	.00	-.04	.06	-.04	-.05
Gender (women)	.11**	.13**	.13**	.11**	.09**	.04
Income (high)	-.02	-.03	-.04	-.05	-.05	.00
Age (high)	.02	.02	.00	.01	.02	-.02
Occupation (low status)	.04	.04	.05	.06*	.06	.03
Own economy retrospectively, better		.11**	.08**	.06*	.06*	.06*
Own economy prospectively, better		.00	-.02	-.02	-.02	.00
National economy retrospectively, better		.07*	.06	.05	.05	.05
Fear of unemployment in future, yes		.03	.05	.05	.06*	.04
Government's handling of financial crisis, good			.32**	.28**	.27**	.14**
Spend more of the oil money, yes				-.25**	-.25**	-.19**
Government performance on school and transport policy, poor					-.14**	-.10**
Government performance on children and family policy and kindergardens, good					.08**	.06**
Public-private index (private)						-.45**
R² (adjusted)	.01	.02	.12	.18	.20	.37

* sig. .05
** sig. .01

By contrast, a positive view of government performance on family policy and kindergardens has a positive effect. However, this block only modestly boosts the explained variance of the model. Finally, introducing the public-private policy index in block 6 almost doubles the explained variance. The items on the financial crisis and the oil money retain significant and strong effects, however, after control for ideology.[50] In other words, economic factors related directly or indirectly to the financial crisis were central for the support for the incumbent government in 2009.

No doubt, the financial means available to the Norwegian government through the oil fund must have been a tremendous asset for the incumbent government in 2009. It gave it the opportunity to show "muscles" in a situation where the economic recession created insecurity among many voters. In so doing, the government was able to meet a long-standing demand by many voters to spend more of the oil money to solve domestic problems. It seems a paradox, therefore, that the more classic economic issues (economic perceptions of the national/private economy, unemployment, and so forth) did not play a more significant role in our comprehensive model. This may be related to the 2009 campaign agenda, in which economic issues did not feature strongly (Narud, 2009; Jenssen/Kalstø, 2011). In addition, we have seen evidence from the election survey that voters had very few concerns about future developments of the labor market and the national or their personal economy. In fact, most voters believed the situation to be the same as earlier. Economic issues did, however, dominate a great part of the public debate in the year leading up to the election, and they certainly formed an important underlying premise in the competition between the political parties. In addition, Jenssen and Kalstø (2011) show that those voters who mentioned economy and labor market policy as the most important issues in the election rated the Labor Party very highly. The "issue ownership" of Labor was not shared by the junior partners of the coalition, the Centre Party and the Socialist Left (in spite of the latter holding the minister of finance portfolio), and this could help explain why Labor was the only incumbent party which seemed to benefit electorally from the crisis. In addition, we should be open to the possibility that the economic recession had a moderating effect on voters' expectations towards the government. These were exceptional circumstances, however, and the question is what will happen when the government returns to a "normal" spending policy in terms of the oil money.

Conclusion

Evidence suggests that the economy affects the vote, but that these effects are moderated by political institutions, contextual factors, and by different aspects of the economy. The importance and direction of economic factors vary between countries, between elections, over time, and with the level of analy-

---

50 I refer to the unstandardized b coefficients when comparing the changing effects from one block to the next.

sis. The main question in this chapter has been which kinds of political and economic contexts are likely to condition the economic vote. I have argued that within the context of the Norwegian welfare system, the impact of the economy is conditioned upon the development of the oil sector. The standard economic indicators have played only a modest role in the vote. One reason may have to do with the country's position as a small nation with an open economy. The influence of the national government on economic development is limited, and voters are thus less likely to hold the government accountable for the economy. Another, but by no means incompatible explanation is suggested by Pacek and Radcliff (1995): in states with generous welfare provisions, economic and social safety-nets lower the saliency of economic issues and make voters less alert to economic fluctuations. In the context of the Norwegian petroeconomy, we have seen that the strong government involvement in the oil sector has strengthened citizens' expectations of benefits they may get from the income from the oil. These expectations are in many ways linked to welfare policies.

The contrasting cases analyzed in this chapter show that the relationship between economic voting and the state of the economy is more complex than the conventional models would predict. A key aspect of voters' decisions to reward or punish the incumbent government seems to be linked to their expectations of government performance, rather than actual government performance. Moreover, voters' expectations are linked to their perceptions of the resources available to the government to solve current issues: voters do not automatically punish the government when the economy dips; instead, their decisions are based on whether governments fulfill expectations, given voters' perceptions of resources, government promises, and the problem at hand. In 2001 and 2005 when the economy was going well, voters' expectations were linked to their perceptions of welfare problems, and the incumbent governments failed to meet these. In 2009 – after the economic downturn – voters' expectations turned toward solving the problems caused by the crisis, and the oil revenues made it possible for the government to live up to these expectations, essentially closing the frustration gap. The break with the four per cent rule was an important prerequisite for this closure.

Due to its advantageous fiscal position, Norway has ridden out the financial crisis better than most OECD countries, and at present the extraordinary stimuli are being tightened to avoid overheating the economy. How likely is it that the government will be able to stick to the 4 per cent rule – or even go below it – in the future? There is no obvious answer to this question. It depends on international development as well as the price of oil (and hence, the growth of the oil fund). Furthermore, it depends on "who" is in government. So far, there has been fairly wide agreement among Norwegian political parties on the implementation of the 4 per cent rule. In 2009, for the first time, the majority of the voters were in line with the parties on this issue.

Only a majority of the Progress Party's voters was still in favor of spending more of the oil revenues, as has been the view of their own party for a number of years. There is no guarantee, however, that the observed changes in public opinion will last. Voters may return to a more expansive view of spending as the waves of the crisis diminish. Such a development will surely place severe constraints on future governments in Norway – and lead to negative incumbency effects – as has been the case in the past.

References

Aalberg, Toril (2002): Norway. In: *European Journal of Political Research 40*: 375-382.
Aardal, Bernt, ed. (2003): *Velgere i villrede. En studie av stortingsvalget i 2001*. Oslo: NKS-forlaget.
Aardal, Bernt, ed. (2007): *Norske velgere. En studie av stortingsvalget i 2005*. Oslo: Damm.
Anderson, Christopher J. (1995): Party Systems and the Dynamics of Government Support. In: *European Journal of Political Research 27*, 1, pp: 93–118.
Anderson, Christopher J. (2000): Economic Voting and Political Context: A Comparative Perspective. In: *Electoral Studies 19*, 2-3, pp: 151–70.
Austen-Smith, David/ Banks, Jeffrey S. (1988): Elections, Coalitions and Legislative Outcomes. In: *American Political Science Review 82*, 2, pp: 405–22.
Auty, Richard M. (1993): *Sustaining Development in Mineral Economies: The Resource Curse Thesis*. London and New York: Routledge.
Bengtsson, Åsa (2004): Economic Voting: The Effect of Political Context, Volatility, and Turnout on Voters' Assignment of Responsibility. In: *European Journal of Political Research 43*, 5, pp: 749-767.
Colomer, Josep (2008): Economic Crisis Favors Incumbent Governments. Josep Colomers Weekely Blog. Comments in insight in political Science. http://jcolomer.blogspot.com/2008_10_13_archive.html
Cronin, Thomas E. (1980): *The State of the Presidency*. Boston: Little and Brown.
Dahl, Robert (ed.) (1966): *Political Opposition in Western Democracies*. New Haven: Yale University Press.
Dalton, Russel (2004): *Democratic Challenges. Democratic Choices*. Oxford: Oxford University Press.
Dorussen Han/ Taylor, Michael (eds.) (2002): *Economic Voting*. London: Routledge.

Duch, Raymond M./ Stevenson, Randolph T. (2008): *The Economic Vote. How Political and Economic Institutions Condition Election Results*. New York: Cambridge University Press.
Epstein, Leon D. (1967): *Political Parties in Western Democracies*. New York: Praeger.
Fiorina, Morris P. (1981): *Retrospective Voting in American National Elections*. New Haven: Yale University Press.
Harrop, Martin/ Miller, William L. (1987): *Elections and Voters*. London: Macmillan.
Hellevik, Ottar (2009): Linear versus logistic regression when the dependent variable is a dichotomy. In: *Qual Quant 43*, 1, pp:59-74.
Jenssen, Anders Todal/ Kalstø, Åshild Male (2011): Reddet finanskrisen den sittende regjeringen i 2009? Om stigende forventningers misnøye og politisk nådetid. In: *Norsk statsvitenskapelig tidsskrift 27*, 1, pp:30-59.
Karl, Terry Lynn (1997): *The Paradox of Plenty: Oil Booms and Petro-States*. Berkeley, California: University of California Press.
Larsen, Erling Røed (2004): *Escaping the Resource Curse and the Dutch Disease?*. Discussion Papers, No. 377, Statistics Norway, Research Department.
Laver, Michael/ Shepsle, Ken (1990): 'Coalitions and Cabinet Government.' In: *American Political Science Review, 84*, 3, pp: 873–90.
Lewis-Beck, Michael (1986): Comparative Economic Voting: Britain, France, Germany, Italy. In: *American Journal of Political Science 30*, 2, pp: 315–46.
Lewis-Beck, Michael/ Paldam, Martin (2000): Economic Voting: an Introduction. In: *Electoral Studies 19*, 2-3, pp:113-121.
Listhaug, Ola (2005): Retrospective Voting. In Thomassen, Jacques. (ed.), *The European Voter A Comparative Study of Modern Democracies*. Oxford: Oxford University Press, pp: 213-234.
Listhaug, Ola (2007): Oil Wealth Dissatisfaction and Political Trust in Norway: A Resource Curse? In Ø. Østerud (ed.), *Norway in Transition*. London and NY: Routledge, pp: 130-147.
Listhaug, Ola/ Narud, Hanne Marthe (2011): The Changing Macro Context of Norwegian Voters: From Centre-Periphery Cleavages to Oil Wealth. In Rosema, Martin/ Denters Bas/ Aarts Kees (Eds.) How *Democracy Works: Political Representation and Policy Congruence in Modern Societies*. Amsterdam: Amsterdam University Press/Pallas Publications, pp: 239-255.
Martinsson, Johan (2009): *Economic Voting and Issue Ownership. An Integrative Approach*. Gothenburg: Department of Political Science.
Müller, Wolfgang C./Strøm, Kaare (eds.) (1999): *Policy, Office or Votes?* Cambridge: Cambridge University Press.

Nannestad, Peter/ Paldam, Martin (1997): The Grievance Asymmetry revisited: A Micro Study of Economic Voting in Denmark. In: *European Journal of Political Economy13*, 1, pp: 81-99.

Narud, Hanne Marthe (1996): Electoral Competition and Coalition Bargaining in Multi-Party Systems. In: *Journal of Theoretical Politics 8*, 4, pp: 499–525.

Narud, Hanne Marthe (1996a): Party Policies and Government Accountability: a Comparison between the Netherlands and Norway. In: *Party Politics 2*, 4, pp: 479–507.

Narud, Hanne Marthe (2009): De små marginenes valg. In: *Norsk statsvitenskaplig tidsskrift 25*, 4, pp: 357-373.

Narud, Hanne Marthe (2011): Et regjeringsvalg i skyggen av finanskrisen. In Aardal, B. (ed.), *Det politiske landskap. En studie av stortingsvalget i 2009*. Oslo: Cappelen-Damm: 221-256.

Narud, Hanne Marthe/ Irwin, Galen A. (1994): Must the Breaker Pay? Cabinet Crises and Electoral Trade-offs. In: *Acta Politica, 29*, 3, pp: 265–84.

Narud, Hanne Marthe/Strøm, Kaare (2000): Norway: A Fragile Coalitional order. In: Müller W. C./ Strøm K. (eds.): *Coalition Governments in Western Europe*. Oxford: Oxford University Press, pp: 158-191.

Narud, Hanne Marthe/ Valen, Henry (2007): *Demokrati og ansvar*. Oslo: Damm.

Narud, Hanne Marthe/ Aardal, Bernt (2007): Økonomisk stemmegivning i oljefondets skygge. In: Aardal, Bernt (ed.), *Norske velgere. En studie av stortingsvalget i 2005*. Oslo: Damm, pp: 173-200.

Narud, Hanne Marthe/ Valen, Henry (2008): Coalition Membership and Electoral Performance in Western Europe. In K. Strøm, W, C. Müller and T. Bergmann (eds.): *Cabinets and Coalition Bargaining. The Democratic Life Cycle in Western Europe*. Oxford: Oxford University Press, pp: 369-402.

Narud, Hanne Marthe/ Strøm, Kaare (2011): Coalition Bargaining in an Unforgiving Environment. In Andeweg R./ de Winter L. (eds.): *Puzzles of Government Formation. Coalition Theory and Deviant Cases*. London: Routledge, pp: 65-87.

Pacek, Alexander/ Radcliff, Benjamin (1995): Economic Voting and the Welfare State: A Cross-National Analysis. In: *The Journal of Politics*, vol. 57 no. 1: 44-61.

Polsby, Nelson/ Wildavsky, Aron (1980): *Presidential Elections*. New York: Charles Scribner's Sons.

Powell, G. Bingham/ Whitten, Guy D. (1993): A Cross National Analysis of Economic Voting: Taking Account of the Political Context. In: *American Journal of Political Science 37*, 2, pp:391-414.

Rokkan, Stein (1970): *Citizens, Elections, Parties*, Oslo: Universitetsforlaget.

Rose, Richard/ Mackie, Thomas (1983): Incumbency in Government: Asset or Liability. In: Daalder Hans/ Mair Peter (eds): *Western European Party Systems: Continuity and Change*. London: Sage, pp: 115-138.

Schattschneider, Elmer E. (1942): *Party Government*. New York: Farrar and Rinehart.

Singer, Matthew M. (2010): Economic Voting and Welfare Programmes: Evidence from the American States. In: *European Journal of Political Research 50*, 4, pp:479-503

Strøm, Kaare (1990): A Behavioral Theory of Competitive Political Parties. In: *American Journal of Political Science 34*, 2, pp: 565–98.

Strøm, Kaare/ Svåsand, Lars (1997): *Challenges to Political Parties*. Ann Arbor: Michigan University Press.

Valen, Henry (1981): *Valg og politikk*. Oslo: NKS-forlaget.

Van der Brug, Wouter/ van der Eijk, Cees/Franklin, Mark (2007): *The Economy and the Vote: Economic Conditions and Elections in Fifteen Countries*. Cambridge: Cambridge University Press.

Chapter 7
Social structure and party choice in Norway and Slovakia: a loosening of ties?

Oddbjørn Knutsen

Introduction

This study is a paired comparison of the relationship between social structure and party choice in Norway and Slovakia.[51] The two countries are different in many respects which are relevant to this research topic. Norway has a fairly stable party system which has developed over more than a century. The social cleavages that have underpinned the party system have long been studied, and it is well-known that socio-structural variables have had a comparatively large impact on how people vote. It has been established that voting behavior is in accordance with the central models developed of social cleavages. Indeed, one of the authors of perhaps the best known model is the Norwegian political scientist, Stein Rokkan. However, in recent decades Norway has witnessed considerable dealignment and, to some extent, realignment. The old structural model no longer explains party choice to the same degree as before, but new structural and issue dimensions have to some extent gained importance in terms of explaining party choice. Electoral volatility has increased significantly.

In Slovakia, the post-communist party system has been characterized by both stability and change. In the early 1990s Slovakia's position within Czechoslovakia was a central political issue; during most of the 1990s, conflicts related to Slovak nation-building were significant. Parties have split and merged, new ones have appeared, while others have disappeared and some of the new ones have proven to be short-lived. Accordingly, there has been considerable instability in the party system. Significant changes in the party system have occurred even since the period studied here. However, there has also been a stable core in the party system (Bakke/Sitter 2005). Within the context of Central and East European (CEE) countries, the issue of party-system stability has been seen in association with the strengthening of the relationship between social structure and party choice. A stronger relation-

---

51 I would like to thank Kevin Deegan-Krause for detailed and very helpful comments on a first draft of this article.

ship has been expected to increase the stability in the party system (Wessels/ Klingemann 2006: 23-24).

An initial hypothesis is thus that social structure has a larger impact on party support in Norway than in Slovakia, but due to the structural dealignment in the Norwegian case, the differences are probably not that great.

A paired comparison allows the researcher access to some descriptive depth and background knowledge. Simultaneously, it is possible to analyze the influence of historical and institutional forms that might explain the differences and similarities between the countries (Tarrow 2010). This is the main rationale for the research design in this chapter.

This chapter is organized as follows: in the following sections, the party systems and the conflict structure in the two countries are outlined. Changes in the party systems after 2006 are not discussed (see below). The survey material which represents the data for examining the relationship between social structure and party choice is then briefly presented. The data are from 2002-06 for Norway, and 2004-06 for Slovakia. The operationalizations of the socio-structural variables are next outlined, and the distributions of several of these variables are shown. The next section – which is the main one – examines the relationship between various social structural variables and party choice. Finally, the relative importance of these variables is examined, and a brief multivariate analysis is performed before conclusions are drawn.

The party systems

The Norwegian party system

The party system in Norway has traditionally been associated with the Nordic five-party system model. According to this, parties that belong to five party families are the dominant ones in the party system. These party families were the Conservatives, the Liberals, the Agrarians, the Social Democrats, and the Communists. The Social Democrats have been the largest party, followed by the Conservatives, while support for the three other parties was smaller, at least in the post-war period (Berglund/Lindström 1978).[52]

Support for the Communist Party declined during the 1950s and a New Left party emerged in the early 1960s. Since 1975 the party has been called the Socialist Left Party and has positioned itself as a supporter of environmentalist positions in addition to traditional concerns for economic equality (Knutsen 1997: 247-248). The party is a socialist left or left-libertarian alter-

---

52 Presentations of the development of the Norwegian party system are found in Rokkan (1967) and Urwin (1997).

native (Kitschelt 1988) in the party system, and replaced the Communist party in the five-party model. The party represents the New Left, in contrast to the Social Democrats which are the Old Left per se.

A significant deviation from the five-party model is the Christian People's Party which emerged in the 1930s. The other deviation is the most significant and is the party considered to be the New or Radical Right, the Progress Party. The party emerged as a protest party against high taxes and public expenditure, but since 1987 the party has focused considerably on immigration and law and order in its political campaigns. It has become the New Right party in the Norwegian party system and has had considerable political success. The Conservative Party is the Norwegian standard-bearer of the Old Right in the party system.

The Slovak party system

Many of the Slovak parties have long names. In Table 7.1 I have indicated the names that will be used in the text below for these parties.

The major questions in the first year after democratization were those of independence from Czechoslovakia, and then – during the period of developing national political institutions – the confrontation between the authoritarian and nationalistic forces and more democratically minded forces. These conflicts are outlined in some detail under 3.3 below.

These dimensions were the basis for the government formations in the period. The parties that articulated authoritarian and nationalist positions were the Movement for a Democratic Slovakia and the National Party, while the parties that opposed these positions were more traditional bourgeois parties according to West European standards, first and foremost the Democratic and Christian Union, the Christian Movement, and the Hungarian Coalition (Bakke 2006: 150). The Citizen's Alliance can also be included in this group.

On the left of the political spectrum, a communist successor party was established. It changed its name to the Democratic Left Party (SDĽ), and adopted a social democratic platform. A breakaway party called "Direction" (Smer) emerged from SDĽ in 1999. This party developed a more centralized party organization than SDĽ, and rapidly gained considerable support. It quickly surpassed the SDĽ and absorbed it and other already marginal center-left parties in 2005 (Rybar/Deegan-Krause 2008). It increased its support and became the largest party in the 2006 election (Rybar 2007).

Table 7.1: Overview of the political orientations of Slovak political parties (2000-06)

Party	Political orientation[1]	Locations on various issue dimensions according to the expert survey [2]
Direction - Social Democracy (Smer-SD) Name used: Direction	A breakaway party from the Party of the Democratic Left (the ex-communist party) in 1999, centre-left, anti-corruption and "law and order" profile, but then defined itself as social democratic (2005).	Left-leaning in general, located as more "leftist" than any other relevant party. Economic leftist, secular and social liberal. Centrist location on urban-rural and nationalism.
Slovak Democratic and Christian Union (SDKU-DS) Name used: Democratic and Christian Union	First and foremost a liberal-conservative party which is not focusing so much on Christian issues even though this is indicated in the name.	Economic rightist, located towards the religious and restrictive pole on social liberal issues, urban and not nationalist.
People's Party - Movement for a Democratic Slovakia (ĽS-HZDS) Name used: Movement for a Democratic Slovakia	Nationalist and authoritarian party with a diffuse ideology. The party's ideology has shifted several times, but has tried to slow down privatisation and economic liberalisation. Several times breakaway leaders from the party.	Centre-left on the economic left-right dimension, located centrist on the religious and social liberal dimension. Fairly nationalistic and is the party that articulate the rural interests mostly.
Hungarian Coalition Party (SMK) Name used: Hungarian Coalition	Party for the ethnic Hungarian minority, liberal-conservative profile	Centrist on economic left-right, fairly religious and restrictive on social liberal issues, rural, opposed to ethnic Slovak nationalism
Christian Democratic Movement (KDH) Name used: Christian Movement	Typical Christian party, fairly economic rightist and conservative, moderate nationalistic	Located to the economic right, religious and restrictive on social liberal issues, rural and nationalist
Slovakian National Party (SNS) Name used: National Party	Classical nationalist party which opposes changes towards broader rights for the ethnical minorities living in Slovakia, first and foremost the Hungarian and the Roma minorities.	Centrist on economic left-right issues, Articulate religious interests restrictive on social liberalism, rural. First and foremost the most nationalist party.
New Citizen Alliance (ANO) Name used: Citizen Alliance	A liberal party, economic rightist, liberal on moral issues	Economic rightist, secular, social liberal, the least nationalist and most urban party.

1) Based on Bakke (2006), Deegan-Krause (2000, 2004), Hlousek and Kopecek (2008).
2) Based on Benoit and Laver (2006: Appendix B).

In Table 7.1 an overview of the parties that were significant in 2004-06 is shown. Based on central, available sources, I have indicated the political orientation of the parties in the period studied. The right-hand column is based on Benoit and Laver's (2006) study based on expert surveys conducted in 2002-2003 in forty-seven countries of the location of political parties on several policy dimensions.

The conflict structure

The Lipset/Rokkan model of structural cleavages

In their analysis of the development of the conflict structure in Western democracies, Lipset and Rokkan (1967: 15-23) focused on the historical origins and the major conflicts between the political parties. They identified four central cleavages which had their basis in the social structure:

1) The center–periphery cleavage was anchored in territorial regions and was related to different ethnic and linguistic groups, as well as religious minorities.

2) The conflict between the church and the state pitted the secular state against the historical privileges of the church and over control of the important educational institutions. This cleavage has more specifically polarized the religious segment against the secular segment of the population.

3) The conflict in the commodity market was between buyers and sellers of agricultural products, or more generally, between the urban and the rural population.

4) Finally, the conflict in the labor market involved owners and employers versus tenants, laborers and workers. This conflict is more generally referred to as the class cleavage.

In this article I examine the impact of all these conflicts on party choice in Norway and Slovakia, in addition to age and gender. The center-periphery conflict will be analyzed by examining the relationship between party choice and region, while the religious conflicts will be analyzed by three variables that tap into different aspects of the religious/secular division. The conflict in the labor market is analyzed by the three class variables of education, social class, and household income. Social class is also relevant for the conflict in the commodity market because of the voting behavior of farmers, but in this work voting differences along the urban-rural territorial axis are the main variable tapping into this conflict.

The Norwegian conflict structure

The Norwegian conflict structure has been multidimensional and crosscutting (Rokkan 1967). The Nordic five-party model is primarily based on the conflicts in the labor and the commodity market. In Lipset and Rokkan's work the two class cleavages were not discussed in relation to each other, but Rokkan developed a more elaborate model based on these cleavages in an important work on the Norwegian cleavage structure (Rokkan 1966: 89-105). His triangular model of electoral fronts located the main party antagonists on the labor market cleavage, Labor and Conservatives, at two poles, together with the trade unions and the employers' organizations, respectively, while the party articulating the interests of the farmers, the Agrarian Center Party, occupied the third pole in the model (Rokkan 1966: 92-105, cf. Knutsen 2004a: 63-70).

Both the Agrarian and the Christian People's Party were splinter parties from the Liberal Party, and the Christian People's Party had its primary anchorage in religious conflict, leaving the remnant of the Liberal Party with a somewhat unclear location on the conflict structure. The focus on environmentalism from the late 1970s, however, gave the Liberal Party a clearer social profile with strongest support among the new middle class and those with higher education (Knutsen 1997).

Central for understanding the religious conflict in Norway is the fact that Norway has a Lutheran State Church. A central aspect of the religious conflict is between the religious fundamentalists organized into various lay organizations within and partly outside the state church on the one hand, and the more tolerant government-appointed priests (civil servants) and the more passive religious population on the other (Lipset/Rokkan 1967: 38). The more fundamentalist lay organizations have been the basis for the Christian People's Party.

Social cleavages in Norway have been studied in details by Rokkan and Valen based on a more specific cleavage model for Norwegian politics (Rokkan 1966; 1967, Rokkan/Valen 1964; Valen/Rokkan 1974) than the more general Lipset/Rokkan model. Studies of changes over time have documented a clear dealignment, a reduced impact of the cleavages in this specific model. This has been most pronounced for the class cleavages and the labor market conflict in particular. Traditional left-right class voting measured by the so-called Alford index (see below) has declined from about forty percentage points in the 1950s and 1960s to close to zero in the 2000s (Knutsen 2009).

In Norway the ideological space is fairly stable and the examination of it has been a central component in election studies. Based on analyses of many political issues, fairly stable attitudinal dimensions have been identified and these have been correlated with party choice. Based on the election studies from 2001 and 2005, the economic left-right dimension is the most important for explaining party choice, followed by three dimensions of about the same strength, namely a religious-secular dimension and two New Politics dimensions. The two New Politics dimensions are one environmentalist dimension, and one libertarian-authoritarian dimension, which is dominated by immigration issues (Aardal 2003; 2007). On these two New Politics dimensions, the Socialist Left Party and the Progress Party have opposite extreme locations.

The Slovak conflict structure

In Slovakia there are few studies based on the Lipset-Rokkan model of the impact of social structure on party choice. Analyses of the impact of issue or value orientations have been more frequent. As mentioned above, issues related to institutional authoritarianism and nationalism were central during the founding years of the Slovak post-communist period. Below, I first outline these issues and then discuss relevant factors for the four structural conflicts in the Lipset/Rokkan model.

The authoritarian-democratic divide was related to various institutional options during the transition from communist rule, and to questions of authority and its proper exercise within a democratic system. Central issues during the 1990s which can be grouped along this dimension are those such as the control of civil society through regime-supported organizations, governmental dominance over the mass media, and the manipulation of electoral laws. The nationalistic divide was related to the attitudes towards Czechoslovakia versus Slovak independence, the rights of the Hungarian minority and other "non-national" Slovaks, and attitudes towards the West (EU) (Bakke 2006: 149-150; Deegan-Krause 2004: 258-267).

Slovakia is an ethnically heterogeneous state in which 9.7 per cent of the population according to the 2001 census are ethnic Hungarians living in the southern regions along the border with Hungary (Hungarians in Slovakia 2011). Conflicts regarding minority rights for ethnic minorities were central in the 1990s and continued to varying degrees in the 2000s.The Hungarian Coalition is a formation devoted to articulating the interests of the Hungarian minorities. There is then an ethnic conflict which is transmitted to the party system.[53]

A religious-secular dimension has been found in analyses of political issues. This dimension is significantly correlated to party choice and has divided the country's governing coalitions, since both the authoritarian coalition of the 1990s and the democratically minded opposition had distinct secular and religious constituent elements (Deegan-Krause 2000: 40).

Social class has not been emphasized as a central cleavage in Slovakia during the 1990s, but it may gradually have increased its role as a central cleavage, especially with the neoliberal reforms of the 2002-2006 govern-

---

53 Slovakia has a significant Roma minority and issues about Roma rights have been significant. Unlike the Hungarian questions, however, these have not become part of the political party system.

ment and the growing strength, in response, of the left-leaning "Direction" party.

Considerable research has documented that authoritarian and nationalist values are more likely to be found within the working class and the lower educated strata.[54] Given that authoritarian[55] and nationalist issues have been central conflicts, class differences in support for the various parties can be expected. These issues have considerably polarized the Movement for a Democratic Slovakia and the National Party against the other parties (Deegan-Krause 2000; 2004).

The increased support for Direction and its clearer social democratic orientation[56] contributed to increasing the significance of the economic left-right dimension around 2004-05 (Bakke/Sitter 2005: 249). The emerging importance of the economic left-right dimension might then contribute to left-right class voting.

Slovakia does not have an agrarian party, but urban-rural contrasts in voting behavior have been observed (Bakke 2006: 149). Traditional values (such as authoritarian, religious, and nationalist values) are more likely to be found in rural than in urban areas. The dominant ideological space in Slovakia can then be expected to contribute to urban-rural contrasts in voting behavior (see the section on "Voting according to territorial variables" below).

The surveys

The data source for this paper is a cumulative data file based on the three first rounds of the European Social Survey (ESS) carried out in 2002, 2004, and 2006. Norway participated in all three rounds, while Slovakia participated in rounds 2 and 3. The data source for the two countries then consists of a large number of cases, 5546 and 3278 for Norway and Slovakia respectively. The party choice variable is based on the respondents' reported party choice in the last national election in their country. For Norway the last general election was in 2001 for those who were asked in 2002 and 2004, and the election in 2005 for those who participated in the third round. For those who participated

---

54 For authoritarianism, see Houtmann (2001); Stenner (2005: chap. 6), and Stubager (2006: chap. 4), and for nationalist values, see Coenders / Scheepers (2003) and Hjelm (2001).
55 It should be underscored that the New Politics authoritarian-libertarian dimension in Norway and the authoritarian-democratic divide in Slovakia are different. In Norway the dimension is related to values and issues on immigration, law and order, and lifestyles, while in Slovakia it primarily is related to support for different institutional solutions after the transition from Communist rule. However, these different types of authoritarianism might be expected to be supported by the same type of voters in terms of social characteristics, and we expect the same to occur for parties that are located close to the authoritarian pole in the two countries.
56 The social democratic orientation is reflected in the change in the party's name in 2005, to Direction – Social Democracy (Rybar/Deegan-Krause 2008: 502-503).

in the second and third round in the Slovak survey, the general elections in 2002 and 2006 respectively were the relevant general elections.[57] The response rates were 65-66 per cent for the three Norwegian surveys and 62.7 per cent and 73.2 per cent, respectively, in Slovakia. 75.3 per cent of the respondents answered the question about party choice in Norway and 55.6 per cent in Slovakia. For Norway the response rates were fairly similar to the turnout in the 2001 and 2005 election, which were 74.5 per cent and 77.4 per cent respectively. For Slovakia, the quite low response rate was fairly similar to the low turnout in the 2006 election (54.7 per cent), but much lower than the turnout in 2002 (70 per cent).Table 7.2 shows the distribution of the party-choice variable for those who indicated a party choice in the surveys.

Table 7.2: Distribution on the party choice variable in the surveys. Per cent

Norway

	N	
Socialist Left P.	541	13,0
Labour P.	1154	27,7
Liberal P.	173	4,1
Christian P. P.	415	9,9
Centre P.	265	6,4
Conservative P.	838	20,1
Progress P.	671	16,1
Other p.	116	2,8
N	4173	100,0

Slovakia

	N	
Movem. Dem.	320	17,5
Dem. And Chr. Union	361	19,8
Direction	527	28,9
Hungarian Coal.	165	9,0
Christian Movement	149	8,2
Citizen Alliance	68	3,7
National Party	97	5,3
Other p.	136	7,4
N	1824	100,0

Movem. Dem. – Movement for a Democratic Slovakia
Dem. And Chr. Union – Democratic and Christian Union
Hungarian Coal. – Hungarian Coalition
For the full names of the parties, see Table 7.1.

---

57 The general election took place in June 2006 in Slovakia, while the data were collected between December 2006 and February 2007.

Social structure

In this section and in the presentation of the impact of socio-structural variables on party choice, the variables are categorized into four groups:
1) ascriptive variables: age and gender
2) territorial variables: region and urban-rural residence
3) religious variables: religious denomination, frequency of church attendance, and degree of religiosity (called religiosity below)
4) class variables: education, social class, and household income.

In this section the operationalizations of the variables in the survey are presented. The distributions on some of variables are also outlined to indicate some interesting differences and similarities between the two countries.

Territorial variables: With regard to the territorial variables, it is relevant to compare the distributions on the variable that tap urban-rural location. Respondents were given a card and asked: "Which phrase on this card best describes the area where you live?" The alternatives and the distributions are shown in Table 7.3A.

Table 7.3: Distribution of urban-rural residence and religious denomination in Norway and Slovakia. Per cent

A. Urban-rural residence

	Norway	Slovakia
A big city	14,6	15,3
Suburbs or outskirts of big city	18,8	5,2
Town or small city	24,8	34,1
Country village	23,2	44,5
Farm or home in countryside	18,6	0,9
Sum	100,0	100,0
N	5541	3251

B. Religious denomination

	Norway	Slovakia
Unaffiliated	48,3	24,4
Roman Catholic	1,0	60,9
Protestant	45,7	7,5
Eastern Orthodox	0,3	0,9
Other Christian denomination	2,4	5,7
Non-Christian religions	2,4	0,6
Sum	100,0	100,0
N	5526	3243

About the same percentage report that they live in a big city, but a considerably larger proportion of the Norwegians report that they live in the suburbs or outskirts of big cities. A larger proportion of Slovaks report that they live in towns or small cities and first and foremost country villages, while a larger proportion of Norwegians report that they live on farms or in the countryside.

Religious variables: Religious denomination was tapped by the respondents being asked: "Do you consider yourself as belonging to any particular religion or denomination?" Those who answered "yes" were then asked which one, and the interviewer was supposed to code the reply into one of several response alternatives. The first of these questions is supposed to tap into identification with a religious community, not official membership.[58] A considerably larger proportion of the people in the Norwegian sample do not consider themselves to belong to a religious denomination compared to Slovakia (see Table 7.3B). Slovakia has a predominantly Catholic population. 7 per cent report that they belong to a Protestant denomination and the same proportion that they belong to other Christian denominations.[59] Less than 50 per cent of the Norwegians consider themselves to belong to the Lutheran State Church, only 1 per cent that they belong to Roman Catholic Church, and 3 per cent that they belonged to other Christian denominations.

The question about church attendance was asked thus: "Apart from special occasions such as weddings and funerals, about how often do you attend religious services nowadays?" The respondents were then shown a card with seven alternatives.[60] The Slovak population seems to be considerably more religious than the Norwegian one: 5 per cent in the Norwegian sample reported that they attended church once a week or more frequently, while the same applies to 32 per cent of the Slovak sample. 88 per cent of the Norwegian sample go to church only on special holy days or less frequently, compared to 58 per cent of the Slovaks.

The question about religiosity was asked thus: "Regardless of whether you belong to a particular religion, how religious would you say that you are?" The respondents are then shown a card with a scale from 0 ("not at all religious") to 10 ("very religious"). The mean score for the Norwegian sam-

---

58 In the source questionnaire the annotation in a footnote is as follows: "Identification is meant, not official membership".

59 According to the Slovak census from 2001 68.9% of the population report that they belonged to the Roman-Catholic Church, 6.9% that they belonged to the Evangelical Church of Augsburg affiliation, 4.1% to the Greek-Catholic Church, 2.0% to the Calvinist Reformed Church and 0.9% to the Orthodox Church which is affiliated to the Eastern Orthodox Church. Other denominations comprised 1.1%, the non-affiliated 13.0% while the denomination of 3.0% was unknown (Religion in Slovakia).

60 These were: 1) every day, 2) more than once a week, 3) once a week, 4) at least once a month, 5) only on special holy days, 6) less often and 7) never.

ple is 4.0, while the mean score in the Slovak sample is 5.9. In sum, different denominations predominate in the two countries, and the Norwegian population is considerably more secular than the Slovak one.

Table 7.4: The Erikson/Goldthorpe class schema and distribution according to social class in Norway and Slovakia. Per cent

		Norway	Slovakia
Higher-level service class	Higher-grade professionals, administrators and officials, managers in large industrial establishments, large proprietors.	15,4	14,4
Lower-level service class	Lower-grade professionals, administrators and officials, higher-grade technicians, managers in small industrial establishments, supervisors of non-manual employees	25,3	16,9
Routine non-manual employees	Routine non-manual employees in administration and commerce, sales personnel, other rank-and-file employees	25,3	16,2
Self-employed / petty bourgeoisie	Small proprietors with and without employees	4,6	5,8
Skilled workers	Lower grade technicians, Supervisors of manual workers, skilled manual workers	13,1	18,2
Unskilled workers	Semi- and unskilled manual workers, agricultural workers and other workers in primary production	14,3	27,7
Farmers/self-employed in the primary sector	Farmers and small-holders, other self-employed in primary production	2,0	0,8
	Sum	100,0	100,0
	N	5133	2728
	Size of the main social classes		
	Service class	40,7	31,3
	Routine non man.	25,3	16,2
	Workers	27,4	45,9

Source for the class schema: Erikson and Goldthorpe (1992: 38-39, Table 2.1).

Social class variables: The education variable differentiates between seven levels of education. The main difference between the countries is that 33 per cent of the Norwegians have a tertiary education compared to 12 per cent of the Slovaks. On the other hand, 65 per cent of the Slovaks have the upper-secondary level as their highest level of education, and only 21 per cent have a lower education than the upper-secondary level compared to 19 per cent of the Norwegians.

Social class can be measured in several ways. I have used the Erikson/Goldthorpe (hereafter EG) class schema (Goldthorpe 1980; Erikson et al. 1979; Erikson/Goldthorpe 1992). The aim of the class schema is to differentiate positions based on the work situation (authority and autonomy) as well as market situations (including income, degree of income security, career prospects, and source of income). Here a seven class version is used. The classes, details regarding how they are conceptualized, and the distributions in the two countries, are shown in Table 7.4.[61] According to the table, we can see that a considerably larger proportion of the Slovaks than the Norwegians belong to the working class, while the service class and the routine non-manual classes are larger in Norway.

Party choice and social structure

Statistical measures

Party choice is here analyzed as a nominal level variable where all significant parties are included. For the bivariate analyses of the relationship between social structural variables and party choice, the correlation coefficients eta and Cramer's V are used. Eta can be used when the conflict variable is a metric variable, while Cramer's V can be used when the conflict variable is a nominal level variable. In addition, I use Nagelkerke's pseudo R^2 from multinomial logistic regression with only one independent socio-structural variable to measure bivariate relationships between party choice and various social cleavages. Although Nagelkerke's pseudo R^2 is not formally a correlation coefficient, I use the notion correlation also for Nagelkerke's pseudo R^2 for the sake of simplicity.

Region, religious denomination, and social class are nominal level variables. The correlation between these variables and party choice is tapped by Cramer's V, and these variables are being treated as so-called factor variables in the multinomial logistic regressions. All the other socio-structural variables are treated as metric variables and the correlations with party choice are tapped by eta, and the socio-structural variables are treated as covariates in the multinomial logistic regressions.

In order to compare the impact of various socio-structural variables on

---

61 In the ESS surveys the respondents' occupations are classified according to ISCO 1988. Leiulfsrud et al (2005) have classified the various occupations according to the ISCO coded into the EG-classes. This classification from ISCO-codes to EG-classes is used here. Their scheme originally contained eleven classes, but I have collapsed these into seven classes according to the schema discussed above.

support for individual parties, log-odds ratios are used. These are not affected by the size of the parties and can be used to compare the impact of various socio-structural variables on support for the various parties. For the mentioned nominal level variables, the kappa index is used for the same purpose. The kappa index calculates several log-odds ratios between a reference category on the structural variable and each of the other categories, and uses the standard deviation of these log-odds ratios as a measure of the impact of the structural variable on support for a given party.

Detailed cross-tabulations are shown only for the relationship between party choice, and region and social class. The patterns for the other variables are outlined in the text.

Voting according to ascriptive variables

Gender differences have changed over time in advanced industrial societies. In Western Europe women tended to vote for religious and conservative parties to a greater extent than men. In the course of the past two or three decades, however, women in many Western countries have changed from being more conservative than men, to becoming more leftist and libertarian. The term *modern gender gap* has been used to characterize these new gender differences (Norris 1999: 150). We expect to find a clear modern gender gap in Norway, while gender differences in Slovakia might be small or of the traditional type.

According to the data, the gender differences in voting behavior are considerable larger in Norway than in Slovakia. In Norway, two parties receive considerably larger support from women, namely the Socialist Left and the Christian People's Party, while the Conservative and the Progress parties receive stronger support from men. The pattern for the Christian People's Party still represents the traditional gender gap, while the patterns for the other parties mentioned are in accordance with the expectations derived from the modern gender gap perspective. The modern gender gap is, however, dominant: gender differences are larger for support for the Socialist Left Party and the two rightist parties than for the Christian People's Party. In Slovakia the correlations between gender and party choice are barely significant (at the 5 per cent level). The Christian Movement and Direction receive stronger support from women while the National Party and the Democratic and Christian Union get stronger support from men. If we consider Direction as a social democratic party there is a slight modern gender gap in Slovakia, but we also find a traditional pattern related to the Christian Movement.

Age or generation is seldom the object of systematic comparative analysis in relation to voting behavior. In Norway age differences can be expected to have several components, but age differences are probably primarily related to the Old and New Left and Right. The New Left and New Right parties are expected to gain stronger support from the younger age groups, while the opposite applies to the old left and right. In addition, the Christian People's Party is expected to gain stronger support from older age groups.

In the context of the CEE countries, older voters have tended to support the ex-communist ruling party of which a significant proportion have been members, while younger voters would tend to benefit from the opportunities associated with the new markets (Evans 2006: 262-263; Kitschelt 1992: 26). However, since the central leftist alternative, Direction, is not a successor party to the Communist Party, we do not expect such age differences to be important in Slovakia.

The value orientations of different parties can again be taken as a point of departure for generating hypotheses about the relationship between a sociostructural variable and party choice. Various findings have shown that authoritarian values are more likely to be found among older age groups (Stenner 2005: 154, 169, 173; Stubager 2006: 90-104). Parties that articulated support for more authoritarian institutional solutions and restrictive policies toward ethnic minorities might therefore be expected to gain stronger support from older age groups. In Slovakia this would first and foremost apply to the National Party and the Movement for a Democratic Slovakia. The other parties which to a larger degree supported full democratic development and a market economy are expected to receive stronger support from the younger age groups.

The correlation with age is somewhat larger in Slovakia than in Norway (see Table 7.5A). In Norway, the Socialist Left Party gains considerably stronger support from the younger age groups.[62] The same applies to the Progress Party and Liberals, but age differences are much smaller for these parties. The Christian People's Party gains relatively strongest support from the older age groups followed, by the Labor and Center parties. Age differences in support for the Conservative Party are minor. The findings are in accordance with the hypotheses, apart from the small age differences for the Conservative Party.

In Slovakia Direction, the Democratic and Christian Union and the Citizen Alliance receive strongest support from the younger age groups, while the Christian Movement and the Movement for a Democratic Slovakia receive stronger support from the older age groups. Differences are large for the Movement for a Democratic Slovakia which gains support from 11-16 per cent from the age groups under forty years old, and 26-32 per cent of the

---

62 The analyses of support for the political parties in different age groups are based on the following grouping of ages: 18-24, 25-29, 30-39, 40-49, 50-59, 60-69 and 70-79 years.

Table 7. 5: Correlations between party choice and socio-structural variables
A. The structural variables grouped into four groups

	Eta or Cramer's V			Nagelkerke's pseudo R^2		
	Norw	Slov		Norw	Slov	
Ascriptive variables						
Gender	0,171	0,087		0,030	0,008	
Age	0,163	0,197		0,028	0,039	
Territorial variables						
Urban-rural resid.	0,298	0,224		0,096	0,050	
Region	0,122	0,166	8 regions	0,084	0,180	8 regions
		0,164	4 regions		0,078	4 regions
Religious variables						
Relig. denom.	0,159	0,144		0,102	0,092	
Freq. of church att.	0,445	0,338		0,164	0,114	
Religiosity	0,351	0,297		0,128	0,099	
Class variables						
Education	0,300	0,258		0,090	0,068	
Income	0,177	0,159		0,034	0,018	
Social class	0,164	0,117		0,129	0,074	

Cramer's V is used for region, religious denomination and social class, eta for the other variables.

Table 7.5 continued
B. Ranking of the correlations according to their strength

Norway	Eta		Nagelkerke's pseudo R^2	Slovakia	Eta		Nagelkerke's pseudo R^2
Church att.	0.445	Church att.	0.164	Church att.	0.338	Region	0.180
Religiosity	0.351	Social class	0.129	Religiosity	0.297	Church att.	0.114
Education	0.300	Religiosity	0.128	Education	0.258	Religiosity	0.099
Urban-rural resid.	0.298	Relig. denom.	0.102	Urban-rural resid.	0.224	Relig. Enom.	0.092
Income	0.177	Urban-rural resid.	0.096	Age	0.197	Social class	0.074
Gender	0.171	Education	0.090	Income	0.159	Education	0.068
Age	0.163	Region	0.084	Gender	0.087	Urban-rural resid.	0.050
		Income	0.034			Age	0.039
	Cramer's V	Gender	0.030		Cramer's V	Income	0.018
Social class	0.164	Age	0.028	Region	0.166	Gender	0.008
Relig. Denom.	0.159			Relig. denom.	0.144		
Region	0.122			Social class	0.117		

support from those over sixty years old. The hypotheses are mostly supported, but the National Party does not gain stronger support from the older age groups.

Voting according to territorial variables

Urban-rural differences in voting behavior may be causes of differences in political orientations and values, differences in general social structural characteristics such as education and income, and differences in economic interests. The population in rural areas is generally more conservative and religious, and probably also more nationalistic and authoritarian than the urban population, and could then be expected to vote for religious parties (Knutsen 2004b: chap. 4). The conflict in the commodity market emphasizes the economic interests of the farmers. This conflict is a central component of possible urban-rural differences in party choice in Norway given the existence of the agrarian Centre Party.

From the premises outlined above, it is hypothesized that parties that have expressed nationalist, authoritarian, and religious policy positions will gain strongest support from the rural areas in Slovakia, i.e. the Movement for a Democratic Slovakia, the National Party, the Hungarian Coalition,[63] and the Christian Movement, while the other parties gain stronger support from urban areas.

The correlation coefficients between urban-rural residence and party choice are as expected larger in Norway than in Slovakia. This is probably due to the agrarian Center Party which to a large degree is concentrated in the category "countryside" where its support is 22 per cent, compared to 1-2 per cent in the three most urban categories. The Christian People's Party also has its stronghold in the less urban categories. Three parties have a distinct urban profile, namely the Socialist Left, the Liberal and the Conservative parties. The most even support across the various categories on the urban-rural variable is found for Labor and the Progress Party.

Two parties are strongly rurally based in Slovakia, namely the Movement for a Democratic Slovakia and the Hungarian Coalition. The National Party gains fairly even support across the various urban-rural categories. The same applies to Direction, while there is a tendency for the Christian Movement to gain strongest support from the big cities contrary to the hypothesis. Support is largest from the big cities (13 per cent) and then from the villages (9 per cent) and smaller for the two categories in between (5-7 per cent). This is a

---

63 The Hungarian Coalition gains most of the votes of the Hungarian minority in Slovakia and most of the party's voters belong to this ethnic group. The findings regarding the support for this party then probably reflect the social composition of this group. However, the findings for this party will be commented upon in the same way as for the other parties.

different pattern to the one found for the Norwegian sister party (the Christian People's Party). The Democratic and Christian Union is the only party that gains considerably stronger support from the most urbanized areas.

The importance of region for party choice in Norway has been examined in the works of Stein Rokkan and Henry Valen (Rokkan 1967, Rokkan/Valen 1964; Valen/Rokkan 1974). Their studies looked at how the regional differences in voting behavior could partly be explained by differences in social structure (religiosity, language, and social class), and differences in the strength of the corresponding cleavages. A major regional variation in voting behavior was for example the one between Southern and Western Norway, and the rest of the country. In Southern and Western Norway the Old Liberal Party and later the Christian People's Party had their strongholds. This could be explained by the strength of three "countercultures", namely Lutheran orthodoxy, the temperance and prohibition movement, and the rural language movements.

The basis for the classification of comparative studies of regions is frequently the classification that has been established by Eurostat (NUTS).[64] For Norway the second level which is used in the ESS surveys comprises seven regions. In Slovakia, the country is divided into four regions along a west-east axis according to NUTS 2, the Bratislava Region, Western, Central and Eastern Region. The ESS data comprises the more detailed third NUTS level with eight regions. The Hungarian minority population is located in these southern regions, and it may be expected that the Hungarian Coalition will gain strongest support from these regions.

Regional differences in voting behavior are somewhat larger in Slovakia than in Norway (see Table 7.5A). In the table, the correlations for both the four and the eight regional variables for Slovakia are shown. Here it is best to rely on Nagelkerke's R^2 which shows a large increase in the correlation from the four to the eight category variable. Table 7.6 shows the voting behavior in different regions in the two countries.

---

64 NUTS is an acronym for *Nomenclature for Territorial Units for Statistics*, which has been established by Eurostat in order to provide a single uniform breakdown of territorial units for the production of regional statistics for the EU (NUTS 2003). For the division of regions in Norway and Slovakia according to different levels of NUTS, see Regions of Slovakia (2011) and NUTS of Norway (2010).

Table 7.6: Party choice and region
Norway

	Centre region	Inner East	South East	South	West	Trøndelag	North	Total
Socialist Left P.	14,7	11,2	13,0	10,5	10,6	16,1	15,5	12,9
Labour P.	27,0	40,4	30,0	18,2	23,0	33,9	30,7	27,7
Liberal P.	6,2	1,1	3,5	3,6	5,1	3,5	3,1	4,2
Christian P. P.	4,7	7,0	10,5	20,0	11,8	7,5	7,0	9,9
Centre P.	2,7	13,5	5,3	4,1	8,6	9,1	7,2	6,4
Conservative P.	29,0	13,8	17,2	21,9	19,7	14,8	13,8	20,1
Progress P.	13,4	11,5	18,8	19,7	17,9	11,8	16,4	16,1
Other p.	2,4	1,4	1,8	2,0	3,3	3,2	6,3	2,8
Sum	100,0	100,0	100,0	100,0	100,0	100,0	100,0	100,0
N	920	356	740	589	782	372	414	4173

	Kappa-index
Liberal P.	0,502
Centre P.	0,501
Christian P. P.	0,435
Conservative P.	0,257
Labour P.	0,243
Progress P.	0,208
Socialist Left P.	0,168

Slovakia

	Bratislava	West	Central	East	Total
Movem. Dem.	8,7	16,9	22,4	16,6	17,7
Dem. And Chr. Union	32,9	16,7	16,2	22,6	19,8
Direction	23,7	29,6	27,9	30,6	28,8
Hungarian Coal.	5,2	18,3	5,3	4,3	9,1
Christian Movement	11,0	6,9	7,1	9,7	8,1
Citizen Alliance	5,2	2,6	4,4	4,1	3,8
National Party	4,0	4,0	8,4	3,9	5,3
Other p.	9,25	4,93	8,38	8,32	7,36
Sum	100,0	100,0	100,0	100,0	100,0
N	173	568	549	517	1807

Kappa-index based on 4 and 8 regions

4 regions		8 regions	
Hungarian Coal.	0,579	Hungarian Coal.	1,790
Movem. Dem.	0,349	National Party	0,520
National Party	0,322	Citizen Alliance	0,412
Dem. And Chr. Union	0,287	Movem. Dem.	0,353
Citizen Alliance	0,250	Christian Movement	0,279
Christian Movement	0,200	Dem. and Chr. Union	0,268
Direction	0,098	Direction	0,172

In Norway support for the three centrist parties, the Liberal, Center and Christian People's Party, varies most between the regions in accordance with expectations. There is a large drop in the kappa values between these three parties and the others. The Christian People's Party still has its strongholds in the Southern region, and then in the Western and the South Eastern regions, while the Center Party has its stronghold in the Inner East. The Liberal and the Conservative Party have their strongholds in the Center Region, while the Labor Party has its stronghold in the Inner East. Regional differences are smallest regarding support for the New Right and the New Left.

For Slovakia only the relationship between the four value regional variable and party choice is shown in the table, but the kappa values for both the four and eight value regional variables are shown. The main pattern in the table is that the Movement for a Democratic Slovakia has its strongholds outside the capital region, while the opposite is true of the Democratic and Christian Union. The Hungarian Coalition gains strongest support from the Western region, while the National Party has its stronghold in the Central region. These parties have the highest kappa values, while Direction has the lowest and subsequently the most even support across the various regions.

The ranking of the parties differs somewhat when the kappa values are calculated based on the eight region variable, but the main difference is that the kappa value for the Hungarian Coalition increases dramatically due to the large variation in support between the Northern and the Southern NUTS 3 regions within three NUTS 2 regions.

Religious voting

Both countries have religious parties and also parties that can be considered basically secular. Religious issues have also been significant in both countries. However, the impact of religion on voting frequently surpasses the impact of issues. Religious values are also related to a wide range of social and political beliefs, and religion signifies a worldview that extends into the political area which frequently implies that religious/secular values underpin party support (Dalton 1990: 86).

The correlation between all religious variables and party choice is larger in Norway than in Slovakia. The difference is smallest for religious denomination.

Religious denomination: In Norway it is mainly the Christian People's Party that receives stronger support from the dominant denomination, namely the Protestant Church (14 per cent), compared to the unaffiliated (3 per cent). Among the other parties, only the Center Party gains stronger support from the Protestant denomination compared to the non-affiliated. There are small differences according to religious denomination for the major parties, the

Progress, Conservative, Labor, and Liberal Parties. Only the Socialist Left Party gains considerably stronger support from the non-affiliated (17 per cent) than from those who consider themselves members of the Protestant church (10 per cent).

However, the Christian People's Party gains extremely high support (57 per cent) from the tiny category of "Other Christian denominations". This is in accordance with the character of the religious cleavage in Norway mentioned above. Support for the Christian People's Party is not highest among the active members of the Lutheran State Churches, but among more fundamentalist groups that are found partly within and partly outside (as Free Churches) the Lutheran Church.

In Slovakia the Christian Movement and the Movement for a Democratic Slovakia receive stronger support from those who belong to the Roman Catholic denomination compared to the non-affiliated. The parties that gain strongest support from the non-affiliated are the Democratic and Christian Union and the Citizen Alliance, while the differences for Direction, the Hungarian Coalition and the National Party are small. The Hungarian Coalition receives, however, strongest support from the Protestants, while this does not apply to the Christian Movement which receives almost no support from the Protestants.

Church attendance and religiosity: In Norway, support for the Christian People's Party is very high in the regular churchgoers. The Christian People's Party gains 66 per cent support from those who attend church once a week or more often, and only 5-3 per cent from those who never or very infrequently attend church. The Center Party and the Liberal Party also gain stronger support from those who attend church more frequently than the average voter. It is accordingly the three parties which are successor parties of the Old Liberal Party that have the most religious voters in Norway. The lowest levels of church attendance are found among voters for the Socialist Left and the Progress Party, and then Labor and Conservative Party voters.

In Slovakia, mainly the Christian Movement receives stronger support from the regular churchgoers. The Movement for a Democratic Slovakia gains even support from voters at all levels of church attendance, apart from those who never go to church whose support is somewhat lower. Direction and the Hungarian Coalition gain strongest support from the irregular churchgoers and smaller support from the regular churchgoers and those who attend church infrequently, while the Citizen Alliance and first and foremost the Democratic and Christian Union gain strongest support from those who never go to church. There are no significant differences in support for the National Party according to church attendance.

We find very much the same patterns as those described above for church attendance for the religiosity variable. In both countries, this variable is not so strongly correlated with party choice as the church attendance variable. The location of the parties is nearly exactly the same as for church attendance.

In sum, in both countries there are religious parties that contribute to fairly strong correlations between religious/secular variables and party choice. The religious/secular conflict cuts across the left-right division of parties in both countries. In Norway this is first and foremost associated with the non-socialist Conservative and Progress Parties which gain strongest support from the secular segments of the population. In Slovakia, this is caused by the liberal Citizen Alliance and first and foremost – because of its larger electoral support – the liberal-conservative Democratic and Christian Union. The Democratic and Christian Union is sometimes described as a Christian party in the literature, although it is also underscored that it has developed from a Christian profile to a more liberal-conservative one. According to the findings here, it is a fairly secular party at the voter level.

Class voting

Traditionally, voting according to class variables has been comparatively very high in Norway and the other Nordic countries (Nieuwbeerta 1995: chap. 3). The left-right division of parties has been very relevant for class voting. Traditional class voting has, however, declined dramatically in Norway (Knutsen 2009). This decline is to some extent explained by the impact of New Politics.

Slovak politics in the post-communist period has been dominated by nationalist and authoritarian-libertarian issues. However, a wide range of opinion surveys have indicated a relatively robust economic left-right dimension among Slovaks, although until 2002 this dimension has been less important than the dimensions mentioned above. With the neoliberal reforms of the 2002-2006 government (Fisher et al. 2007), and the rising social democratic inclination of Direction, the economic left-right dimension has become more significant. We can then expect some degree of left-right class voting in Slovakia and that Direction will gain stronger support from the lower educated strata and working class. However, we also expect that the nationalist and authoritarian parties, the Hungarian Coalition, the National Party, and the Movement for a Democratic Slovakia, due to their ideological profile, will gain stronger support from the lower educated and the working class.

All three class variables are more strongly correlated with party choice in Norway than in Slovakia, but the differences between the two countries are not very large (see Table 7.5A).

Education: In Norway the impact of education seems to largely cut across the left-right division of parties. The Old Left (the Labor Party) and the New Right (the Progress Party) gain strongest support from the lower educated strata, while the Old Right (the Conservative Party) and the New Left (the Socialist Left Party) gain strongest support from the higher educated strata.

The Center Party and the Christian People's Party also gain strongest support from the lower educated strata, while the opposite is the case for the Liberal Party. The average education level is highest among voters for the Liberal, the Socialist Left and then the Conservative Parties and lowest among voters for the Progress Party and then Labor, the Centre Party and the Christian People's Party.

Two parties gain considerably stronger support from the lower educated strata in Slovakia, namely the Movement for a Democratic Slovakia and the Hungarian Coalition, while the Democratic and Christian Union and the Citizen Alliance gain considerably stronger support from the higher educated strata. For the other parties, Direction and the Christian Movement, support is fairly similar from voters at different education levels. The average educational level is highest among voters for the Democratic and Christian Union and the Citizen Alliance and then the National Party, the Christian Movement, and Direction and lowest among voters for the Hungarian Coalition and the Movement for a Democratic Slovakia.

Social class: Studies of class voting have undergone significant changes and one can differentiate between three stages or 'generations' (Knutsen 2007: 459–461; Nieuwbeerta 1995: chap. 1):

1) "Traditional (left–right) class voting" examines the left-right division of parties and incorporates only two social classes (the manual/non-manual division). Traditional class voting has been measured by the Alford index which is based on a percentage difference measurement.

2) "Overall or total left-right class voting" examines the left-right voting of all social classes.

3) "Total class voting" considers class differences (based on a detailed class schema) in voting between all the parties in the party system

Let us first examine class voting according to the first generation of class voting, the Alford index[65]: there is no significant traditional class voting in Norway or Slovakia, with one per cent and three per cent respectively.

Then we can examine left-right class voting based on all the EG classes. In Norway, the farmers are less inclined to support the leftist parties, followed by the petty bourgeoisie. Differences in leftist support from the other numerically most significant classes, two levels of workers, and two levels of service class and routine non-manuals are very small, in the range of 41-48 per cent.

---

65 Left-right class voting is tapped by grouping the leftist party families (social democrats, socialist left and communist parties) in the leftist group, and parties belonging to all other party families in the non-leftist group.

Table 7.7: Party choice and social class

Norway

	Hi serv class	Lo serv class	Rout non-m	Petty bour	Skilled worker	Unskilled worker	Farmer	Total
Socialist Left P.	15,2	15,2	18,0	4,7	9,5	7,1	2,7	13,4
Labour P.	26,3	27,2	27,8	21,8	35,3	33,4	14,7	28,4
Liberal P.	6,5	5,6	2,9	3,6	2,3	1,6	4,0	4,1
Christian P. P.	8,0	10,3	10,5	9,3	5,7	12,1	10,7	9,6
Centre P.	2,6	4,6	5,4	7,3	6,3	6,3	50,7	5,9
Conservative P.	31,1	22,8	16,6	29,0	13,9	8,1	8,0	19,8
Progress P.	7,6	11,2	16,0	24,4	23,9	27,7	9,3	16,0
Other p.	2,7	3,1	2,8	0,0	3,2	3,6	0,0	2,8
Sum	100,0	100,0	100,0	100,0	100,0	100,0	100,0	100,0
N	659	1099	942	193	476	494	75	3938

Slovakia

	Hi serv class	Lo serv class	Rout non-m	Petty bour	Skilled worker	Unskilled worker	Farmer	Total
Movem. Dem.	12,9	12,9	13,1	13,2	20,1	25,1	6,7	17,4
Dem. And Chr. Union	33,5	21,8	22,4	26,4	10,9	11,1	26,7	19,3
Direction	20,9	32,7	29,5	28,6	35,4	28,7	40,0	29,5
Hungarian Coal.	5,4	5,8	8,4	6,6	10,2	13,1	13,3	9,0
Christian Movement	8,3	9,9	9,7	9,9	6,5	6,6	0,0	8,0
Citizen Alliance	5,4	3,4	5,5	3,3	2,7	2,9	0,0	3,8
National Party	4,7	6,8	4,6	5,5	6,5	3,8	6,7	5,2
Other p.	9,0	6,8	6,8	6,6	7,8	8,6	6,7	7,8
Sum	100,0	100,0	100,0	100,0	100,0	100,0	100,0	100,0
N	278	294	237	91	294	442	15	1651

Explanations

Hi serv class – Higher-level service class, Lo serv class – Lower-level service class, Rout non-m – Routine non-manuals, Petty bour – Petty bourgeosie

In Slovakia, support for Direction varies between 29 per cent and 35 per cent for all social classes apart from the higher-level service class where support is lower, and the tiny group of farmers. The kappa index for leftist voting is then fairly small in both countries, but somewhat lower in Slovakia (0,270 versus 0,348).

Finally, we examine total class voting where we take support for all significant parties into account. This is shown in Table 7.7. In Norway, we find as expected that the Old Right and Old Left gain strongest support from the service class and the petty bourgeoisie, and the workers, respectively. This pattern is, however, much more pronounced for the Old Right than for the Old Left. The Liberal Party resembles the Conservative Party in the sense that support is strongest among the service class. The New Right, the Progress Party, gains strongest support from workers and from the petty bourgeoisie, and then from the routine non-manual workers. Support from farmers and the service class is considerably smaller. For the Socialist Left Party we find an opposite pattern with strongest support from the service class and the routine non-manuals. The most significant class party is, however, the Center party which gains support from about 50 per cent of the farmers, and less than 3-7 per cent from all the other social classes.

This is expressed by the kappa index (not shown) which indicates that the Center Party has the most uneven support among the various classes, followed by the Socialist Left and the Conservative and Progress Party. The Labor Party has one of the lowest kappa values, only the Christian People's Party has a considerably lower value.

In Slovakia we have already commented upon the pattern for Direction since it is the only leftist party in the material. As for many other sociostructural variables, differences in voting behavior among the various social groups are first and foremost found among the non-leftist parties.

The Movement for a Democratic Slovakia and the Hungarian Coalition gain strongest support from the working class, in particular from the unskilled workers. This does not apply to the National Party, which has very even support from the various social classes. On the other hand, the Democratic and Christian Union gains strong support from all classes other than the workers, in particular the petty bourgeoisie and the higher-level service class. The Citizen Alliance and the Christian Movement also gain stronger support from all classes other than workers.

Class voting according to the kappa index (not shown) is largest for the Democratic and Christian Union and the Movement for a Democratic Slovakia, and then for the Hungarian Coalition and the Citizen Alliance, and lowest for the Christian Movement, the National Party and Direction. Class voting is then mainly associated with parties other than the social democrats in both countries.

Household income is considerably lower correlated with party choice than the other class variables in both countries. We find roughly the same ranking of the parties for the income variable as for the education variable above.

The relative importance of socio-structural variables for explaining party choice

In Table 7.5B the various variables are ranked according to the strength of the correlations. Since eta and Cramer's V cannot be compared, the ranking based on these coefficients is in two groups. For the correlations based on Nagelkerke's R^2, the correlations for all variables can be compared.

If we first examine the ranking of the variables based on eta, we find a striking similarity between the two countries. The two religious variables are most highly correlated in both countries, followed by education and urban-rural residence. Indeed, only age has a different ranking in the two countries. The ranking of the three nominal level variables based on Cramer's V shows a more diversified pattern. Here the ranking of the variables is completely opposite although the differences between the strength of the correlations are not large in any of the countries.

The similarity in the relative impact of the various variables is also striking when we examine the ranking based on Nagelkerke's R^2. The most important difference is that region (based on the 8 category variable) is the most influential variable in Slovakia, while it is ranked toward the lower end in Norway.

In Table 7.8 the explanatory power of the four groups of variables which we have outlined above are shown based on multinomial logistic regressions. In the first column the explanatory power of the variable groups is shown without any controls. In the second column the variables are included in a sequential order according to causal considerations. The territorial variables can be considered as quasi-ascriptive variables and are therefore included before the religious and class variables. The religious variables can be considered as traits that are established in formative years and have therefore been included before the class variables.

If we first examine the "bivariate" explanatory power without any controls, we can see that the religious variables are most important in Norway, followed by the class and then the territorial variables, while the ascriptive variables have least explanatory power. In Slovakia the territorial variables are most important, but then the ranking is the same as in Norway: religious, class, and finally ascriptive variables.

Table 7.8: The explanatory power of the four groups of variables. Results from multinomial logistic regressions. Nagelkerke's R^2

Norway

	Bivariate	Cumulative	Unique
Ascriptive variables	0,055	0,055	0,055
Territorial variables	0,152	0,187	0,132
Religious variables	0,215	0,337	0,150
Social class variables	0,187	0,420	0,083

Slovakia

	Bivariate	Cumulative	Unique
Ascriptive variables	0,046	0,046	0,046
Territorial variables	0,209	0,247	0,201
Religious variables	0,174	0,346	0,099
Social class variables	0,122	0,423	0,077

Explanations

"Bivariate" – The explanatory power of a given variable group without any controls

Cumulative – The explanatory power of the variable groups that are entered into the analysis so far

Unique – The unique explanatory power of the variable group in addition to the other variable groups already included in the analysis

The next columns show the explanatory power when the variables are entered into the model in accordance with the mentioned causal model. We note that the total explanatory power is fairly similar in the two countries. The third column shows the additional explanatory power of a given variable group when (prior) variable groups already have been included in the model. In particular the impact of the class variables in Norway reduces their explanatory power compared to the bivariate analyses, and the territorial variables have larger explanatory power than the class variables in this analysis. Apart from this the relative importance of the four variables group remains the same compared to the bivariate analysis. The same applies without exceptions to the results from Slovakia.

Conclusions

The main comparative findings can be summed up as follows: Quite surprisingly, the explanatory power of social structure for party choice is fairly similar in the two countries. The initial hypothesis from the introduction is then not supported. However, most of the variables have a somewhat greater impact in Norway. The main exceptions to this are age and region which have a much larger impact in Slovakia. The large impact of region in Slovakia is probably due mainly to the existence of the Hungarian Coalition for the Hungarian minority which has a regional base.

The impact of the religious variables is fairly large in both countries. In both countries there are parties that define themselves as Christian, and there are also secular parties which oppose these parties on important issues. This is clearly reflected at the voter level. The strong correlations in Norway must be seen against the fact that the distributions on the religious variables tapping the religious cleavage are skewed. A small segment of the population is religious, but this segment votes largely for the Christian People's Party, and this produces a strong correlation.

The analysis revealed that there is little left-right class voting in Slovakia, but (still) some in Norway based on analyses of all the EG classes. Most of the class voting that exists in the two countries does not follow the left-right division of parties. In this article this is explained by the impact of authoritarian, nationalist, and New Politics dimensions.

The two countries belong to different groups of democracies with regard to social cleavages and electoral politics. In Norway the social cleavages examined here have for several decades had a large explanatory power for party choice. Dealignment is the term used to characterize the weakening connection between social structure and party choice, and has been associated in particular with the reduced and transformed impact of class variables.

In Slovakia, the instability and high volatility in the party system, and weak internal party structure that causes frequent splinters and mergers of parties could be associated with a weak relationship between social structure and party choice. Developments of persistent alliances between social groups and political parties are central to the legitimacy and stability of political processes. For some authors crystallization and politicization of the social structure are important processes in this respect. Crystallization includes a constrained relationship between social structure and interests; politicization includes a constrained relationship between the interaction of the social structure, social interests, and political parties (Wessels/Klingemann 2006: 23-24).

But we have seen that it is not weak in an absolute sense or when compared to Norway. However, it seems reasonable to explain many of the findings regarding social structure and party choice in Slovakia by the dominance of nationalist and authoritarian issues. In this article, central aspects of the voting pattern related to age, urban-rural residence, and the class variables have been explained by these issues. So far these issue dimensions have not produced a stable party system. It remains to be seen whether these issues will dominate also in the future. Since these issues to some extent are related to nation-building in Slovakia, they might be expected to decline in importance. If some other issue dimensions become significant, a transition period with continued instability will occur, and it is difficult to predict whether these dimensions will produce greater stability in the party system.

The strong impact of dimensions of New Politics in Norway is fairly different from the issues that have dominated in Slovak politics, although they have some similarities related to authoritarian values. Parties that focus on growth-oriented instead of environmental values and on restrictive immigration policies in a polity where New Politics issues are important gain stronger support from the lower educated strata and the working class. New Politics is then probably a major reason for the left-right class dealignment in *Norway*, and this dealignment is to a considerable degree associated with support for the Progress Party and the Socialist Left Party. However, this class dealignment has not hindered the endurance of the economic left-right dimension as the most important issue dimension for explaining party choice. This creates greater stability in the system than the structural dealignment indicates.

References

Aardal, Bernt (2003): Ideologi og stemmegivning. In: Aardel, Bernt (ed.): *Velgere i Villrede .... En Analyse av Stortingsvalget 2001*. Oslo: N.W. Damm & Søn, pp. 83-106.
Aardal, Bernt (2007): Ideologiske Dimensjoner og Stemmegivning: Gir store Velgervandringer Nye Mønstre? In: Bernt Aardal (ed.): *Norske Velgere. En Studie av Stortingsvalget 2005*. Oslo: N.W. Dam & Søn, pp. 81-109.
Bakke, Elisabeth (2006): Slovakia: Den Kronglete Veien til Demokrati. In: Bakke, Elisabeth (ed.): *Sentral-Europa og Baltikum etter 1989*. Oslo: Samlaget, pp. 138-158.
Bakke, Elisabeth/ Sitter, Nick (2005): Patterns of Stability. Party Competition and Strategy in Central Europe Since 1989. In: *Party Politics 11*, 2, pp. 243-263.
Benoit, Kenneth/ Laver, Michael (2006): *Party Policy in Modern Democracy*. London & New York: Routledge.
Berglund, Sten/ Lindström, Ulf (1978): *The Scandinavian Party System*. Lund: Student-litteratur.

Coenders, Marcel/ Scheepers, Peer (2003): The Effect of Education on Nationalism and Ethnic Exclusionism: An International Comparison. In: *Political Psychology 24*, 2, pp. 313-343.

Dalton, Russell J. (1990): Religion and Party Alignment. In: Sänkiaho, Risto et al.: *People and Their Polities. Jyväskylä: The Finnish Political Science Association*, pp. 66-88.

Deegan-Krause, Kevin (2000): Public Opinion and Party Choice in Slovakia and the Czech Republic. In: *Party Politics 6*, 1, pp. 23-46.

Deegan-Krause, Kevin (2004): Slovakia. In: Berglund, Sten et al. (eds.): *The Handbook Of Political Change in Eastern Europe*. Chetlenham: Edward Elgar, pp. 255-287.

Erikson, Robert/ Goldthorpe, John H./ Portocarero, Lucienne (1979): Intergenerational Class Mobility in Three Western European Societies: England, France and Sweden. In: *British Journal of Sociology 30*, 4, pp. 415-441.

Erikson, Robert/ Goldthorpe, John H. (1992): The Constant Flux. A Study Of Class Mobility In *Industrial Societies*. Oxford: Clarendon Press.

Evans, Geoffrey (2006): The Social Bases of Political Divisions in Post-Communist Eastern Europe. In: *Annual Review of Sociology 32*, pp. 245-270.

Fisher, Sharon/ Gould, John/Houghton,Tim (2007): Slovakia's Neoliberal Turn. In: *Europe-Asia Studies 59*, 6, pp. 977-998.

Goldthorpe, John H. (1980): Social Mobility and Class Structure in *Modern Britain*. Oxford: Clarendon Press.

Hjelm, Michael (2001): Education, Xenophobia and Nationalism: A Comparative Analysis. In: *Journal of Ethnic and Migration Studies 27*, 1, pp. 37-60.

Houtman, Dick (2001): Class, culture, and conservatism. Reassessing education as a variable in political sociology. In: Clark, Terry Nichols/Lipset, Seymour Martin (eds.): *The Breakdown Of Class Po-litics. A Debate on Post-Industrial Stratification*. Baltimore and London: The John Hopkins University Press, pp. 161-195.

Hungarians in Slovakia (2011).
http://en.wikipedia.org/wiki/Hungarians_in_Slovakia. (2011-01-03)

Kitschelt, Herbert (1988): Left-Libertarian Parties: Explaining Innovation in Competitive Party Systems. In: *World Politics XL*, 2, pp. 194-234.

Kitschelt, Herbert (1992): The Formation of Party Systems in East Central Europe. In: *Politics and Societies 20*, 1, pp. 7-50.

Knutsen, Oddbjørn (1997): From Old to New Politics: Environmentalism as a Party Cleavage. In: Strøm, Kaare/Svåsand, Lars (eds.): *Challenges to Political Parties: The Case of Norway*. Ann Arbor: The University of Michigan Press, pp. 229-262.
Knutsen, Oddbjørn (2004a): Voters and Social Cleavages. In: Heidar, Knut (ed.): *Nordic Politics. Comparative Perspectives*. Oslo: Universitetsforlaget, pp. 60-80.
Knutsen, Oddbjørn (2004b): *Social Structure and Party Choice in Western Europe – A Comparative Longitudinal Study*. Houndsmills, Basingstoke: Palgrave Macmillan.
Knutsen, Oddbjørn (2007): The Decline of Social Class? In: Dalton, Russell J./Klingemann, Hans-Dieter (eds.): *The Oxford Handbook of Political Behavior*. Oxford: Oxford University Press, pp. 457-480.
Knutsen, Oddbjørn (2009): Sosiale Klasser og Velgeradferd. In: Malnes, Raino (ed.): *Prekær Politikk*. Oslo Gyldendal Akademisk, pp. 139-161.
Leiulfsrud, Håkon/ Ivano Bison/ Jensberg, Heidi (2005): Social Class in Europe. *European Social Survey 2002/3*. Trondheim: NTNU Social Research Ltd.
Lipset, Seymour Martin/ Rokkan, Stein (1967): Cleavage Structure, Party Systems, and Voter Alignments: An introduction. In: Seymour Martin Lipset / Rokkan,Stein (eds.)*: Party Systems and Voter Alignments*. New York: The Free Press, pp. 1-64.
Nieuwbeerta, Paul (1995): *The Democratic Class Struggle in Twenty Countries 1945–1990*. Amsterdam: Thesis Publishers.
Norris, Pippa (1999): Gender: A Gender-Generation Gap? In: Evans, Geoffrey/ Norris, Pippa (eds.): *Critical elections. British Parties and Voters in Long-Term Perspective*. London: Sage, pp. 148-163.
NUTS (2003): Regions. Nomenclature of Territorial Units for Statistics. Luxembourg: European Communities.
NUTS of Norway (2010). http://en.wikipedia.org/wiki/NUTS_of_Norway (2011-01-04)
Regions of Slovakia (2011).
http://en.wikipedia.org/wiki/Regions_of_Slovakia.(2011-03-01)
Religion in Slovakia. http://www.slovensko.com/about/religion/
(2011-30-03)
Rokkan, Stein (1966): Norway: Numerical Democracy and Corporate Pluralism. In: Dahl, Robert A. (ed.): *Political Oppositions in Western Democracies. New Haven and London:* Yale University Press, pp. 70-115.

Rokkan, Stein (1967): Geography, Religion, and Social Class: Crosscutting Cleavages in Norwegian Politics. In: Lipset, Seymour Martin/ Rokkan, Stein (eds.): *Party Systems and Voter Alignments*, New York: The Free Press, pp. 367–444.

Rokkan, Stein/ Valen, Henry (1964): Regional Contrasts in Norwegian Politics: A Review of Data from Official Statistics and from Sample Survey. In: Allardt, Erik/ Littunen. Yrjö (eds.): *Cleavages, Ideologies and Party Systems: Contributions to Comparative Political Sociology, Helsinki: Westermarck Society*, pp. 162–238.

Rybar, Marek (2007): The Parliamentary Election in Slovakia, June 2006. In: *Electoral Studies 26*, pp. 699-703.

Rybar, Marek/Deegan-Krause, Kevin (2008): Slovakia's Communist Successor Parties in Comparative Perspective. In: *Communist and Post-Communist Studies 41*, 4, pp. 497-519.

Stenner, Karen (2005): *The Authoritarian Dynamic*. Cambridge: Cambridge University Press.

Stubager, Rune (2006): *The Education Cleavage*: New Politics in Denmark. Århus: Politica.

Tarrow, Sidney (2010): The Strategy of Paired Comparison: Towards a Theory of Practice. In: *Comparative Political Studies 43*, 2, pp. 230-259.

Valen, Henry/ Rokkan, Stein (1974): Conflict structure and Mass Politics in a European Periphery. In: Richard Rose (ed.): *Electoral Behaviour: A Comparative Handbook*, New York: The Free Press, pp. 315–370.

Urwin, Derek W. (1997): The Norwegian Party System from the 1880s to the 1990s. In Strøm, Kaars/Svåsand, Lars (eds.): *Challenges to Political Parties: the Case of Norway*. Ann Arbor: The University of Michigan Press, pp. 33-59.

Wessels, Bernhard/ Klingemann, Hans-Dieter (2006): Parties and Voters – Representative Consolidation in Central and Eastern Europe. In: *International Journal of Sociology 36*, 2, pp. 11-44.

Chapter 8
The appeal of populism

Ol'ga Gyárfášová and Anders Ravik Jupskås

Introduction

In the last three decades, "populist" parties have increasingly gained support and influence in Europe[66]. While parties belonging to what has been labeled the "extreme right", the "populist radical right", the "far right" or "national populists" polled around three per cent of the votes in national elections at the beginning of the 1980s, their support was thrice as much in 2006 (Ellinas 2010: 5). Some parties have even entered government coalitions (e.g. the Freedom Party in Austria, the Lega Nord in Italy, and parties in a some other Central and Eastern European countries), or acted as a stable support party for those in office (e.g. the Danish People's Party, and the Freedom Party in the Netherlands). Although populism is no new phenomenon at times of worldwide economic crises, global and national turbulence may bring new populist impetus to democratic societies.

Both Norway and Slovakia have witnessed the growth of populist parties. Although these two countries differ in many respects, parties claiming to speak on behalf of 'the people' and against the elite have been quite successful in both of them, at least electorally, in the last two decades. What makes populism such a potent political force in both countries, and to what extent do such parties have the same consequences?

By populist parties we mean ones that maintain the thin-centered ideology of populism. Such parties consider "society to be ultimately separated into two homogenous and antagonistic groups, 'the pure people' and 'the corrupt elite'", and they argue "that politics should be an expression of the *volonté general*" (Mudde 2007: 23, see also Canovan 2002; Stanley 2008). The most successful contemporary populist parties often mobilize on anti-establishment sentiments, tapping into a distrust in politics and politicians, and using a confrontational rhetoric against immigrants and/or minorities. Unlike other types of populism such as social or neoliberal populism, the populist appeal is largely an "appeal to *our people*, often in the sense of our ethnic kith and kin" (Canovan 1999:5). However, as the Norwegian Progress

---

66 Thanks to Peter Učeň for comments.

Party exemplifies, combining the nationalist and neoliberal populist appeal is possible (see below).

A number of explanations for the rise of this new party family have been presented (e.g. Taggart 2000, Mudde 2007, Eatwell 2003). However, as noted by Mudde (2007), the notion of "modernization" is never far away when discussing the rise of this party family. Processes of globalization and technological development have led countries in Western Europe into the post-industrial era. In Norway, the size of the traditional working class has shrunk from forty-four per cent in 1965 to eighteen per cent in 2005 (Bjørklund 2009). To some extent this has led to a reorientation of labor parties all over Western Europe and to the depoliticization of economic issues. Combined with increased immigration, new issues such as multiculturalism and national identity have become more salient in the public discourse and among voters. In Norway, these issues have largely been addressed only by a populist party. In Central and Eastern Europe, similar profound societal changes have been caused by the transition from a planned economy and authoritarian rule to the market economy and liberal democracies. Slovakia, like any other post-communist country, has had to cope with the phenomenon of populism. Since the "Velvet Revolution", populist politics has demonstrated various faces and contents, and the extent to which it has affected the country's development has varied.

In this chapter we will examine different aspects of populist parties in Slovakia and of the only populist party in Norwegian party politics since the end of the Second World War, the Progress Party (FRP). While some scholars might claim that the Socialist Left Party in Norway also displays populist characteristics, such claims are more likely to rest on an oversimplified definition of populism.[67] Though populist appeals could be identified in practically all parties in Slovakia, here we will focus mainly on the parties which represent national populist cases and which exhibit consistent populist features across time. These are the Movement for a Democratic Slovakia, the Slovak National Party and the Smer Party (see table 8.1).

Our analysis follows a 'most different system design' (MDSD) as our comparative strategy focuses on a rather limited number of variables and on just one phenomenon within political life (populism). While a few scholars have systematically compared these parties in Western and Eastern Europe (Mudde 2007), such analyses are usually restricted to large N-studies. Our approach is more qualitative, and the text outlines basic comparisons between

---

67 Some scholars seem to juxtapose populism with the politics of protest in general. This is incorrect, however, as many parties are against the establishment without necessarily making any appeals to "the people". Green parties might be a good illustration. Another misunderstanding occurs when populism is defined as impracticable policy proposals. Such a definition tends to see all radical policy as populist. Again, this has nothing to do with the appeals to "the people", and is therefore not populism.

Norwegian and Slovak populisms based on five categories: actors, issues, appeals, strategies, and voters.

Actors: the Norwegian Progress Party and the Slovak populist parties

The only party in Norway almost always labeled populist is the Progress Party (Betz 1994, Bjørklund 2003, Jupskås 2009, Kitschelt/McGann 1995). Ideologically, it has been defined as "neoliberal populist" (Andersen/Bjørklund 2000, Mudde 2007), and it is indeed located further to the right on socio-economic issues than other populist parties in the Nordic countries (Jupskås/Jungar 2010). Nevertheless, it has to some extent repositioned itself in the last two decades, focusing on immigration, welfare issues, and law and order.

The party – first called *Anders Lange's Party for the Strong Reduction in Taxes, Duties and Public Interventions* – entered party politics in 1973. Inspired by a similar development in Denmark, its seemingly charismatic leader, Anders Lange, was able to mobilize on anti-tax issues and anti-establishment sentiments (Bjørklund 1981, Harmel/Svåsand 1993). The failure of the Conservative Party to pursue a more traditional right-wing policy after entering office in the mid-1960s in combination with the erosion of party loyalty in the aftermath of the referendum on Norwegian EU membership in 1972, have been put forward as explanations for the emergence of a electoral niche for a new right-wing party (Bjørklund 2000). Only six months after the party had been established, it polled five per cent of the votes in a national election, thereby achieving the electoral threshold of four per cent. It won four parliamentary seats (see table 8.1). Due to internal struggles, a lack of organization, and the death of the party leader, FRP was not able to win any seats at the next national election. Subsequently, in 1977 another "charismatic outsider", Carl I. Hagen, was elected party leader. The party was simultaneously renamed *The Progress Party* (again inspired by Denmark). With a stronger organization, a youth wing and Hagen's skills, it was again able to profit from an available right-wing niche. In 1981 it had its "second breakthrough".

Nevertheless, it remained a fringe party nationally until 1989. Its *real* electoral breakthrough came in the 1987 local elections, later dubbed Norway's first "immigration election" (Bjørklund/Bergh 2005), when it obtained 12.3 per cent. Although it was plagued by internal disagreement over both its main ideological foundation and preferred strategic behavior throughout the 1990s and 2000s, this does not seem to have affected its popularity: indeed, its electoral support has usually steadily increased. In 2006 Hagen stepped down, and Siv Jensen became party leader. Although some observers thought FRP would decline without Hagen (e.g. Svåsand/Wörlund 2005: 278), it did not. In the parliamentary election of 2009, the FRP received a record high with 22.9 per cent of the vote. Currently, the party has forty-one of 169 MPs, and it is represented in all counties, and in more than 350 municipalities (of 431). In terms of organizational strength, the party has grown substantially in the last two decades. From 1995 to 2009, its membership increased by 450 per cent, from about 5000 in 1995 to about 23 000 in 2009 (see table 8.1). It is Norway's fourth largest party in terms of membership.

Table 8.1: Populist parties in Norway and Slovakia: National election results, parliamentary seats, municipalities and county elections results

FRP					
Yr	N	S	L	C	M
73	5	4	-	-	-
75	-	-	0.8	1.4	-
77	1.9	0	-	-	-
79	-	-	1.9	2.5	-
81	4.5	4	-	-	-
83	-	-	5.3	6.3	-
85	3.7	2	-	-	-
87	-	-	10.4	12.3	-
89	13.0	22	-	-	-
91	-	-	6.5	7.0	-
93	6.3	10	-	-	-
95	-	-	10.5	12.0	4 976
97	15.3	25	-	-	6 816
99	-	-	12.1	13.4	11 224
01	14.6	26	-	-	16 746
03	-	-	16.4	17.9	17 660
05	22.1	38	-	-	19 581
07	-	-	17.5	18.5	20 961
09	22.9	41	-	-	22 876

Table 8.1 continued

Yr	SNS			HZDS			Smer		
	N	S	M	N	S	M	N	S	M
90	13.9	22		X			X		
92	7.9	15		37.5	74		X		
94	5.4	9		35.0	61		X		
98	9.1	14		27.0	43		X		
02	3.3¹	0		19.5	36		13.5	25	
06	11.7	20		8.8	15		29.1	50	
10	5.1	9	1 500	4.3	0	35 000	34.8	62	16 000

Sources: Norway Statistics; Progress Party's party members is taken from Jupskås (2009:67) and annual report 2010; Election results from Slovakia from Statistical Office of the Slovak Republic. Party abbreviations: FRP: The Progress Party, SNS: Slovak National Party, HZDS: Movement for a Democratic Slovakia, Smer: The Direction. Table abbreviations: Y: Year, N: National elections results in per cent of valid votes. S: Number of seats in the national parliament, L: Results in the local elections in per cent of valid votes, C: Results in the county elections in per cent of valid votes M: Party members, X: the party did not exist. 1: SNS was split in this election; the spring-off -"True SNS"- received 3.7 per cent of votes, summed votes would be enough for entering the parliament.

The flora of Slovak populist parties is much more diverse, and not one has experienced the same stability as the FRP. The most obvious Slovak populistparty is the Movement for a Democratic Slovakia (HZDS), founded in 1991 due to internal rifts within the broad anti-communist civic movement Public against Violence. HZDS and its leader Vladimír Mečiar have played a significant role in Slovak politics. First, as a driving force behind Czechoslovakia's split in 1992. Secondly, as the main political force which brought Slovakia from the main transition path and was responsible for a domestic "democracy deficit" which caused Slovakia to lag behind in the European integration processes. It was defeated in the 1998 general election, with its electoral support eroding significantly during the 2000s and its failure in 2010 to reach the threshold of five per cent. This party seems to be undergoing its political closing stage (see table 8.1). Accordingly, we will focus on more recent actors – the most popular party Smer (Direction), and the Slovak National Party (SNS).[68]

---

68 Deegan-Krause and Haughton have quantified populist appeals and, based on an expert survey, scored Slovak parties during the period 1990-2006. As for the 2002/2006-period, the parties which scored above average are: the Slovak National Party with the highest degree of populist appeals, followed by the Communist Party of Slovakia (since the 2006

Smer has grown to be the most popular party in Slovakia. Labeling it populist may seem controversial since it does not display such strong authoritarian attributes as HZDS did, but many authors agree that it displays populist features (Deegan-Krause/Haughton, 2009; Mesežnikov 2009; Učeň 2009; Gyárfášová 2010). It has the position of a broadly defined mainstream party, which above all combines two strands of populist agenda: national populism and social demagogy. The party was established in late 1999 by a maverick from the transformed post-communist party, Robert Fico. Initially it avoided any ideological profile using self-styled characteristics such as "pragmatic" or "third way alternative". The party also offered itself as a fresh, uncorrupt alternative. After a moderately successful result in the 2002 general election, the party turned left and started the process of its "social democratization" and added "SD" to its name, standing for social democracy.[69] This was accompanied by the nationalization of the party's agenda.[70] In 2006, thanks to the party's heavy criticism of the ongoing economic reforms at the time, it won thirty per cent of the vote and became the governing party. Four years of governing with junior partners the SNS and the HZDS, strengthened public support. However, its 2010 electoral victory (thirty-five per cent of the vote) was not enough to build a coalition as there were no available partners. Smer's rule has meant the "etatization" and "ethnization" (ethnocentrism was an important binding agent of the coalition) of the political discourse. The party leader's rhetoric has been based on "taking care of the common people", offering a protective hand to those who feel left behind and defending "national interests". Compared to HZDS and the nativist nationalism of the Slovak National Party, Smer represents the instrumentalization of national populism. Although Smer does not rely on mass membership, early on it merged with the Party of Democratic Left (SDĽ), the transformed former Communist party, and all the smaller left-wing parties, thereby enabling it to take over the electorate and the infrastructure of these parties

The Slovak National Party was established soon after the breakdown of communist rule. It is a typical single-issues party and belongs to the family of radical right-wing parties. The core components of its ideology and appeal are authoritarianism, xenophobia, nationalism, and populism (Učeň 2007).[71] It ran in the first democratic elections[72] in 1990 and won fourteen per cent of the vote. It was a strong advocate of Slovakia's secession from the Czecho-

---

election no longer in parliament), Smer, and HZDS (Deegan-Krause – Haughton, 2009).
69 Since then the official name of the party has been Smer-Sociálna Demokracia (Smer-Social Democracy, Smer-SD). However, in this study we use the name "Smer" throughout.
70 For more details: Orogváni, 2006.
71 Peter Učeň includes the Slovak National Party in one group along with parties such as the League of Polish Families; ATAKA – Coalition Attack (Bulgaria), Hungarian Life and Justice Party, or the Greater Romania Party (Učeň 2007: 52).
72 SNS presents itself as the "oldest Slovak party", and claims continuity with the Slovak National Party established back in 1871.

slovak federation, and the most fundamentalist and militant promoter of the nationalist agenda. Later it became a junior coalition partner alongside the HZDS, but during the electoral cycle of 2002-2006 its political role was marginalized due to internal frictions. The 2006 general election marked its "triumphant comeback", winning almost twelve per cent of the vote and joining the ruling coalition lead by Smer. It performed more weakly in the 2010 national election with only 5.1 per cent of the vote and is now in opposition.[73]

Issues: similarities and differences

There appear to be quite a few interesting similarities between populist parties in Norway and Slovakia. These are most visible in such parties' perception of democracy, and their focus on nationalism, immigration/ minorities, and law and order. There are important difference in tax policy and opinions on the European Union.

A populist democracy?

FRP has been critical of the quality of Norwegian democracy, but has moderated the view it had in the early 1980s. The 2009 official manifesto seems much more sophisticated and more thoroughly prepared. Under the section on democracy, the FRP is more concerned with its own principles than with describing the failures of the current system. Nevertheless, the party still sees "weaknesses in [Norwegian] democracy". FRP demands the inclusion of referendums in the constitution, ones which can veto political decisions taken by legislative authorities

In Slovakia, the discourse on liberal democracy took place within the frame of "nativist democracy", under what Mudde (2007: 139-40) calls the national populists slogan: "our own state for our own nation". This mainly had consequences for minority rights and the political representation of minorities (mainly the ethnic Hungarians). In 1998, an electoral law amendment adopted by the ruling HZDS and SNS changed the conditions for coalitions. This amendment mainly targeted the Party of Hungarian Coalition (SMK).

---

73 Populist appeals appear also in other political parties in Slovakia regardless of their ideological positions. For example in the 2010 general election a political grouping called "Common People" entered Parliament by way of the candidate list of a liberal party, Freedom and Solidarity (SaS). Its representatives use anti-establishment and anti-elite rhetoric. This grouping may develop into a consistent populist party. Moreover, features of national populism could be observed also in appeals of the Party of Hungarian Coalition (SMK), the political representation of ethnic Hungarians in Slovakia.

The Slovak National Party continued its attacks on SMK: in 2006, for example, it campaigned with the slogan: "Slovak government for the Slovaks", implying that the representatives of the Hungarian minority should not be part of the ruling coalition.

National identity, immigration, and minorities

One of the most visible features of the populist parties in Norway and Slovakia is the distrust of either minorities (HZDS, SNS, and to a lesser extent Smer) or immigrants (FRP). Table 8.2 clearly shows that the voters for these parties stand out on these issues. FRP voters are substantially more likely to believe that "immigration is a serious threat to national identity". In Slovakia, meanwhile, voters sympathetic to populist parties are more likely to prefer confrontation with different minorities in the country, rather than accommodating them.

Nationalism is not explicitly used very often by the FRP. However, it is highly critical of immigration in general and Muslims in particular. Quite a substantial part of the party elite thinks immigration is a serious threat to national identity. In Norway, immigration issues received increasingly more media attention due to a rise in asylum seekers in the mid-1980s (Hagelund 2003), and Hagen immediately realized the mobilization potential of this specific issue. During the 1987 campaign, he presented a letter, allegedly signed by a Muslim, containing allegations that the Muslims would slowly but surely destroy Christian heritage and transform Norway into a Muslim state.

Although 'playing the immigration card' was a highly successful strategy for the party, the party elite still consisted of many young liberals who disliked this new immigration profile (Iversen 1998). The anti-immigration message was not really articulated again until 1995. Basically, FRP sees immigration as a burden: the increasing number of non-western immigrants is often associated with crime, social disorder, and the survival of the Norwegian welfare system.

In Hagen's own words,

> instead of being realistic, the other parties are cheering and idealizing the multicultural and multireligious society [...] They want a multicultural society where we reject the traditional values that our forefathers have developed and preserved through centuries (Hagen 2007: 241).

Table 8.2: Attitudes towards ethnic minorities and immigrants. Mean scores

Norway		Slovakia	
Parties	Immigration-skepticism	Parties	Minorities-skepticism
SV	4.4*	Most-Híd	5.5*
V	4.0	SaS	4.7*
KrF	4.0*	**All**	**4.3**
Ap	3.9*	SDKÚ	4.2
H	3.7	KDH	4.1
All	**3.7**	Smer	4.0*
Sp	3.4	HZDS	3.5*
Frp	2.7*	SNS	3.5*

Source: Survey among Norwegian voters, June 2009; CSES Slovakia, July 2010.
Note: Statement in the Norwegian survey: "Immigration is a serious threat against national identity" (1 is very much, 5 is not at all). In the Slovak survey attitudes towards minorities and immigration are measured by three indicators: A. "The ethnic Slovaks should have a superior status within the state" vs. "Slovakia should guarantee equal rights to all citizens, regardless of their ethnicity." B. "In a democracy, the majority has the right to decide also at the expense of the minorities" vs. "In a democracy, the rights of the minorities must be respected." C. "The immigration to Slovakia should be severely restricted" vs. "Slovakia should be open to everybody who is interested in working and living in our country." (Confrontation is (1) and accommodation is (7)).
Party abbreviations: Most-Híd: Bridge Party; SaS: Freedom and Solidarity, SDKÚ: Slovak Democratic and Christian Union, KDH: Christian Democratic Movement, Smer: Direction Party, HZDS: Movement for a Democratic Slovakia, SNS: Slovak National Party.
* The mean value for each party is significantly different from average (α=0.05).

In recent years immigration in general and Muslim communities in particular are seen as a threat to "Norwegian values", such as freedom of speech, gender equality, and tolerance (see also (Akkerman/Hagelund 2007).

In Slovakia, however, the migrant community is very small, less than one per cent of the population as of 2010. A large proportion of migrants are EU citizens and not third-country nationals. Consequently, nationalistic and xenophobic parties in Central and Eastern Europe tend to target the traditional native minorities. For instance, SNS used a variety of national issues in the 2006 electoral campaign – using slogans such as "Slovakia to the Slovaks" it attacked the SMK, which was a member of the center-right coalition government for two electoral terms. SNS was questioning the loyalty of ethnic Hungarians. Such rhetoric escalated during the presidential election in 2009[74] and before the 2010 parliamentary elections. In the campaign SNS

---

74 The anti-Hungarian campaign before the 2009 presidential elections heavily contributed to the victory of the incumbent president, Ivan Gašparovič, supported by Smer and the SNS. Its main element was the accusation, supported by all opposition parties including the SMK, of Iveta Radičová of favoring Hungarian interests at the expense of Slovakia's.

spread an image of "the Hungarian enemy" and called for vigilance. SNS also portrayed the Roma as a threat to all "decent" Slovaks. Smer, however, employed "softer" rhetoric; the main issue in this respect was the defense of "the interests of the nation-state". But as a main coalition partner, Smer was responsible for specific political steps against minorities, such as the Language Act, which introduced restrictions on using the minority language. It also approved the Patriotic Act and the passage of the Dual Citizenship Act reacting to a new nationality law introduced in Hungary.[75]

Quest for order and a firm hand

Elements of authoritarian policy are to be found in Slovakia and Norway, with a focus for instance on law and order, and increased spending on the police force and the military. However, while the FRP tends to focus on law and order, populists in Slovakia have also argued for the need for strong leaders.

Law and order is a key issue for FRP. It would increase police officers' pay, reorganize the police so it can deal more effectively with organized crime, ensure fewer early releases from prison, and stop alternative forms of penalties such as community service. The party also wants to increase the maximum prison sentence from twenty-one to thirty years (Weiby 2010). They would also increase penalties in general. In their own words: "Today, the punishment for many types of crimes in Norway is so feeble that it offends against the sense of justice of the general population. Therefore, we desire stricter punishments and sentencing in accordance with the letter of the law. Crime should not pay!" (Fremskrittspartiet 2010). According to Per Sandberg, the party would also lower 'the age of criminal responsibility to 13 or 14 years' (Weiby 2010). Moreover, FRP politicians recently called for the reintroduction of the death penalty for raping women and killing children. An up-and-coming star, Sylvi Listhaug, disagreed, arguing that prisoners should be 'tortured in prison, so to speak, rather than getting away with the death penalty' (NTB 2010).

In Slovakia, the change of regime in 1989 and the transition process brought feelings of uncertainty, the loss of a familiar social order and a kind of "value vacuum" for many people. There was a demand from some for

---

75 The new Hungarian nationality law was passed shortly after the electoral victory of Viktor Orbán in spring 2010, and came into force by January 2011. According to this law, every person who was a Hungarian citizen or is a descendant of a person who was a Hungarian citizen before 1920, and speaks Hungarian may apply to become a Hungarian citizen even if he or she does not live in Hungary. In reaction the Slovak Citizenship Act has been modified and restricted dual citizenship. The amendment provides that if a Slovak citizen acquires the citizenship of another state "by an act of will", the person will automatically lose Slovak citizenship.

strong political leaders showing a firm hand. The strong authority of Vladimír Mečiar seemed appealing to many voters in the 1990s. In 2010, Smer appealed by offering "certainty in hard times", referring to the economic crisis. Slovak society continues to prefer social security to political and civil liberties.[76] The Fico administration strongly encourages people to "stick" to social security and material values.[77]

Euroskeptics?

Although euro-skepticism has become an important mobilizing issue for populist radical right parties,[78] both Norway and Slovakia are exceptions to this general pattern. Judging by voter attitudes, none of the populist parties in these two countries is particularly euroskeptic. Although the two big nationalist populist parties in Slovakia are indeed the two most euro-skeptical ones (see table 8.3), neither has a majority of euro-skeptics because the Slovak public is largely enthusiastic about the EU. In Norway, however, around half of the population is against EU membership. Despite having a good number of EU skeptics among its rank and file, however, the Progress Party is far from being the most skeptical party. In fact, the two other large parties – the Labor Party and the Conservatives – are either at the same level of skepticism (Labor), or more EU-friendly (Conservatives). In Norway the opposition to the EU is largely represented by the agrarian Center Party, the Christian People's Party, and the Socialist Left Party.

The FRP has always been fundamentally divided *and* highly polarized on the question of Norwegian EU membership. In 1992, two years before the Norwegian referendum, two-thirds of delegates were pro-EU, while one-third was against membership (Iversen 1998: : 118).

---

76 Based on the standard question: "Imagine that somebody in Slovakia intended to curb political and civil freedoms while somebody else aimed to restrict social security. What would you personally consider less acceptable?" 56 per cent were concerned with social security, 24 per cent with civil freedoms (IVO, May 2008. For more details see: Mesežnikov/Gyárfášová, 2008: 39).
77 For more details see: Mesežnikov/Gyárfášová, 2008.
78 The situation has not always been thus, however. Before the broader and deeper integration of the European Union, parties that belonged to the populist radical right party family used to be euro-enthusiasts rather than euro-skeptics (Mudde 2007: 181). This illustrates, of course, that parties, also populist ones, pay attention to societal development and change their policy accordingly. Nowadays, these parties usually support close European cooperation while being skeptical of the current direction of the EU and its supranational tendencies.

Table 8.3: Public attitudes towards EU membership. Per cent of respondents in support of respective positions

	Norway			Slovakia	
Parties	Euro-enthusiasts	Euro-skeptics	Parties	Euro-enthusiasts	Euro-skeptics
H	65	24	SaS	94	4
Ap	40	45	SDKÚ	90	5
Frp	40	49	Most-Híd	87	7
All	**35**	**49**	KDH	84	10
V	33	41	**All**	**81**	**12**
SV	18	56	Smer	80	12
KrF	14	70	SNS	53	47
Sp	4	89			

Source: Norwegian Voter Survey 2009; CSES, Slovakia 2010.
Note: Statement in Norway: "Norway should become a full member of the European Union". Euro-enthusiasts are defined as "agree completely" and "agree somewhat", while Euro-skeptics are defined as "disagree completely" and "disagree somewhat". Question in Slovakia: "If you were to vote in a referendum today, would you vote for Slovakia's accession to the European Union or against it?" The respondents are voters of parliamentary parties after 2010 election. Euro-enthusiasts is defined as "definitely and 'rather for'" while Euro-skeptics are defined as "definitely and 'rather against'".

The slogan during Norway's second referendum on EU membership tried to satisfy both these factions: "Yes to EU – no to the Union". Accordingly, support for FRP was halved in 1993 as many potential FRP voters felt safer voting for the Center Party, whose anti-EU message was unmistakable (Aardal/Valen 1995: 143). Today, the FRP is neither skeptical about Europe in general, nor about supranational arrangements in particular. According to the manifesto (Fremskrittspartiet 2009), the party wants to work for closer cooperation between Norway and Europe, also by introducing and participating in "supranational solutions" on security issues, environment protection, and criminal policy. However, the party is still split with regard to Norwegian membership into two almost identical factions at all levels within the party – i.e. among voters, members, and MPs (see figure 8.1).

Figure 8.1: Attitudes towards Norwegian membership in the EU: Four levels in the Frp 2009

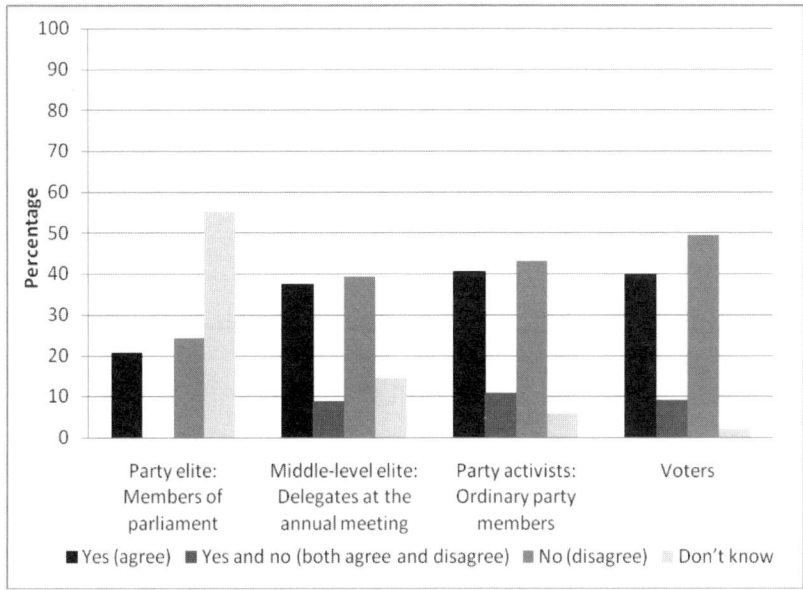

Source: Fossum 2009; Norwegian party members and delegate study 2009; Voter survey 2009

Notes: The response rate in the MP-survey was 76.3 % and 47.7 % the delegate survey. For the MPs the question was: Do you think that Norway should join the EU (yes, no or don't know), while for the delegates, members and voters were asked to agree or disagree with the following statement: Norway should become a full member of the European Union. (Response options were 1 to 5, the two positive and two negative categories are combined)

This division could also explain why FRP is the only party in Norway with no official policy on EU membership. As the manifesto states: the FRP will respect the will of the people, and the party will thus free its MPs in the debate on Norwegian membership. The party sees

> [...] itself as a receiver, rather than a shaper, of popular opinion on this important issue (Fossum 2009).

In Slovakia, however, there is simply no potential for politicizing the issue of EU membership since the general public maintains a strong pro-EU bias (Mattila/Raunio 2007). Although the three populist parties in question are the most euro-skeptic of all parties in Slovakia, opposition to the EU is no higher than thirteen per cent, which is the case with HZDS (see figure 8.2). However, in HZDS and SNS, there is no majority in favor of the EU. As shown in figure 8.2, only slightly more than forty percent is pro-EU – quite a substantial share of the voters seems to think that Slovak membership is "neither a good nor a bad thing".

Figure 8.2: Party affiliations and attitudes towards Slovakia's EU membership

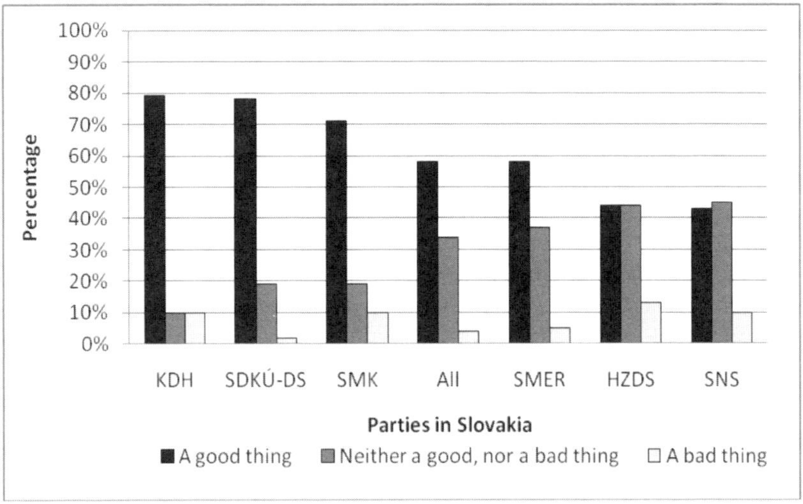

Source: European Parliament Election Study 2009, [Voter Study].
Note: "Do not know" replies add up to the total of 100 %. Statement "Membership in the EU is…"

Moreover, the European agenda is not salient for voters – the EU arena is still perceived as a sphere in which less is at stake; the main political battlefield and source of power consist of politics at the national level. The SNS has recently faced the challenge of closing the gap between the national political realm and that of Europe. In the 2009 European Parliament election campaign, the SNS did not tackle whether European and national interests are conflicting or complementing priorities, selling them instead as a "single package". It sought to demonstrate that being of a nationalist orientation did not require being euro-skeptical. Nevertheless, this form of ethnic appeal did not break the SNS adherents' indifference to the EU.

Two important differences: anti-tax and anti-corruption

Although several of the populist parties in Western Europe initially advocated parts of a neoliberal agenda (e.g. Betz 1993, Kitschelt/McGann 1995), most of the parties belonging to the current populist radical right party family seem to have abandoned this policy. This does not mean they have become socialist; rather, they increasingly adjust to the slogan of Jörg Haider: "social, not socialist" (quoted in Mudde 2007). However, FRP does still seem to adhere to its neoliberal agenda. Since its establishment, FRP has emphasized the need for tax cuts, privatization, and less state intervention.

The context-specific issue for populist parties in Central and Eastern Europe is the anti-corruption agenda. Most populist parties utilize the dissatisfaction and detachment of the electorate, and thus nurture the expectation that populist politics and politicians "may be different".

Appeals: the common people against the elite

The appeal to "the people" and "against the elite" is at the heart of populist ideology, and all of the main leaders of the FRP have presented themselves as spokespeople for ordinary people. The founder of FRP, Anders Lange, used to speak of "real people", those who did "honest work" (Eide/Lange 1974: 55). His main enemies were "the socialist states, political parties, organizations and trade unions and monopoly tendencies in private capitalism" (Bjørklund 2003:130). He also loathed intellectuals:

> I despise intellectuals; I am a man who, I hope, has the common sense to be able to express myself the way people think (Eide/Lange 1974: 54).

Another traditional invocation is the appeal to hard-working tax payers. This neoliberal populist appeal long prevailed in FRP. In Hagen's worldview, 'the people' are the equivalent of 'tax payers' – ordinary people who work hard but who are "taxed to death". In the party leader debate in 1985, Hagen presented a classic FRP appeal:

> We politicians, we do not own the money that the state has at its disposal – it is you who owns the money the state has at its disposal (Jupskås 2008: 100).

In this respect Hagen was truly inspired by Thatcher and Reagan (Hagen 2007: 83-84). Nevertheless, the statements also echo other populists who were neoliberal at that point such as the Freedom Party of Austria [FPÖ].

Due to governmental ambitions, FRP has slightly moderated its anti-establishment discourse. Nevertheless, the idea of being fundamentally different from the other parties is still prevalent:

> FRP is the only party which represents a real change and a real alternative to the current red-green government. With FRP in office, the voters can feel confident that they have a party which serves as an ombudsman for ordinary people (Fremskrittspartiet, 2010b).

Moreover, an anti-tax doctrine is also a key feature of the modern, professionalized FRP. In the recent English-language self-presentation, *A Change for the Better* (Fremskrittspartiet 2010a), the FRP states that the party wants to "... transfer political and economic power from the government to the people". The argument is that "limited government is about respect [...] for the decisions made by the people". During the last decade, two more appeals have been frequently employed to mobilize specific segments of the electorate. First, after having obtained a stable level of support from a fairly large group of traditional working-class voters, Hagen declared at the annual meeting in 2003 that the FRP was the "new Labor party". This image as the "real" Labor party has been an important part of the appeal ever since. Second, the party has combined its defense of Israel and Christian-Judeo values with critical remarks about Islam and Muslim culture. In the tradition of the Dutch populist leader, Pim Fortuyn, the current party leader, Siv Jensen, has argued that Norway is experiencing the "crafty" islamization of society.

In Slovakia, meanwhile, SNS always seems to appeal based on ethnicity. It addresses "Slovaks", and refers to "us" (Slovaks) and "them" (Hungarians and gypsies). 2010 campaign slogans included: "We will not give up Slovakia!", implying not giving up Slovakian territory to Hungary. Territorial integrity and raising the specter of irredentism – one of the constitutional parts of national populism – were transferred into the slogan "That our borders remain our borders". However, when Smer appeals to "people" it means ordinary, hardworking, decent people. "For the people, for Slovakia" was the title of the 2010 party manifesto.

Blaming and scapegoating are also typical of populist appeals in Slovakia. Despite Smer's position as a main coalition party, it used to shift responsibility to others – be they the media (biased for the opposition); the opposition parties (acting against the interests of Slovakia); monopolies (acting anti-socially); the Hungarian minority in Slovakia (not being loyal enough); the Hungarian Republic (harming the Slovaks by bickering with them in international forums).

Those who vote for the populist parties in Slovakia are often concentrated on a charismatic party leader. Smer Chairman Robert Fico is the most trusted politician for almost ninety per cent of party supporters. He is also perceived as the main factor behind the party's election success. Mr. Fico also displays other hallmarks of a populist leader, such as direct and unmediated communication with the public and constant campaigning against 'enemies'.

Party strategies: from protest to office seeking?

Kaare Strøm (1990) argues political parties have three fundamental goals: votes, policy, and office. The argument is not that parties prioritize only one (or two) of these goals, but that the importance of the three goals might vary between parties and over time. Most interesting when analyzing populist parties is the extent to which they de-radicalize to become "acceptable".

The FRP started out as a classical protest party, purely seeking votes. Almost none of the people close to the party's founder, Anders Lange, had any political skills (Bjørklund 2000:435) and, according to (Iversen 1998: 191), Lange was not really interested in traditional parliamentary work. However, the autobiographies of the next leader Carl I. Hagen (2007) show a politician eager to have real influence in national politics. Accordingly, in the 1985 election campaign Hagen promised to support the non-socialist government. However, already in 1986 he was forced to vote against a governmental proposal to raise taxes on gas. The event illustrates a recurring dilemma for the FRP: how much of its policy can be an object of political compromise?

After a successful election in 1997, and Siv Jensen's election as vice-chairman in 1999, the party started to prepare more systematically for government (Mo 2011). Although the distribution of parliamentary seats and legislative weight of the FRP had made the party the stable supporter of the non-socialist government with regard to the state budget (Narud/Valen 2007: 223), it was not satisfied with its position as an opposition party. But there seems to be no alternative. Although the FRP was accepted as a potential governmental partner by the Conservatives in 2009, and the party collaborates with many different parties locally, the two other smaller center-oriented non-socialist parties, the Christian People's Party and the Liberals, still reject forming a coalition with the FRP due to perceived insuperable ideological differences. The Conservatives and the FRP would thus need a majority to enter government together.

SNS and Smer, however, are not just protest parties. They are office-seeking and have participated in government: SNS as a coalition party with HZDS in 1990, and with Smer in 2006-2010. Smer focused on areas such as restrictions on the use of the minority language in textbooks, and the adoption of the Patriotic Act which included the use of national symbols in public. Although Smer was impatient to enter office from its very formation, it did not succeed at first. In 2006, however, it formed a coalition with "unusual" partners – nationalists and populists (SNS and HZDS). In 2010 it won the most votes, but it lacked coalition partners and was outweighed by the center-right parties which built a fragile coalition.

Several studies have analyzed the impact of government participation on populist parties. One general assumption is that these parties lose public support once they participate in government and lose their protest appeal. In Slovakia the results are mixed. Of those new parties which emerged, six managed to win seats in Parliament and participate in government. Three of them had dramatically worse electoral performances after their first election, while three improved (Deegan-Krause/Haughton 2009). The most illustrative example is Smer in the 2010 election – after being the governmental coalition leader for four years, the party received significantly more votes than before.

The voter perspective: populist radical right as 'new labor' parties?

In many social milieus, it was long unacceptable to express any sympathy for the FRP. Even today its supporters are frequently vilified by academics, commentators, journalists, and writers. Yet almost one-quarter of Norwegian voters vote for this party.

FRP has mainly attracted voters who used to vote for the Conservatives and the Labor Party (see table 8.4). In every election since the late 1980s, a rather large proportion of FRP's voters has come from these two parties; 16.4 per cent from the Conservatives and 9.7 per cent from the Labor Party. FRP also seems to attract more voters from the Christian People's Party. It also mobilizes young voters and voters that would otherwise not vote. A substantial part of FRP voters comes from first-time voters and non-voters

Table 8.4: Distribution of the Progress Party's voters in relation to what they voted in the previous election: 1989-2005 . Per cent

Party/Year	Frp	H	Ap	KrF	Sp	SV	Ftv[1]	Nv[2]	(N)
1989	24.7	29.2	13.7	0.9	1.4	0.9	12.3	11	(219)
1993	65.1	8.4	4.8	3.6	1.2	1.2	10.8	3.6	(83)
1997	45.6	16.9	11.8	3.1	7.7	1.5	7.2	3.6	(195)
2001	55.6	9.1	10.2	7.0	1.1	0.5	5.3	5.3	(187)
2005	44.7	18.5	7.9	4.3	0.9	0.9	7.9	8.5	(329)
Mean	*47.1*	*16.4*	*9.7*	*3.8*	*2.5*	*1.0*	*8.7*	*6.4*	

Source: Norwegian Elections Studies. Note: 1: First Time Voters, 2: Non-voters
Party abbreviations: Frp: The Progress Party, H: The Conservatives, Ap: The Labour Party, KrF: The Christian People's Party, Sp: The Centre party, SV: The Socialist Left Party

Second, with regard to the socio-economic and demographic characteristics of FRP voters, the early voter profile was characterized by "[...] working class or private sector employed, average education, low or middle income, man, under 30 years old [...], passive with regard to religious activity and located in the Oslo fjord area" (Valen et al. 1990: 106).

Analyses of the three latest available election surveys (1997, 2001 and 2005) largely confirm this pattern (see table 8.5). The FRP attracts voters from the working class and to some lesser extent from the private sector, and the party is unpopular among people in the public sector and students. The party is still predominantly supported by voters with low or middle incomes. Men are more likely to vote for the FRP than women, a pattern which is consistent with more or less all the radical right parties in Europe (Norris 2005).

However, there have been some interesting changes in the voter profile. Consistent with the 'petty bourgeoisie revolt thesis', the party used to be supported by the self-employed. But in terms of the self-employed, from being overrepresented by five percentage points in 1997, the party in 2005 was underrepresented by three percentage points. As the party has grown, its electorate has thus become proletarianized. This means that an increasingly larger share of the voters belongs to the traditional working class. FRP's share of working-class voters in 1989 was already closer to that of the Labor Party than any other Norwegian party (Valen, et al. 1990: 106). However, while the support of working-class voters from 1993 to 2005 has dropped by ten percentage points for Labor (52 to 42 percent) and 12 points for the center parties (30 to 18 per cent), support has increased by 22 percentage points for the FRP (5 to 27 per cent) (Bjørklund 2009). Labor still has the largest support, but the FRP has a more working-class profile (because the party is smaller). Moreover, at the election in 2005, the FRP was for the first time ever the largest party among the unskilled working class (37 per cent from this group: 7 per cent more than Labor).

With regard to religion, region and the city/rural-dimension there are also some interesting developments. The party is no longer a predominantly Oslo-based party or an urban party; in fact it is now underrepresented around the capital city, with support equally distributed between towns and more rural areas more generally. However, one stronghold is now Western Norway, partly because of a reorientation from non-religious rhetoric to a staunch promotion of Christian values and the Christian heritage of Norway, and partly because the party is the only one which almost unreservedly defends Israel. This is something the FRP has in common with many other right-wing

Table 8.5: Voter profile for the Progress party: 1997-2005. Per cent

	1997	Deviation 1997	2001	Deviation 2001	2005	Deviation 2005
Electoral support	*15.3*		*14.6*		*22.1*	
Occupation						
Working class	27	4	28	11	26	8
Public sector	15	-10	22	-8	19	-9
Private sector	31	2	30	-3	36	4
Farmers/fishermen	4	0	2	-2	1	-1
Self-employed	11	5	8	1	7	-3
Students	3	-4	5	-2	7	-3
Others	9	3	4	2	2	0
Education						
Primary and High school	19	0	26	12	19	4
College	65	8	59	2	55	10
University/College university	16	-8	14	-14	26	-14
Income						
High	29	-6	28	-10	25	-5
Middle	37	5	37	2	40	5
Low	34	1	35	7	35	0
Gender						
Men	62	9	64	14	59	6
Women	38	-9	36	-14	41	-6
Religion						
Member	7	-3	6	-3	2	1
Moderately active	17	2	16	0	10	-3
Low activity	15	-3	16	-3	13	-4
Passive	61	4	61	6	66	6
Region						
Around the Oslo fjord	31	0	24	-8	31	-3
Eastern Norway	14	-2	11	-6	15	-2
Southern Norway	6	0	5	-1	4	-1
Western Norway	31	4	46	18	34	9
Trøndelag	8	-1	6	-3	8	-2
Northern Norway	10	-1	9	0	8	-1
City/rural						
Rural	24	-9	34	1	31	-1
Cities	76	9	66	-1	69	1

Political trust						
High	13	-14	7	-10	13	-10
Medium	53	-7	46	-12	51	-6
Low	35	21	47	23	36	16
Political knowledge						
High	-	-	28	-12	15	-10
Medium	-	-	21	-5	24	-4
Low	-	-	51	17	61	14
Political interest						
Very much interested	12	2	9	1	6	-3
Somewhat interested	45	-10	53	-8	52	-9
Little interest	38	5	37	7	40	11
Not at all interested	5	3	2	0	2	1

Source: Aardal et.al. (2007: 20) and Norwegian Election Studies 1997-2005. The author's own calculations. Notes: The information for the variable *education 2005* is based on interviews. In 2001 and 1997 information is taken from the education database of Norwegian Statistics.

populist parties in Europe, especially after 9/11 (Mudde 2007: 295). Other right-wing populist parties in Northern Europe – the Danish People's Party, the Dutch Freedom Party, the Swedish Democrats and Vlaams Belang – also support Israel, while Front National and FPÖ are more ambivalent towards Israel due to (mild) anti-Semitism. In the 2005 election one of the parties that lost most voters to the FRP was the Christian People's Party. 15 per cent of those who voted for the Christian People's Party in 2001 preferred the FRP in 2005 (Aardal 2007: 26). Thus FRP is now slightly overrepresented among members of religious communities. But the party is still more popular among those who are passive with regard to religious activity.

There are significant differences between the three populist parties in Slovakia. HZDS voters were typical frustrated "transition losers" (the elderly, rural dwellers, those with low education with lower cultural and social capital). They also viewed the past nostalgically and regarded the previous regime as better than the post-1989 one. They also tended to value the firm hand of authority, and were rather narrow-minded; relying on the protective hand of the state (Gyárfášová et al. 2001).SNS is typically more successful with men than women. In established democracies this type of party is usually favored by blue-collar workers. In Slovakia the class alignment is difficult to identify but if we look at the educational structure, SNS is above-averagely popular with voters who have a vocational education. Although it used to be a party for younger voters, many younger voters (even former SNS voters) have changed to a more radical alternative – a small extreme right-wing party, the People's Party – Our Slovakia. Paradoxically, SNS voters are more leftist when it comes to socioeconomic views and clearly anti-

minorities on the l relevant issues. As for attitudes to the EU, SNS voters are on the most euro-skeptical end of the scale, but only a few of them think that EU membership is a bad thing. Nonetheless, a majority of them would vote t for Slovakia's EU membership. SNS voters see nationalist issues as salient but – above all for the 2010 election – they prioritize social and economic issues. The electorate of SNS is rather volatile, substantial in- and outflows between the elections could be observed, and its electoral performance depends very much on the party being the only "issue owner". If a stronger party appears offering the "defense of national interests", as was the case in 1994 or 2010, SNS's gains may be threatened.

Smer, as a newly established party, was able to attract voters from both sides of a polarized society. In its first election in 2002 it attracted former voters of the post-communist left party (SDĽ), voters of the nationalist HZDS and SNS, and voters of its main political rival, the center-right liberal SDKÚ (see table 8.6). Later, inflow voters mainly came from HZDS. The best result ever in the 2010 general election was achieved by a combination of a high share of loyal core voters (70 per cent), and an ability to attract voters from other parties – in particular from its coalition partners.

Table 8.6: Distribution of the Smer Party's voters in relation to what they voted in the previous election: 2002-2010. Per cent

Party /Year	Smer	SNS	HZDS	SDKÚ	KDH	SDĽ	Other parties	Ftv[1]	Nv[2]	(N)
2002	-	13	15	16	-	22	19	14	1	103
2006	30	3	13	8	1	-	31	8	6	159
2010	70	1	2	1	1	-	5	6	14	699

Sources: Institute for Public Affairs, 2002, 2006; FOCUS agency 2010. Note: 1: First Time Voters, 2: Non-voters. Party abbreviations: SNS: Slovak National Party, HZDS: Movement for a Democratic Slovakia, SDKÚ: Slovak Democratic and Christian Union, KDH: Christian Democratic Movement, SDĽ: Party of Democratic Left.

Also, as a new party it was an attractive alternative for young voters, but since 2002 the party's electorate has grown older (whereas in 2002 the deviation in the age group 18-34 was + 12, in 2010 it was – 11), and has become more rural and less educated (see table 8.7). These structural changes reflect a large segment of HZDS' electorate moving to Smer.

Smer voters purport to be leftists. In their attitudes to the role of the state, they emphasize the need for a strong social state which compensates for the negative social impacts of free market competition. The adherents of center-right liberal parties, however, underscore the need for individual responsibility and the freedom for entrepreneurship and economic competition.

The views of Smer's party supporters regarding cultural-ethical issues are more conservative than would be expected from left-leaning voters. On the axis of minority rights, the status of minorities, and attitudes

Table 8.7: Voter profile for the Smer party: 2002-2010. Per cent

	2002	Deviation 2002	2006	Deviation 2006	2010	Deviation 2010
Electoral support	*13.5*		*29.1*		*34.8*	
Age						
18-34	48	+12	33	-2	21	-11
35-54	37	-1	39	+2	41	+3
55+	15	-11	28	-	38	+8
Education						
Primary	18	-18	22	-2	18	+2
Vocational	32	+2	30	-2	35	+5
High school	40	+14	38	+4	37	-2
University/College university	10	+2	10	-	10	-5
Gender						
Men	40	-8	46	-2	46	-2
Women	60	+8	54	+2	54	+2
City/rural						
Rural (up to 5 000 inhab.)	38	-6	42	-2	49	+7
Middle (5 – 50 000 inhab.)	32	+1	31	-1	30	-1
Cities (more than 50 000 inhab.)	30	+5	27	+3	21	-6

Source: Institute for Public Affairs (2002, 2006); FOCUS agency (2010). The author's own calculations.

toward the Hungarian minority, they show above-average intolerant views but are not as nationalistic as SNS voters. They are pro-EU but not as enthusiastic as the center-right voters. In many respects, Smer voters occupy average or centered positions. This is partly due to the broad constituency; moreover, such a position makes possible expanding in the future into other social groups.

Concluding remarks

Though Norwegian and Slovak populist politics differ in many respects, recent global turbulence has posed parallel challenges to both small states. In a comparative perspective, the Norwegian party system has been and still is characterized as extremely stable (Lipset/Rokkan 1967), although the emergence of FRP has challenged the traditional "five-party model" in Norway. After the Left Socialist Party (SV) joined the government in 2005, the FRP is currently the only true outsider – defined as a lack of governmental experience – in Parliament. So far the FRP has been able to challenge the other parties through its more generous inclinations regarding the use of state's oil revenues. How the populist reflex of the party would deal with governmental responsibility, however, remains to be seen.

Slovakia, as a relatively newly formed democracy, has not only a very unstable political system with a volatile electorate, but also weak socioeconomic ties between political parties and their constituencies (see chapter 7). One of the structural factors of the post-communist political development is ethnic heterogeneity. National issues have been strongly politicized and national populism has become one of the most effective populist appeals in the past twenty or so years. Unlike in Norway, the populist parties have all been in office, and their impact on Slovakia's consolidation of democracy and ambitions to join the EU has been enormous, above all in the 1990s. Many issues and appeals favored in populist politics reflect nationalistic concerns, based on the distinction between "us" and "them", inclusion and exclusion. However, in contrast to Norway, migration as such and new, non-Western minorities are not salient issues in Slovakia. In the near future, populist appeals will continue to draw on the dominant ethnic cleavage with a possible shift to the issue of the Roma minority, combining ethnicity with social chauvinism.

There are also significant differences in political culture between the two countries. A distinctive feature of the Norwegian political culture has been its consensus orientation. The anti-establishment feature of FRP has therefore been a new element in Norwegian post-war party politics. Nevertheless, the party has served as a reliable partner in the process of forming state budgets. Moreover, FRP is no extremist, defined as anti-democratic, party. But the party argues that the system is malfunctioning, and that measures have to be taken to restore true "popular sovereignty". While it can be difficult to substantiate the populist argument that contemporary democracy is not controlled by the popular will, a substantial volume of research in recent decades has sought to document a growing 'democratic deficit', in which the reach of the ballot is supposedly reduced (Selle/Østerud 2006, Østerud et al. 2003, Holst 2009).

Slovakia's political culture, meanwhile, is polarized and fragmented. The extent of polarization is indicated by a full alternation of power after almost every general election (Szomolányi 2011). Furthermore, voter volatility largely occurs within the respective blocs (intra-bloc, shallow volatility) and not across the blocs (deep, inter-bloc volatility, see Kitschelt et. at. 1999). On the other hand, a broad, national consensus going beyond the political dividing lines was reached with regard to the integration issues (accession to the European Union and NATO in the early 2000s, similarly for the adoption of the euro), but not for other reforms.

Despite these differences, both Slovakia and Norway live with populist politics under the conditions of transitional and established democracy respectively, which means that in both cases the populist parties are neither absorbed by the mainstream nor pushed to the margins of the political scene.

References

Aardal, Bernt (2007): *Norske velgere: En studie av stortingsvalget 2005*. Oslo: NW Damm og Søn.
Aardal, Bernt/ Valen, Henry (1995*): Konflikt og opinion*. Oslo: NKS-forlag.
Akkerman, Tjitske/Hagelund, Anniken (2007): 'Women and children first!'Anti-immigration parties and gender in Norway and the Netherlands. In: *Patterns of Prejudice 41*, 2, pp. 197-214.
Andersen, Jørgen Goul (2007): Restricting access to social protection for immigrants in the Danish welfare state. In: *Benefits 15*, 3, pp. 257-69.
Andersen, Jørgen Goul/ Bjørklund, Tor (2000): Radical right-wing populism in Scandinavia: from tax revolt to neo-liberalism and xenophobia. In: Hainsworth, Paul (ed): *The politics of the extreme right: From the margins to the mainstream,* London: Pinter, pp. 193-223.
Betz, Hans-Georg (1993): The two faces of radical right-wing populism in Western Europe. In: *The Review of Politics 55*, 4, pp. 663-86.
Betz, Hans-Georg (1994): Radical right-wing populism in Western Europe. Basingstoke: Macmillan.
Bjørklund, Tor (1981): *Anders Lange og Fremskrittspartiet: Norges svar på Glistrupianismen. Arbeidsnotat*. Oslo: Institutt for samfunnsforskning.
Bjørklund, Tor (2000): Om Anders Lange og ideen om et nytt parti. In: *Historisk tidsskrift 79*, 4, pp. 435–56.
Bjørklund, Tor (2003): Fremskrittspartiet gjennom 30 år. In: *Nytt Norsk Tidsskrift 20*, 2, pp. 129–45.

Bjørklund, Tor (2004): Norsk populisme fra Ottar Brox til Carl I. Hagen. In: *Nytt Norsk Tidsskrift*, 3-4, pp. 410-20.

Bjørklund, Tor (2009): To mål på arbeiderklasse: Yrke og klassetilhørighet – Norske velgere og partier fra 1965 til 2005. In: *Norsk statsvitenskapelig tidsskrift*, 1, pp. 5-27.

Bjørklund, Tor/ Bergh, Johannes (2005): Innvandrere i lokalpolitikken – En suksesshistorie? In: Saglie, Jo/Bjørklund, Tor (ed.): *Lokalvalg og lokalt folkestyre*. Oslo: Gyldendal Akademisk, pp. 178-94.

Canovan, Margaret (1999): Trust the people! Populism and the two faces of democracy. In: *Political Studies 47*, 1, pp. 2-16.

Canovan, Margaret (2002): Taking politics to the people: populism as the ideology of democracy. In: Meny, Yves/Surel, Yves (ed.): *Democracies and the Populist Challenge*. Basingstoke: Palgrave MacMillan, pp. 25-44.

Deegan-Krause, Kevin/Haughton, Tim (2009): Toward a More Useful Conceptualization of Populism: Types and Degrees of Populist Appeals in the Case of Slovakia. In: *Politics & Policy 37*, 4, pp. 821-841.

Eatwell, Roger (2003): Ten theories of the extreme right. In: Merkl, P./ Weinberg, L. (ed.): *Right-Wing Extremism in the Twenty-First Century*. London: Frank Cass, pp. 45-70.

Eide, Martin (2001): *Til dagsorden!: journalistikk, makt og demokrati*. Oslo: Gyldendal akademisk.

Eide, Torbjørn/Lange, Anders (1974): *Anders Lange som han var*. Drammen: Lyche.

Ellinas, Antonis A. (2010): *The media and the far right in Western Europe: playing the nationalist card*. Cambridge: Cambridge University Press.

Fossum, John Erik (2009): Norway's European conundrum. In *ARENA Working Paper no. 4*, February 2009, pp. 1-22: University of Oslo.

Fremskrittspartiet (2009): Handlingsprogram 2009-2013. Oslo: Fremskrittspartiet.

Fremskrittspartiet (2010a): A Change for the Better. Oslo: Fremskrittspartiet.

Fremskrittspartiet (2010b): "Vi mener".
URL: http://www.Frp.no/no/Vi_mener/ (2010-01-12)

Gyárfášová, Oľga/Krivý Vladimír/Velšic, Marián (2001): *Krajina v pohybe. Správa o politických názoroch a hodnotách ľudí na Slovensku*.[Country in a Motion. Report on Political Views and Values of People in Slovakia]. Bratislava: Inštitút pre verejné otázky.

Gyárfášová, Oľga (2010): Voľby a voliči [Elections and Voters]. In: Bútora, Martin/ Kollár, Miroslav/ Mesežnikov, Grigorij/Bútorová, Zora: *Kde sme? Mentálne mapy Slovenska*. [Where we are? Mental Maps of Slovakia]. Bratislava : Inštitút pre verejné otázky/ Kalligram, 2010, pp. 72-94.

Hagelund, Anniken (2003): A matter of decency? The Progress Party in Norwegian immigration politics. In: *Journal of Ethnic and Migration Studies 29*, 1, pp. 47-65.

Hagen, Carl I. (2007): *Ærlig talt: memoarer 1944-2007*. Oslo: Cappelen.

Harmel, Robert/ Svåsand, Lars (1993): Party leadership and party institutionalisation: Three phases of development. In: *West European Politics 16*, 2, pp. 67-88.

Holst, Cathrine (2009): Når ombudet ordner opp. In: *Nytt Norsk Tidsskrift 25*, 3-4, pp. 395-407.

Iversen, Jan Martin (1998): *Fra Anders Lange til Carl I. Hagen: 25 år med Fremskrittspartiet*. (Oslo): Millennium.

Johansen, Anders (2001): Enkeltpersoner og kollektivpersoner. In: Eide, Martin (ed.): *Til dagsorden! Journalistikk, makt og demokrati*. Oslo: Gyldendal Akademisk, pp. 167-96.

Jupskås, Anders Ravik. (2008) Populisme på norsk: en typologi med belegg fra partilederdebatter 1973-2005. Institutt for statsvitenskap, p. 135 s. Oslo: Universitetet i Oslo.

Jupskås, Anders Ravik (2009): Høyrepopulisme på norsk. Historien om Anders Langes Parti og Fremskrittspartiet. In: Kjøstvedt, Anders Granås/Simonsen, Tor Espen/ Randin, Katrine (ed.): *Høyrepopulisme i Vest-Europa*. Oslo: Unipub Forlag, pp. 27-79.

Jupskås, Anders Ravik/ Jungar, Ann-Cathrine (2010): En *populistisk partifamilie? En komparativ-historisk analyse av nordiske populistpartier*. Paper presented at Statsvetenskapliga förbundets årsmöte. Göteborg.

Kitschelt, Herbert/ McGann, Anthony J. (1995): *The radical right in Western Europe: a comparative analysis*. Ann Arbor: University of Michigan Press.

Kitschelt, Herbert/ Mansfeldova, Zdenka/ Markowski, Radoslaw/ Tóka, Gábor (1999): *Post-Communist Party Systems – Competition, Representation, and Inter-Party Cooperation*. Cambridge: Cambridge University Press.

Lipset, Seymour Martin/ Rokkan, Stein (1967): Cleavage structures, party systems, and voter alignments: an introduction. In: Lipset, Seymour Martin/ Rokkan, Stein (ed.): *Party Systems and Voter Alignments*. New York: Free Press.

Mattila, Mikko/ Tapio, Raunio (2007): From Consensus to Competition? Ideological Alternatives on the EU Dimension. In Marsh, Michael/Mikhaylov, Slava/Schmitt, Hermann (eds.): *European Elections after Eastern Enlargement. Preliminary Results from the European Election Study 2004*. The CONNEX Report Series No 1, Mannheim, pp. 277-296.

Mesežnikov Grigorij/ Gyárfášová Oľga (2008): *National Populism in Slovakia*. Bratislava: Institute for Public Affairs.

Mesežnikov Grigorij (2009): National Populism in Slovakia – Defining the Character of the State and Interpreting Select Historic Events. in: Petöcz, Kálmán (ed.) *National Populism and Slovak-Hungarian Relations in Slovakia 2006-2009*. Šamorín: Forum Minority Research Institute, pp. 39-66.

Mo, Geir (2011): Interview with general secretary in the Progress Party, Geir Mo. Interview conducted by Anders Ravik Jupskås. Duration 1 hour.

Mudde, Cas (2007): *Populist radical right parties in Europe*. Cambridge: Cambridge University Press.

Narud, Hanne Marthe/ Valen, Henry (2007): *Demokrati og ansvar. Politisk representasjon i et flerpartisystem*. Oslo: NW Damm & Søn.

Norris, Pippa (2005*): Radical right: voters and parties in the electoral market*. Cambridge: Cambridge University Press.

NTB (2010): "Frp-velgere vil ha dødsstraff i Norge" http://www.aftenposten.no/nyheter/iriks/article3881217.ece.(2010-30-10)

Orogváni, Andrej (2006): Strana Smer – pokus o novú definíciu slovenskej ľavice [The Party 'Smer' – An Attempt at a New Definition of Slovakia's Left]. In: Mesežnikov, Grigorij/Gyárfášová, Oľga/Kollár, Miroslav (eds.): *Slovenské voľby '06. Výsledky, príčiny, súvislosti* [Slovak Elections of 2006: Results, Causes, Context]. Bratislava: Inštitút pre verejné otázky, pp. 95 – 109.

Selle, Per/ Østerud, Øyvind (2006): The eroding of representative democracy in Norway. In: *Journal of European Public Policy 13*, 4, pp. 551-68.

Strøm, Kaare (1990): A behavioral theory of competitive political parties. In: *American Journal of Political Science 34*, 2, pp. 565-98.

Svåsand, Lars (1998): Scandinavian right-wing radicalism. In: Betz, Hans-Georg/Immerfall, Stefan (ed.): *The new politics of the right: Neo-populist parties and movements in established democracies*. New York: St. Martin's Press, pp. 77–93.

Svåsand, Lars/ Wörlund, Ingemar (2005): Partifremvekst og partioverlevelse: Fremskrittspartiet og Ny Demokrati. In: Demker, Marie/Svåsand, Lars (eds.): *Partiernas århundrade*. Stockholm: Santérus Förlag, pp. 253-79.

Stanley, Ben (2008): The Thin Ideology of Populism, *Journal of Political Ideologies 13*, 1, pp. 5-110.

Statistisk Sentralbyrå (2010): "Medlemmer i trus- og livssynssamfunn utanfor Den norske kyrkja, etter religion/livssyn. 1. januar. 2005-2010. Absolutte tal og present".
http://www.ssb.no/trosamf/tab-2010-12-13-01.html.(2011-12-06.)
http://www.ssb.no/emner/02/01/10/innvbef/tab-2011-04-28-01.html. (2011-12-6)

Taggart, Paul (2000): *Populism*. Buckingham: Open University Press.

Szomolányi, Soňa (2011): Two Decades of Free Elections in Central Europe: What do they Tell us about the Quality of and Future for Democracy? In: Gyárfášová, Oľga/Mesežnikov, Grigorij (eds.): *Visegrad Elections 2010: Domestic Impact and European Consequences*. Bratislava: Intitute for Public Affairs, pp. 9 – 32.

Učeň, Peter (2004): Centrist Populism as a New Competitive and Mobilization strategy in Slovak Politics, in: Gyárfášová, Oľga/ Grigorij Mesežnikov (eds), *Party Government in Slovakia: Experience and Perspectives*. Bratislava: Institute for Public Affairs, 2004, pp. 45–73.

Učeň, Peter (2007): Populist Appeals in Slovak Politics Before 2006 Elections, in: Bútora, Martin/Gyárfášová, Oľga/Mesežnikov, Grigorij/Skladony, Thomas, W. (eds) *Democracy and Populism in Central Europe: The Visegrad Elections and Their Aftermath*. Bratislava: Institute for Public Affairs 2007, pp. 131-47.

Učeň, Peter (2009): Approaching National Populism, in: Petöcz, Kálmán (ed.) *National Populism and Slovak-Hungarian Relations in Slovakia 2006-2009*. Šamorín: Forum Minority Research Institute, pp. 13-38.

Valen, Henry/ Aardal, Bernt/ Vogt, Gunnar (1990): *Endring og kontinuitet: stortingsvalget 1989*. Sosiale og økonomiske studier. Oslo: Statistisk sentralbyrå.

Weiby, Hans Erik (2010) *Vil straffe de unge strengere*. NRK http://www.nrk.no/nyheter/norge/1.6942338 (2009-24-09)

Chapter 9
Why are there so few female MPs in Slovak parliaments?

Elisabeth Bakke

Introduction

In July 2010, Iveta Radičová became the first female prime minister in Slovak history[79]. Her party, the center-right Slovak Democratic and Christian Union (SDKÚ-DS), had the highest share of female MPs at twenty-one per cent, which is around the European average. However, aggregate female representation in Slovakia is below the European average, and far below average female representation in the Nordic countries (Women in National Parliaments, 2011). It is also lower than during communism, and has not increased substantially since the 1990s.

The social composition of the political elite in a society depends on the pool of candidates (the able and willing), nomination procedures, and electoral behavior. However, the relative importance of these three elements depends on the institutional context. The research questions in the present chapter are first, whether Slovakia's low share of female MPs can be explained by institutional factors such as the electoral or party system, and second, whether variations between parties can be explained by the voting behavior of the electorate, the nomination procedures and the selection criteria of the 'gatekeepers', or the supply of female candidates. The analysis is based on a unique dataset covering all MPs that have served in Slovak parliaments since the end of communism, and on party interviews.[80] Both are a part of a larger elite project covering the four Visegrád countries (in coopera-

---

[79] An earlier draft was presented to the National Political Science Conference in Bergen 7–9 January 2011. I would like to thank especially Hanne Marthe Narud and Anders Todal Jenssen for useful comments.

[80] I wish to thank the Information Service of the Slovak parliament and Slovak party headquarters for generous assistance and provision of information, and Ondrej Gažovič for research assistance. The dataset is based on printed sources (*Slovenská Národná rada 1986, 1990, 1992; Národná rada Slovenskej Republiky* 1996, 1999, 2003; *Federální shromáždění* 1986, 1991, 1992), as well as electronic data and biographical information supplied by the parliament's information service website (www.nrsr.sk). Candidate information is also available at the website of the Slovak statistical office (http://portal.statistics.sk/showdoc.do?docid=3090).

tion with Professor Nick Sitter, BI Norwegian Business School and Central European University).
The chapter is divided into four. First, I briefly present the elite literature, with the main emphasis on parliamentary elite recruitment. Second, I provide a brief introduction to the Slovak party system since 1989, including an overview of the electoral system. In parts three and four, I present and analyze female recruitment patterns in Slovakia. Finally, I present my conclusions.

Elite research

A central point in the elite literature is that societies and organizations are run by elites, and all empirical research shows that these elites are generally not representative of the population as a whole. In Western Europe MPs admittedly lost some of their original 'social elite' character with the extension of suffrage to new social groups, but this 'democratization of the elite' was later reversed as the parliamentary elite became increasingly professionalized (Putnam 1976, Best/Cotta 2000, Norris 1997, Narud/Valen 2007). According to Best & Cotta, the typical (West) European MP is very middle class. A clear majority of the MPs in all countries studied – with the striking exception of Norway – has a university degree. In the 1800s and early 1900s, lawyers comprised on average twenty to twenty-five per cent of MPs, up to nearly fifty per cent (Italy, early 1900s), but since the 1960s teachers and professors have increased their share, and they now comprise fifteen to twenty per cent (Best/Cotta 2000: 497–503).

In Central Europe the social elite character of the MPs increased after the fall of communism and the transition to democracy, as the quota system that had ensured some social representativeness was abolished and the legislatures became real democratic decision-making bodies. During communism, MPs had not been professional politicians – they were given paid leave of absence from their ordinary jobs to meet for a couple of days a few times a year, and only had their expenses covered (Interview, Hoření 2007). After the Velvet Revolution, the educational level of the MPs in Slovakia thus rose abruptly. Over ninety per cent of current MPs have a university degree – which is among the highest in Europe – and more than a third of these again have technical-economic education. The share of teachers and professors is currently around the European average, as is the share of lawyers (Bakke/Sitter dataset). Although Slovak MPs have increased their educational and occupational skills, the social composition of the parliamentary elite in Slovakia does not differ much from the European average.

The part of the elite literature that focuses on the recruitment of parliamentary elites uses aspects of the recruitment process to explain the socially

187

biased composition of the elite, as well as cross-country variations in elite composition and re-election rates. Analyses tend to focus on the institutional aspect of the recruitment process (the political system, electoral laws, other legal regulations, party financing), on the role of parties in this process (how candidate screening and nomination are organized, and what qualifications the 'gatekeepers' emphasize), and, to a lesser extent, on the supply of candidates (Best/Cotta 2000, Fox/ Lawless 2004, Gallagher/Marsh 1988, Narud/Valen 2007, Norris 1997, Ranney 1981). In recent years this research includes a growing body of gender studies (e.g. Lovenduski/ Norris 1993).

The distinction between the supply of candidates, the gatekeepers, and the electorate is a useful analytical point of departure for studying female recruitment to legislatures. The underrepresentation of women can be explained by: a) an insufficient supply of eligible (and willing) female candidates; b) recruitment criteria and nomination procedures that directly or indirectly discriminate against female candidates; and/or, c) voter preferences in favor of male candidates. The relative importance of these sets of factors depends on the institutional context: the party system (number and size), the election system (majority versus PR system, constituency size, open versus closed lists, electoral thresholds), and other laws regulating recruitment to the parliament. Comparative research shows that PR elections in large constituencies tend to further female representation, because this makes list-balancing easier, while the effect of preference voting is less conclusive (Narud/Valen 2007: 71–72).

The supply of female candidates is hard to assess (Fox/Lawless 2004), but in countries where parties control the nomination process and most of the candidates are party members, the share of female party members may serve as a proxy.

Institutions and party system in Slovakia since 1989

Slovakia is a parliamentary democracy with a unicameral legislature, the *National Council of the Slovak Republic*. The 150 MPs are proportionally elected. Slovakia was originally divided into four large constituencies, but since 1998, the whole country has been one constituency. The present electoral threshold is five per cent for parties and seven to ten per cent for electoral alliances, making it impossible for independent candidates (and small parties) to enter parliament on their own. Parties thus control the nomination process, but voters have the right to give preference votes to individual candidates.

Slovakia has a multi-party system, with between five and seven subjects (parties and/or electoral alliances) winning representation in the National Council in every election (table 9.1). A total of seven parties have won representation in three elections or more. A set of five parties dominated Slovak politics in the 1990s, with the Movement for a Democratic Slovakia (HZDS) as the largest. In the 2000s two parties founded around the turn of the millennium came to dominate, the center-right Slovak Democratic and Christian Union (SDKÚ-DS) and Smer Social Democrats (Smer-SD). Smer took over as the biggest party in the 2006 election.

The *Movement for a Democratic Slovakia* split from the opposition movement Public against Violence (VPN) in 1991, and was the kingpin of most governments until 1998. It has remained ideologically diffuse, but has always been left-leaning in economic policy (Hloušek/Kopeček 2004: 157). The party owed much of its success in the 1990s to the charisma of its founder and chairman Vladimír Mečiar, but it is now reduced to a shadow of its former self, and fell below the threshold in 2010.

The *Christian Democratic Movement* (KDH) was founded by leading Catholic dissidents in February 1990 (Kosteleck□2002: 47), and is the only party that has been represented in all parliaments since 1990. It is ideologically right of center in cultural as well as in socioeconomic terms.

The *Slovak National Party* (SNS) is a classical nationalist party founded in March 1990. In the 1992 election, the SNS was the only party to advocate Slovak independence; since independence, its main focus has been on the struggle against (Hungarian) minority rights. It fell below the threshold in 2002 after a split, but the reunited party returned to parliament in 2006.

The *Hungarian Coalition Party* (MKP) is a 1998 merger of three center-right Hungarian parties founded before the first democratic elections. Two of the parties had run together since 1990, the third since 1994. The merger took place in response to the introduction of a new, higher electoral threshold for electoral alliances that would have left the Hungarians without representation[81]. The MKP used to be the electorally most stable party in Slovakia, until it fell below the threshold in 2010, due to a party split in 2009. (The new party, the Most–Híd (bridge), won representation).

The *Democratic Left Party* (SDĽ) was the successor of the former communist regime party. Upon parting with their Czech comrades, the reform-oriented Slovak communist elite adopted a social democratic platform and easily won the bid for the social democratic left. However, after falling below the threshold in 2002, the party merged with *Smer*-SD in 2005.

---

81 The electoral threshold was 5 per cent per party for electoral alliances with up to four participants in the 1998 election only. After the election, it reverted to the original seven to ten per cent.

Table 9.1: Election results, Slovak National Council, 1990-2010 (per cent)

Parties that received mandates	1990	1992	1994	1998	2002	2006	2010
Democratic Left Party (SDĽ) – to Smer	13.4	14.7	10.4	14.7	(1.4)	†	
Movement for a democratic Slovakia (HZDS)		37.3	35.0	27.0	19.5	8.8	(4.3)
Hungarian Coalition Party (MKP)	8.7	7.4	10.2	9.1	11.2	11.7	(4.3)
Slovak National Party (SNS)	13.9	7.9	5.4	9.1	(3.3)	11.7	5.1
Christian Democratic Movement (KDH)	19.2	8.9	10.1	*	8.3	8.3	8.5
Smer – Social Democrats (Smer-SD)					13.5	29.1	34.8
Slovak Democratic and Christian Union (SDKÚ-DS)					15.1	18.4	15.4
Public against Violence (VPN)	29.4	†					
Greens (SZ)	3.5	(2.1)	**	*			
Democratic Party (DS) – to SDKÚ-DS	4.4	(3.3)	(3.4)	*		†	
Labor Union of Slovakia (ZRS)			7.3	(1.3)			
Democratic Union (DÚ) – to SDKÚ-DS			8.6	*	†		
Slovak Democratic Coalition (SDK)				26.3	†		
Party of Civic Understanding (SOP) – to Smer				8.0	†		
Alliance for the New Citizen (ANO)					8.0	(1.4)	†
Communist Party of Slovakia (KSS)					6.3	(3.9)	
Bridge (Most–Híd)							8.1
Freedom and Solidarity (SaS)							12.1

Parties that have crossed the five per cent electoral threshold (three per cent in 1990) in at least one election. MKP is a merger of three Hungarian parties that ran together also in 1994, and two of them even in 1990. Results in grey = the party was not represented in the parliament that period.

† Party had ceased to exist.
* Ran in the Slovak Democratic Coalition (SDK) in 1998.
** Ran in Common Choice (SpV) in 1994, with the SDĽ, the historical social democrats SDSS, and the Agrarian movement.

Smer Social Democrats (Smer-SD), originally a centrist populist party, was founded by former SDĽ MP Robert Fico in 1999. In the run-up to the 2006 election it adopted a social democratic platform, merging with the ex-communist SDĽ, the historical social democrats SDSS, and the Party of Civic Understanding (SOP).

The second largest party in the 2006 and 2010 elections was the *Slovak Democratic and Christian Union* (SDKÚ-DS), which formed the backbone of center-right government coalitions in the 2000s. It originated in the Slovak Democratic Coalition (SDK), a five-party alliance organized as a party, formed before the 1998 election to oust Mečiar. After an unsuccessful attempt to turn the SDK into a normal political party, the circle around Prime Minister Dzurinda founded the SDKÚ in 2000. The SDKÚ elites mainly came from the most liberal part of the KDH and the liberal Democratic Union (DÚ), which merged with the new party. In 2006 the Democratic Party (DS) followed suit, and DS was added to the SDKÚ acronym. The SDKÚ-DS has over time developed in the direction of a liberal conservative party, much like the Czech Civic Democrats.

In addition to these seven parties, a number of parties have been represented in the parliament once. I will here focus mainly on the seven parties that dominated Slovak politics in the 1990s and/or 2000s, both because these are the parties for which we have interview data,[82] and because these parties together account for a majority of the MPs that have been elected since the transition to democracy.

Female representation in Slovakia – an overview

Let us now have a brief look at the main trends. First, female representation in the Slovak parliament is consistently lower than before the transition to democracy, and among the lowest in Europe. In the 2010 election, fifteen per cent of the MPs in Slovakia were women, while the Nordic average is forty-two per cent, and the European average without the Nordic countries is twenty per cent (*Women in National Parliaments* 2011).[83] Of the four Visegrád countries only Hungary scores lower (figure 9.1). Second, although the average is slightly higher in the 2000s than in the 1990s, the increase in female representation since 1990 has been modest. In contrast, the share of female MPs has increased substantially in the Czech Republic and Poland since 2000. Third, there are still substantial differences between parties

---

82 We started to collect party data for our elite project only in 2007, and historical data are hard to come by, especially for parties that no longer exist. Fortunately, Richter (Smer-SD) also used to be the general secretary of the SDĽ and was able to provide me with some information about that extinct party.

83 As per March 2011, only seven European countries had a lower share of female MPs than Slovakia: Ireland, Slovenia, Russia, Romania, Montenegro, Hungary, and Ukraine. In comparison, Norway's share of female MPs is forty per cent as per 2011.

Table 9.2: Female MPs in the National Council, 1990–2010 (per cent)

Parties that received mandates	1990	1992	1994	1998	2002	2006	2010	Average
Total for all parties	13.3	15.3	14.7	11.3	14.7	16.0	15.3	14.4
Democratic Left Party (SDĽ)(SpV in '94)	13.6	17.2	16.7	8.7				14.1
Movement for a Dem. Slovakia (HZDS)		21.6	21.3	14.0	13.9	26.7		19.5
Hungarian Coalition Party (MKP)	7.1	7.1	5.9	6.7	5.0	15.0		7.8
Slovak National Party (SNS)	18.2	6.7	22.2	21.4		15.0	11.1	15.8
Christian Democratic Movement (KDH)	9.7	0.0	5.9	(7.7)	13.3	14.3	13.3	9.4
Smer – Social Democrats (Smer-SD)					20.0	12.0	16.1	16.0
Slovak Dem. & Chr. Union (SDKÚ-DS)					21.4	19.4	21.4	20.7
Public against Violence (VPN)	8.3							
Greens (SZ)	33.3		(0.0)					
Democratic Party (DS)	42.9							
Labor Union of Slovakia (ZRS)			7.7					
Democratic Union (DÚ)			6.7	(0.0)				
Slovak Democratic Coalition (SDK)				4.8				
Party of Civic Understanding (SOP)				23.1				
Alliance for the New Citizen (ANO)					13.3			
Communist Party of Slovakia (KSS)					9.1			
Bridge (Most–Híd)							0.0	
Freedom and Solidarity (SaS)							18.2	
Difference between highest and lowest %	35.8	21.6	16.3	16.4	16.4	14.7	21.4	20.4

1994: The SpV had three female MPs, of these two belonged to the SDĽ (15.4%).
1998: SDK as a whole had two female MPs. Of these, one belonged to the KDH. The DÚ got ten MPs elected, none female.

across elections (table 9.2), although there seems to be a certain convergence, at least between the *Slovak* parties. Finally, a high share of female MPs does not seem to be related to a leftist position, as it is in the Nordic countries. On the contrary, the center-right SDKÚ-DS has the highest average share of female MPs, followed by the ideologically diffuse HZDS, while the track record of the SNS varies the most. The Christian Democrats and the Hungarian parties score lowest, with the social democrats in the middle.

Why are there so few women in Slovak parliaments?

In the first subsection below I will address whether Slovakia's low share of female MPs can be explained by institutional factors such as the electoral or party system. In order to do so, I will compare Slovakia to the three other Visegrád countries. In the next three subsections I turn to the voting behavior of the electorate, the selection criteria of the gatekeepers, and the supply of female candidates, to see whether one of these factors alone or these factors in combination can explain the variations between parties across elections set out in table 9.2.

Institutional factors

To what extent can differences in *electoral systems* explain that Slovakia has higher female representation than Hungary, but lower than the Czech Republic and Poland? Based on earlier research, I would expect the country with the most benevolent electoral system (PR elections in large constituencies) to score highest. However, while Hungary's mixed electoral system may in part explain why Hungary has the lowest share of female MPs, the electoral system cannot explain why Slovakia has lower female representation than Poland and the Czech Republic. All three countries have PR systems, and Slovakia has larger constituencies than the other two: originally four (on average thirty-seven mandates per constituency) – and from 1998, one constituency. Poland has forty-one constituencies (on average eleven mandates per constituency), and the Czech Republic fourteen (on average fourteen mandates per constituency).

In fact, the overall share of female MPs in Slovakia seems to be quite unrelated to the change in constituency size: female representation has increased by a meager 0.5 per cent since the whole country became one constituency, and more importantly, Slovakia reached its all-time low in terms of female MPS in 1998, the first election after one constituency had been introduced (figure 9.1).

Figure 9.1: Share of female MPs in Visegrád countries, 1990-2010 (%)

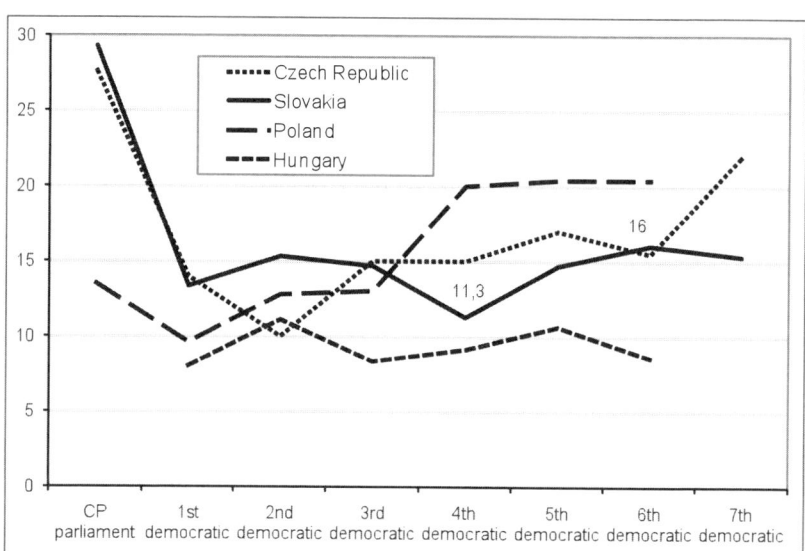

The next question is whether differences in *party systems* can explain the patterns of female representation in the Visegrád countries. According to Narud and Valen (2007: 72), it is more difficult for a party to balance the list if it has few 'secure' mandates. We would therefore expect countries with many (small) parties in the parliament to have a lower share of female MPs than countries with fewer and bigger parties. However, of the Visegrád four, Poland has the highest average number of parliamentary parties as well as the highest share of female MPs, while Hungary scores lowest on both. Slovakia does have a higher average number of parties than the Czech Republic, but because Slovakia is one constituency, even the smallest party in Slovakia wins more seats in that one constituency than the biggest parties do in the average Czech constituency. The difference in female representation cannot thus be convincingly explained by the logic of small parties.

Moreover, even within each country the number of parties explains next to nothing: omitting the (rather exceptional) first democratic elections in all four countries, I calculated Pearson's R using the number of effective parties and the share of female MPs in each election from 1992. I found a weak correlation in the expected direction for the Czech Republic (-0.13) and Hungary (-0.02), and a weak correlation in the opposite direction for Poland (0.06). The strongest correlation was found for Slovakia (-0.22) where fewer effective parties were correlated with higher female representation. However, when I recalculated Pearson's R using the actual number of subjects in the Slovak parliament in each election, the correlation decreased to -0.09.

Finally, there is no obvious connection between party size and female representation in Slovakia. Figure 9.2 shows the average share of female MPs for the two biggest and the two smallest parties: in three of seven elections, the two smallest parties had higher average female representation than the two biggest. The Slovak record is held by the Democratic Party, the second smallest party in 1990. Two parties have had all male parliamentary groups: the Christian Democrats in 1992, and Most–Híd in 2010. Neither party was the smallest in that election.

Figure 9.2: Female MPs by party size (per cent)

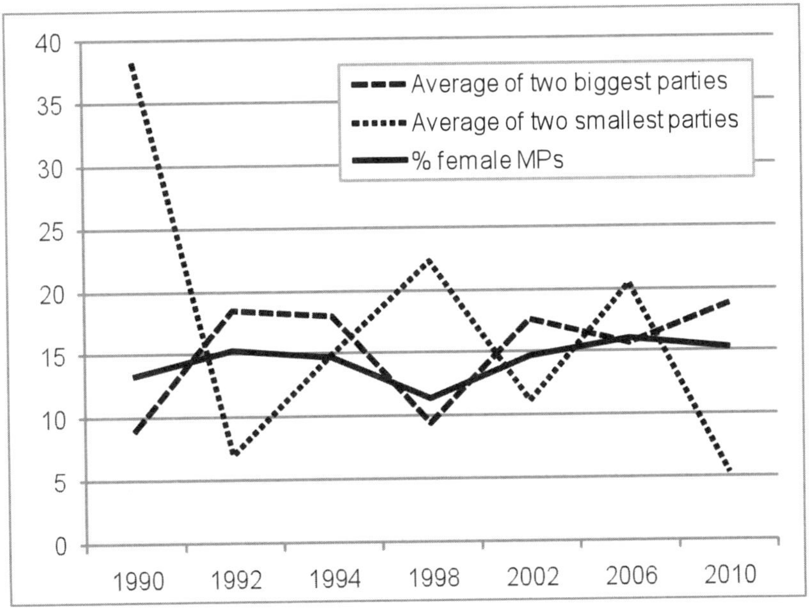

Voting behavior

The analysis so far has shown that institutional factors explain little. The same can be said of voting behavior, to the extent that preference voting is an indication of whether voters prefer men to women. First, a very limited number of MPs have been elected because of preference votes in *any* election in Slovakia (table 9.3), and second, the net effect of preference voting on female representation is neutral or slightly positive.

195

Table 9.3: The effect of preference voting on female representation (in MPs)

Number of MPs (total=150)	1990	1992	1994	1998	2002	2006	2010
MPs with sufficient percentage of preference votes*	14	82	98	29	31	63	63
MPs elected due to preference votes	4	9	11	0	1	7	11
Net effect on female representation	0	0	+1	0	-1	+2	-1
– of these: female candidates for Hungarian parties				0	-1	-1	-1

* Percentage needed to advance on the party list: over fifty per cent in 1990; ten per cent in 1992, 1994, 1998, and 2002; and three per cent in 2006 and 2010.

In 1990 one female candidate was elected and one deselected because of preference votes, in 1994 one female was elected, in 2002 one was deselected, in 2006 three were elected and one deselected, and in 2010 one was elected and two deselected. In short, the voters elected the MPs the parties wanted them to; they neither favored nor disfavored women. However, three of the four deselected women in the 2000s represented Hungarian parties; the Hungarian voters can therefore be blamed for the low percentage of female MPs in the MKP and Most–Híd, and hence for their lagging behind the Slovak parties. On the other hand, without preference votes, the KDH would have been left without any female MPs in 2006.

Gatekeepers and selection criteria

Because the electoral threshold rules out individual candidates, the parties (and in some instances, alliances of parties) control the nomination process in Slovakia. Who the actual 'gatekeepers' are depends on how centralized and inclusive the nomination process is. Centralized processes make list-balancing easier, and should therefore promote female representation. On the other hand, open processes with many participants (members and/or voters) may disadvantage women. However, the findings of the research literature are inconclusive (Narud/Valen 2007: 72–74). I will return to this shortly.

A second important aspect of the nomination process that potentially affects female representation is which criteria the gatekeepers employ, and gender quotas are especially important. According to Narud and Valen (2007: 89), the strong increase in the share of female MPs in Norway from the 1970s onwards can be attributed to gender quotas in leftist parties, while the share of female MPs is consistently lower in rightist parties. In fact, this is the key to understanding the abrupt fall in female representation since the last Communist parliament elected in 1986 to the first democratically elected parliament in 1990, as well as the difference in female representation between the Czech Republic and Slovakia in the 2000s (figure 9.1).

During communism, groups such as women, national minorities, and of course workers, had fixed quotas (Interview, Hoření 2007). After the transition to democracy, this quota system was abolished, and gender quotas are today totally absent on both sides of the left–right divide in Slovakia. In contrast, the orthodox Communist Party (KSČM) in the Czech Republic reintroduced gender quotas in the mid-1990s. The party recommends that thirty-three per cent of the candidates be women (every third place on the list, and one female among the top three candidates). And this works: in the period 1998–2010 the average share of female MPs was 32.4 per cent for the KSČM, compared to 14.8 per cent for the rest of the Czech parties. Excluding the former communist regime parties (figure 9.3), we find that the average Slovak female representation for the entire 1990–2010 period is slightly higher than the Czech one (and on a par with the Polish one, but Poland had a higher average in the 2000s).

Figure 9.3: Female MPs excluding ex-communist parties, 1990-2010 (per cent)

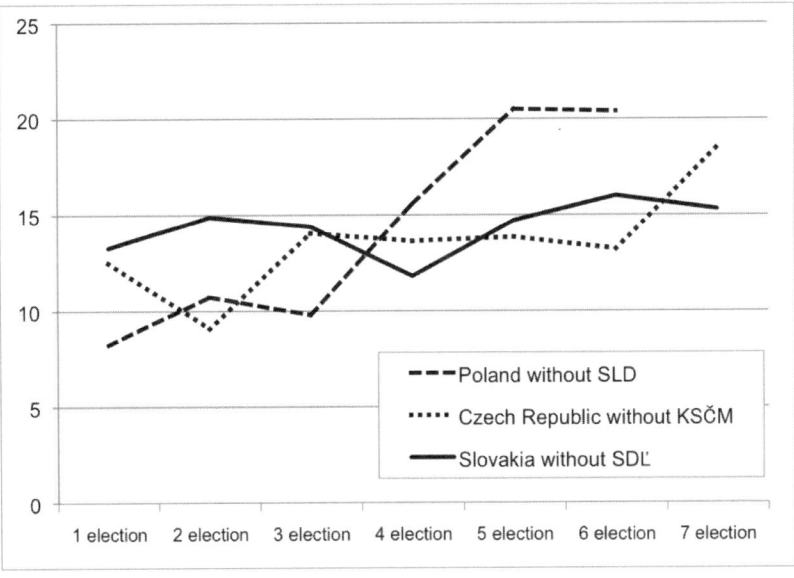

Next, can different selection criteria explain the variation in female representation between parties across elections *within* Slovakia? In the party with the highest average, the SDKÚ-DS, the women 'do not want quotas' (Interview, Homoľa 2008). In the party with the second highest average, the HZDS, 'clever women and youth have priority' (Interview, Mečiar 2008). The Smer-SD is the only party with an explicit target (thirty per cent) but this has so far not been within reach (Interview, Richter 2008). Several of my informants stated that they personally would like to see more women in politics, but argued that 'competence is more important than gender' (the SNS), or that recruiting women is difficult (the KDH and MKP) (Interviews, Benková, Abrhan, and Bárdos, 2008).

The parties' attitudes to female representation do not seem to differ much. My general impression is that gender equality is secondary to other, more important criteria – in particular professional competence and region. With one list for the whole country, the parties need mechanisms to ensure that all regions are represented, while doing justice to party strongholds. Most of the parties give priority to candidates from regions where the party performed particularly well in the last election, and some even have formal rules about this. This is clearly more important than gender. Since women on average have a slightly higher level of education than men in Slovakia, emphasis on professional competence should not in itself disadvantage women, (Gyárfášová et al 2008: 257–58). Figure 9.4 supports this.

As for the parties' nomination procedures, all candidate lists for parliamentary elections are adopted by *central* party organs, and this was the case even when the country was divided into four constituencies, but the *inclusiveness* of the nomination process varies between parties (see also Appendix 1). Most of the parties have some sort of convention system. Of these, the HZDS involves the largest number of people. A personnel committee (the party chairman, the chairman of the parliamentary group, and the chairmen of the regional branches) proposes the ranking, and a nomination congress decides (the congress has 5–600 delegates, including local representatives, incumbent MPs, and candidates proposed for the new list). In practice, however, Mečiar has much influence over the outcome (Interview, Mečiar 2008). The SNS has the most centralized and least inclusive process, as the narrow party leadership (seven people) decide the composition as well as the ranking of the list, after regional screening (Interview, Benková 2008). The rest of the parties fall somewhere in-between: in Smer-SD, the chairman (Fico) proposes the ranking of the candidates, and the wider party leadership (thirty-five people, including the chairmen of the regional branches) approves the list (Interview, Richter 2008). In the case of the KDH and the MKP, the party leadership proposes the ranking of candidates only at the beginning of the list, and the Council (eighty and ninety-four people respectively, in both cases dominated by the regional level) approves the list by secret ballot (Interviews, Abrhan and Bárdos, 2008).

Figure 9.4: Slovak MPs with high education by gender (per cent)

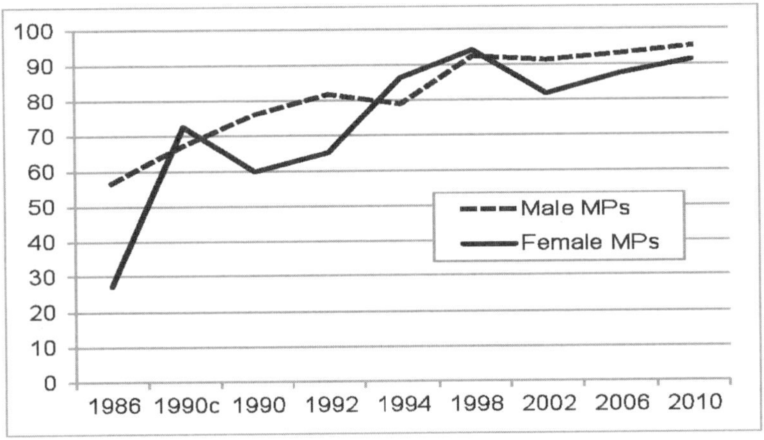

[Line chart showing percentages from 0 to 100 on the y-axis and years 1986, 1990c, 1990, 1992, 1994, 1998, 2002, 2006, 2010 on the x-axis, with dashed line for Male MPs and solid line for Female MPs]

1990c: coopted MPs in the spring of 1990.

The odd party out is the SDKÚ-DS, where the list leader is elected first by secret ballot by all party members. In the next step the rest of the candidates are elected through a complicated system, where the eight regions, the party presidium, the youth and women's organizations propose one list each (eleven lists put together), and the party members are allocated fifteen votes each, but must vote for at least one candidate per list. The ranking on the final list depends on how many votes each candidate wins, and what list he or she is on (places 2–6 for instance are given to the most popular candidates on the presidium list) (Interview, Homoľa 2008). In practice, this is preference voting with a twist that ensures representation for the regions as well as for women and youth.

Based on this, it is difficult to judge the effect on female representation. If anything, the correlation between inclusiveness and *average* female representation is curvilinear: the parties with the most inclusive process (the SDKÚ-DS and the HZDS) score highest, followed by the two parties with the most centralized and exclusive process (the SNS and the Smer-SD). The KDH's and the MKP's intermediate sized nomination bodies (with stronger regional involvement) resulted in the lowest average female representation. In both cases, the regions usually negotiate deals between themselves. A possible explanation could be that when regions have a strong say, regional concerns trump other concerns, including gender. However, for the parties that have been represented since the early 1990s the average masks variation in the ten to fifteen per cent range, suggesting that female representation is not particularly strongly connected to the inclusiveness of the nomination process.

One final aspect of the nomination process that deserves to be mentioned is list-balancing in electoral alliances and other cases where more parties or factions are involved. The most obvious example is the Slovak Democratic Coalition (SDK), but also Public against Violence (VPN), Common Choice (SpV), the Hungarian Coalition, and Smer-SD (in 2006) involved several political currents. In all the cases for which I have interview data, efforts were made to ensure that all parties/currents would have their candidates elected. In the case of newly merged parties (the MKP in 1998 and Smer-SD in 2006), efforts were made to ensure that all the original parties had candidates high enough on the list to be elected. In the case of the electoral alliances (the SDK, and the Hungarian Coalition before the merger), the participating parties first put together separate lists, and then the distribution of the various parties' candidates on the final list was decided through negotiations, while respecting the original ranking within each party (Interviews, Bárdos, Homoľa, and Richter 2008).

Multiple political factions in one party or electoral alliance seem to have had a negative effect on female representation in all but one case. The mechanism is probably that when an extra list-balancing concern is added, gender becomes even less of a priority. Of the cases mentioned above, the Slovak Democratic Coalition had the largest (negative) effect on female representation in Slovakia as a whole. When excluding the SDK, female representation in Slovakia is on a par with the Czech Republic in 1998, and the dip in figure 9.1 more or less disappears. The single exception is Common Choice, an alliance comprising social democrats, Greens and Agrarians (all three female MPs were social democrats).

Supply of female candidates

Finally, can low female representation and variations between parties be explained by an insufficient supply of eligible and willing female candidates? It is tricky to assess how large the pool of eligible women really is, but as a minimum we can assume that female list candidates are qualified *and* willing to run for office. Party lists are easily accessible at the Statistical Bureau of the Slovak Republic. Furthermore, since most of the MPs in Slovakia are party members, the discrepancy between the percentage of female party members and female MPs may be an indication of the parties' 'unused potential'. Unfortunately, only four of the seven parties under investigation were able to provide such data, and only for 2010: HZDS, Smer-SD, SDKÚ-DS, and KDH.

If we combine these data, we find that all four parties have an unused potential in terms of female party members, while there is a better match between the parties' average share of female list candidates and their average share of female MPs (this masks variation across elections). The HZDS and the KDH had the largest unused potential, in terms of list candidates as well as party members, while the SDKÚ-DS actually had a slightly higher average share of female MPs than candidates. Only the KDH has a female majority among its members: in all other cases, the predominance of males on the party lists and among the MPs corresponds to male dominance in party members. This is probably also the case for the SNS, which is known to attract more male than female voters (Gyárfášová et al 2008: 246).

Figure 9.5: Average share of female MPs, list candidates and party members, 2000s (per cent)

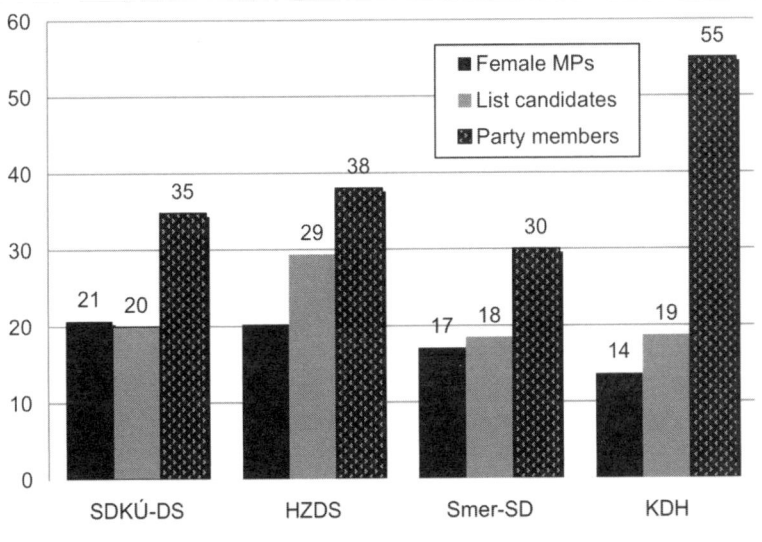

Of the three parties for which I have only candidate data, the variations across elections are largest for the SNS: in 1992, its share of female MPs was almost nine per cent lower than the share of female candidates; in 1994, it was almost nine per cent *higher*. Also the ex-communist SDĽ had a higher share of female MPs than candidates in two elections (1992 and 1994). On average, however, there was not a great discrepancy between the share of female list candidates and female MPs for either party. In contrast, the MKP had an unused potential, with a higher share of female candidates than MPs in all but the 2006 election.

Concluding discussion

On average, female representation in Slovak parliaments since 1989 is less than half of the female representation in the last communist National Council elected in 1986, and it has not increased much since the turn of the millennium. The parties of the Hungarian minority have consistently had the lowest average share of female MPs and the lowest share of female list candidates. Of the Slovak parties, the Christian Democrats have had the lowest average female representation, and the largest main-stream center-right party, the SDKÚ-DS, the highest. Slovakia's two social democratic parties have been slightly above (Smer-SD) or slightly below average (the SDĽ), while the HZDS and the SNS have had the most uneven female representation, albeit above average.

My first research question was whether Slovakia's low share of female MPs can be explained by institutional factors such as electoral systems or party systems, and the answer to this is no. First, Slovakia has the most proportional electoral system of all the four Visegrád countries: if PR elections in large constituencies favor female representation, Slovakia should have had a *higher* share of female MPs than the Czech Republic and Poland in the 2000s. Second, the size and number of parties explain very little. The share of female MPs is only weakly correlated with the number of parliamentary parties, and there is no obvious connection between party size and female representation in Slovakia (cf. figure 9.2). Finally, Slovakia's low average share of female MPs cannot be blamed on the voters. Few MPs are elected because of preference voting, and the net effect on female representation is actually slightly positive (one extra female MP across elections).

However, two factors associated with the nomination process seem to explain much of the difference in average female representation between communist and democratic parliaments in Slovakia, as well as between Slovakia and the Czech Republic (and to a lesser extent Poland) in the 2000s. First, and most importantly, the Communist Party of Czechoslovakia – and from the mid-1990s its successor, the Communist Party of Bohemia and Moravia – employed gender quotas. In contrast, such quotas have been totally absent across the left–right divide in Slovakia since the transition to democracy. When controlling for the ex-communist parties on both sides, the difference between Slovakia and the Czech Republic in the 2000s disappears. Second, electoral alliances and newly merged parties have lower average female representation when they attempt to represent multiple political currents simultaneously. When controlling for the SDK and the ex-communists in 1998, the difference between Slovakia and the Czech Republic disappears altogether.

My second research question was whether variations between parties across elections can be explained by the supply of female candidates, the voting behavior of the electorate, or the nomination procedures and selection criteria of the gatekeepers. First, an insufficient supply of eligible and willing female candidates is not a credible explanation for the low share of female MPs in Slovakia, and certainly not for the variation between parties. In fact, the Slovak party with the lowest share of female MPs, the KDH, has a female majority among its party members, and also the other three parties I have membership data for have a female share of thirty per cent or more. All the parties thus had an unused potential in terms of female party members, female list candidates, or both.

Second, different nomination procedures seem to have mattered more for the female representation of the individual parties than the gatekeepers' selection criteria. Perhaps a little surprisingly, the correlation between the inclusiveness of the nomination process and average female representation was found to be curvilinear: the parties with the most inclusive process had the highest average, followed by the parties with the most centralized and exclusive process, while intermediate sized nomination bodies (where the regions have a strong say) go together with the lowest average female representation. My general impression, based on party interviews, is that gender equality is secondary to other, more important criteria – in particular professional competence and region – in *all* the parties.

Third, although voting behavior cannot explain the low overall female representation in Slovakia, it did matter in two cases: the Hungarian parties (MKP and Most-Híd) have a lower average share of female MPs because of preference voting than they would have had otherwise, and the Christian Democrats a slightly higher share.

Finally, it is an open question what role ideology played. The low female representation of the Christian Democrats fits well with the argument that the hierarchical political culture of Catholic countries affects the willingness of women to run for office (Narud/Valen 2007:88). The center-left parties' female representation which is near or above average is also largely as expected. From a Norwegian point of view, the most surprising is perhaps that the center-right SDKÚ-DS has the highest average share of female MPs, while it is less surprising that its close ideological allies, the MKP and, from 2010, the Most-Híd, have the lowest. Part of the explanation for this may be that gender concerns are institutionalized in the SDKÚ-DS through a women's organization with the right to propose one of eleven lists. Yet, I suspect that region also played a role here: the SDKÚ-DS has its major strongholds in urban areas (especially the two largest cities), and attracts (younger) voters with university education, while the MKP has its major strongholds in the Hungarian-speaking rural border areas and attracts (older) voters with lower education (Gyarfášová et al 2008: 246). Gender equality tends to find more support among the urban, young, and educated all over the Western world. In the case of the MKP (and Most-Híd), their predominantly rural voters contributed to the low female representation by giving preference to male candidates.

Interviews

Abrhan, Pavol (2008): Interview with Pavol Abrhan, General secretary and MP for KDH, Bratislava, 21 May, 2008.
Benková, Jana (2008): Interview with Jana Benková, spokesperson for SNS, Bratislava, 26 May, 2008.
Bárdos, Gyula (2008): Interview with Gyula Bárdos, chairman of the MKP parliamentary Club, Bratislava, 23 May, 2008.
Homoľa, Kamil (2008): Interview with Kamil Homoľa, General secretary of the SDKÚ-DS, 28 May, 2008.
Hoření, Monika (2007): Interview with Monika Hoření, PR manager of the Communist Party in Bohemia and Moravia (KSČM), 2 May, 2007.
Mečiar, Vladimír (2008): Interview with Vladimír Mečiar, chairman of the HZDS, 28 May, 2008.
Richter, Ján (2008): Interview with Ján Richter, General secretary and MP for Smer-SD, Bratislava, 26 May, 2008.

References

Best, Heinrich/Cotta, Maurizio (eds 2000): *Parliamentary Representatives in Europe, 1848-2000: Legislative Recruitment and Careers in Eleven European Countries*. Oxford: Oxford University Press.
Federální shromáždění ČSSR, (1986): V. volební období. Praha.
Federální shromáždění České a slovenské federativní republiky (1991): VI. volební období, Praha.
Federální shromáždění ČSFR (1992), VII. volební období (Praha).
Fox, Richard L./Lawless, Jennifer L. (2004): Entering the Arena? Gender and the Decision to Run for Office. In *American Journal of Political Science 48*, 2 2004: 264–280.

Gallagher, Michael/Marsh, Michael (1988): *Candidate Selection in Comparative Perspective*. London: Sage.

Gyarfášová, Oľga/ Bútorová, Zora /Filadelfiová, Jarmila (2008): Women and Men in Public Life and Politics. In: Zora Bútorová (ed.): *She and He in Slovakia. Gender and Age in the Period of Transition*. Bratislava: Institute for Public Affairs.

Hloušek, Vít/Kopeček, Lubomír (2004): *Konfliktní demokracie. Moderní masová politika ve střední Evropě*. Brno: IIPS.

Kosteleck☐ Tomáš (2002): *Political Parties after Communism. Developments in East-Central Europe*. Washington D.C.: Woodrow Wilson Center Press.

Lovenduski, Joni/Norris, Pippa (1993): *Gender and Party Politics*. London: Sage.

Národná rada Slovenskej Republiky. I., II., III. volebné obdobie (1996, 1999, 2003). Bratislava: Kancelária Národnej rady Slovenskej Republiky.

Narud, Hanne Marthe/Valen, Henry (2007): *Demokrati og ansvar. Politisk representasjon i et flerpartisystem*. Oslo: Damm.

Norris, Pippa (ed. 1997): *Passages to Power: Legislative Recruitment in Advanced Democracies*. Cambridge: Cambridge University Press.

Putnam, Robert (1976): *The Comparative Study of Political Elites*. Englewood Cliffs, NJ: Prentice-Hall.

Ranney, Austin (1981): Candidate Selection. In David Butler; Howard R. Penniman/Austin Ranney (eds.): *Democracy at the Polls. A Comparative Study of Competitive National Elections*. Washington: American Enterprise Institute for Public Policy Research.

Slovenská Národná rada. VIII., IX., X. volebné obdobie (1986, 1990, 1992). Bratislava: Kancelária Slovenskej národnej rady.

Women in National Parliaments (2011). the Inter-Parliamentary Union (data as per 31 March, 2011) at http://www.ipu.org/wmn-e/world.htm [4 May, 2011].

Appendix 1: The parties' nomination process in parliamentary elections

Party	Right to propose candidates	Final rank order proposed by	Decision making body	Criteria
Smer-SD	District branches. Regional branches screen and put together ranked list	Party chairman (Fico)	Presidium. Any member can demand a secret ballot if multiple candidates – did not happen in 2006	no gender quotas, but 30% target
KDH	District branches, members of the Council, presidium, expert groups	Presidium, but only for the candidates the party can hope to get in.	The Council decides the ranking by secret ballot. Candidates need > 50% of the votes to win.	no gender quotas
MKP	All party members, local branches, district branches (hierarchical)	Presidium proposes 15 and the regions 15 of the first 30 on the list.	The Council decides the ranking by secret ballot. Candidates need > 50% of the votes to win.	no gender quotas
SDKÚ-DS	Presidium, regional branches, 300 members can propose candidates for list leader	8 regions, the presidium, the women's org. and the youth org. set up ranked lists = 11 lists	First candidate: secret ballot among all members. The rest: The same. Each party member has 15 votes and must vote for at least 1 candidate per list	no gender quotas, but women's org. set up one list
SNS	Local, district, and regional branches; regional branches screen candidates	Not formalized	Presidium members decide by raising their hands.	no gender quotas
HZDS	Members, district branches, regions, parliamentary club, expert groups	Personnel committee (party chairman, leader of parliamentary club, region leaders)	Nomination congress (5-600) = delegates from local branches + 150 incumbent MPs + 150 proposed candidates. Can replace candidates or change ranking, by secret ballot or raising hands	no gender quotas, but 'clever women and youth get priority'

Appendix 2: Party organizations of main parties as per 2010

	Smer-SD	SNS	HZDS	KDH	MKP	SDKÚ-DS
Membership	16869	1839	28873	15360	10349	7318
– in per cent of 2010 votes	1.9	1.4	26.4	7.1	9.4	1.9
Local organizations	955	107	1427	1010	493	529
District organizations	79	79	79	38	18	0
Regional organizations	8	8	8	8	5	8

Source: Information provided by party headquarters. SNS data are from 2008 (membership data 2010)

Chapter 10
Regionalization of governance: testing the capacity for reform

Harald Baldersheim and Ľudmila Malíková

Introduction

Reforming territorial governance may amount to tinkering with the very identity of a state; little wonder, therefore, that such attempts are usually steeped in controversy, and often founder due to resistance. However, reforming territorial governance – although risky – may appear unavoidable for reasons of administrative efficiency and high politics. Over the last decade, territorial governance has been a source of continuous debate, political conflict, and reform initiatives in both Norway and Slovakia. Why should small countries such as these pursue decentralization policies in the first place? Why was reform in this field of governance so difficult to achieve?

The classical distinction between federal and unitary states no longer suffices to exhaustively classify European states. A category of *regionalized* states has emerged in recent decades. Regionalized states are halfway houses between federal states and unitary, decentralized states. Territorial units in federal states play a constitutionally stipulated role in national decision-making and legislation, while in decentralized, unitary states they are local governments. The territorial units of regionalized states often enjoy *secondary* or *devolved legislative powers*, entailing less autonomy than the territorial units of a federal state, but more autonomy than those of unitary states. The latter may have competencies and functions of their own, but no legislative powers. Regionalization usually also implies the introduction of fairly large-scale units of territorial governance, either through the amalgamation of existing units or the establishment of a new tier of governance in-between the central state and local government. Spain and Italy are among the better-known examples of regionalized states. The United Kingdom may now be added to this category since directly elected parliaments or assemblies were introduced for Scotland, Wales and Northern Ireland in 1998. France has also taken steps in this direction. For some years a *Conference of Regions with*

Legislative Power (REGLEG) has existed. It has seventy-three member regions drawn from eight European countries, all of which are members of the European Union.[84]

However, 'regions' may mean different things in different countries. REGLEG may represent the vanguard of regionalization. Marks et al. (2008a) suggest that regionalization should be treated as a variable that may characterize a polity to a larger or lesser extent. They distinguish first of all between *self-rule* and *shared rule*. The former denotes units with powers that may be exercised only in geographically limited jurisdictions, whereas shared rule means that regions partake in government in the nation at large, i. e. there are legal channels through which regions can influence national decision-making. The more regions are involved in shared rule, the more the country has the features of a federation. Neither Norway nor Slovakia has elements of shared rule and scores nil on this part of the assessment. However, they do both have many features of regional self-rule, which is measured by the number of functions performed by regions and their political, administrative, and fiscal independence. Political independence means the direct election of regional assemblies, administrative independence means regions have their own executive bodies directly accountable to the elected assemblies, while fiscal independence denotes the right to levy regional taxes. With regard to self-rule today Norway scores somewhat higher than Slovakia. This is mainly due to the greater fiscal autonomy enjoyed by Norwegian regions. However, even the extent of Norwegian regionalization is modest in comparison to the vanguard regions of REGLEG (Marks et al. 2008b).

Both countries sought to reform their overall structures of territorial governance in the 2000s. After an intricate and arduous process of reform, Slovakia established its regions in 2001-2002 as a part of its pre-accession adjustment to EU requirements. In Norway, directly elected county councils have a long history, and an initiative to transform them into larger, more powerful regions was launched in 2005 but resulted only in modest change. In both cases controversy and resistance surrounded the initiatives. Why was Slovakia able to overcome or accommodate resistance and establish regions, while Norway's regional initiative came to (almost) nothing? Could the outcomes of the regional reform initiatives in the two countries be accounted for by *forces of region-building* or by features of the *reform processes*?

Students of regionalization have invoked a variety of forces of region-building to account for the recent surge of regionalization in Europe. These include:

---

84   Available at
    http://www.regleg.eu/index.php?option=com_content&view=article&id=96&Itemid=9.
    (2011-03-28).

- 'The Return of History' thesis, or the revival of regional identities (Harvie 1994, Keating 1996). Many European countries have areas characterized by specific cultural traditions and regional identities that may differ from the rest of the country. Such regional specificities may become the basis for regional political mobilization and movements that claim wider regional autonomy (Rokkan/ Urwin 1983). Such movements have grown in force in many countries since the 1970s, and especially since the end of the Cold War, and have driven institutional regionalization. The UK, Belgium or Italy may exemplify this trend. Such forces could also, conceivably, drive regionalization in Norway and Slovakia. Slovakia has a sizeable Hungarian minority located along its border with Hungary. Norway has regions in its West and North which have specific cultural and political traditions, and it also has a Sami minority which has pressed for extended rights in territorial governance in recent years.
- 'The Rise of Competitive Regions' thesis: in response to economic globalization and the new information economy, regions are increasingly pursuing endogenous development strategies. Under labels such as learning regions, Triple Helix partnerships, and so forth (Annoni/ Kozovska 2010, Boekema et al, 2000) regions are chasing foreign investments in the hope of creating jobs for their population in times when capital and industries can easily move from country to country. These development strategies may require more agile regional bodies which again may mean more autonomous regions.
- European integration, which has provided incentives to develop or establish regions to act as conduits for development funds set up by the EU (Cohesion fund, Interreg, etc); new member countries have either overhauled their regional structures or established them from scratch in order to comply with accession requirements (Scherpereel 2010, Scully/Jones 2010). This is a likely source of Slovak regionalization, but EU regional policy modalities have also had repercussions beyond EU member states. Norway is in fact economically integrated with the inner market through the EEA[85] mechanism, which gives Norwegian companies access to the markets of the EU member countries; in return, Norway has to implement all EU directives; through the EEA mechanism, Norwegian public administration is also exposed to the European alignment which takes place in member countries, and also with regard to regional institutions.
- Democratic revival, i.e. an increasing insistence on democratic procedures and transparency in public affairs as part of "the good governance" movement. In many countries this has been taken to mean a need to debureaucratize public administration and transfer functions and powers to levels of government closer to the people, including regions. The democ-

---

85 European Economic Area, the members of which are Norway, Iceland and Lichtenstein.

ratic impetus could be expected to work with special force in Slovakia given its experiences of a communist regime in its recent past.

Reform processes necessary for establishing or enhancing the status of regions may be handled in a variety of ways. There is no one best way to implement regional reforms (Baldersheim/Rose 2010b). However, reforms requiring the consent of several levels of government are vulnerable to the *"joint-decision trap problem"* (Scharpf 1988), i. e. the mutual blockage of reform proposals resulting in stalemate or an outcome that regresses to the lowest common denominator. Given its already existing regions with their own pressure groups and decades of fragmented parliamentary politics, joint-decision traps could be expected to be a more likely feature in Norway than in Slovakia. However, Slovakia has also had pressure groups in the field of territorial governance (e. g. the Association of Towns and Villages of the Slovak Republic), and a politically fragmented polity; accordingly, in Slovakia decision-making on regions could also be expected to be difficult.

Processes of regionalization in Norway and Slovakia

SLOVAKIA

Understandably, considerable attention is paid to the meso-level of government in Slovakia since it was part of the post-socialist transformation process. It included decentralization and deconcentration, as well as institution building at the regional level (see Surazska et al 1997, Wollman 1997). The meso-level of Slovak government – eight regions – was established in 2001. The first regional elections were held in December 2001, and regional self-government began functioning in January 2002.

1990-1998
In the first period of post-communist democracy in Slovakia from 1990-1998, regional structures had not yet been established. There had been a dual model of public administration with state administration and municipal self-government since 1990, although the boundaries and allocation of competencies were frequently unclear.

At the local level, there was a high number of very small municipal self-governmental units which lacked sufficient finance and infrastructure, and which were thus highly dependent on state subsidies. By 1995, there were 2839 municipal self-governmental units at local level (communes), but only 123 of them had a population above 5000; 1195 communes had fewer than

500 people[86]. This situation did not provide most communes with the opportunity to create and realize their own local policy. There was no meso-level of self-government, but there were numerous political disputes about the formation of regional units. These involved both political parties and experts among the emerging agents of local reform, such as the new Association of Towns and Villages of the Slovak Republic (ZMOS). ZMOS was an important actor in the discussions, partly because it comprises the mayors of all towns and villages, and since they are directly elected, they are fairly powerful actors in local politics. In spring 1992, before the division of Czechoslovakia, the Slovak government proposed dividing Slovakia into sixteen regions (to be called 'provinces') and seventy-seven districts. It was assumed that the meso-level boundaries would be the same for state administration and for self-governmental units, but there were disagreements about the number of regions and what they should be called, with some preferring the term 'zupa' which had been used for regions in the Austro-Hungarian empire and interwar Czechoslovakia. The proposal's opponents claimed that the division into sixteen regions was an inappropriate resurrection of pre-communist traditions which took no account of the new population centers and the contemporary location of industry, infrastructure networks, and services. Some preferred the four regions that had been established under communism, while the proponents of sixteen provinces were determined to abolish all traces of the previous regime and return to the pre-communist territorial divisions which they considered 'natural'.

After the 1992 elections, which led to a change of government and Slovak independence, the new government of Vladimir Mečiar rejected the 'provincial' proposal as economically backward, and started to prepare a new proposal for territorial division, with emphasis placed on the economic ramifications of the reform, with a consequent preference for larger regions. In 1995, after Mečiar had been briefly removed from power and then was returned to it after new elections, the government decided state administration would have two levels: 'districts' at the lower level, and eight regions (*kraje*) at the meso-level. However, it failed to deal with the question of transferring powers, in part because after all the years of discussion about redistributing competencies, it had given up any hope of resolving the issue. ZMOS became reconciled to the idea of eight regions and eighty districts for state administration since this was not incompatible with its preferred option of having sixteen self-governing 'provinces' (Obecné Noviny, 1996).[87] It had been weakened by internal division among its members, who supported various different numbers of regions. However, the reforms were distrusted by many

---

86 Statistical yearbook of SR 1995 . Bratislava, SU SR 1995.
87 *Obecné Noviny*, 12. March 1996.

self-government representatives and opposition parties: their impression was that the content of public administration reform was changing in the direction of strengthening state power at the local level.

The proposal was finally passed in July 1996 and the parties in the government coalition all supported the law. It had originated from the Movement for a Democratic Slovakia (HZDS) of Prime Minister Mečiar, which was by far the largest party in parliament, and its two smaller partners – the Slovak National Party (SNS), and the maverick extreme left Association of Workers of Slovakia (ZRS) – voted for the bill because they opposed having a large number of regions, and would even have supported a return to the communist-era division into four regions (East Slovakia, Central Slovakia, Western Slovakia, and Bratislava).

Among the opposition parties, the Christian Democratic Movement (KDH), which had supported sixteen self-governing regions when leading the government in 1992, remained particularly concerned with the transfer of competencies from the state administration. The party had good representation throughout Slovakia and could benefit from the exercise of regional power. However, the parties representing Slovakia's ten per cent Hungarian minority were primarily interested in the shape rather than the number of regions. Hungarian speakers were concentrated in the south of Slovakia, along the border with Hungary, and wanted regions that did not reach too far north so that at least one of them would have a Hungarian majority and guarantee ethnically Hungarian politicians a regional bastion. They justified this on the basis that these would be 'natural' historical regions, but this was precisely what the parties of the nationalistically inclined Mečiar government wanted to avoid since the historical period when Slovaks were ruled by Hungary was one to which they did not want to return. Slovaks living in the south of Slovakia were also concerned that if there were a 'Hungarian' region, Slovaks living there could be completely excluded from public life on the grounds that they did not speak Hungarian. Consequently, the eight state administrative regions were arranged so that none had a Hungarian majority, and in all future debates on self-governing regions, the Party of the Hungarian Coalition (SMK) was the strongest opponent of these being the same as the state administrative regions.

1998-2006

The 1998 parliamentary election in Slovakia is known as having been crucial for the country as the ousting of Mečiar changed Slovakia's direction in both domestic and foreign affairs, and led to its accession to the EU and NATO in 2003 and 2004 respectively. It was also important for the future of public administration reform, and the introduction of regional self-government was linked to the country's new striving toward European integration. The new government's program focused on the need to transfer competencies from state government offices to self-government, and this was agreed to by all the parties in the broad right-left government coalition, and by non-governmental organizations such as ZMOS. In 2001, when a number of constitutional amendments were adopted (many to facilitate EU accession), one of them strengthened the constitutional requirement to have regional self-government (Ústava Slovenskej Republiky).[88]

However, there was still a heated discussion between the five government parties which was related to the number of self-governing regions, and whether these should be the same as the state administrative regions. The Hungarian SMK insisted on a compact region encompassing the area where Hungarian speakers live, while the post-communist Party of the Democratic Left (SDĽ) was inclined, for reasons of economy, to adopt the four regions that had existed during the communist period, but was also willing to consider having eight regions.

In 2000, the government finally approved a new administrative-territorial division of the Slovak Republic with twelve regional self-government units (Nižňanský 2001).[89] This was supported by the two center-right parties, Prime Minister Mikuláš Dzurinda's Slovak Democratic Coalition (SDK), and the Christian Democratic Movement (KDH). This proposal was also supported by representatives of local self-government such as ZMOS. However, when the bill containing this solution finally came to parliamentary vote in July 2001, it unexpectedly failed to be passed, despite the fact that the governing coalition had a majority of over sixty per cent of deputies. During the second reading of the bill, the opposition introduced an amendment reducing the number of regions from twelve to eight, and both the leftist government parties suddenly voted for it. This prompted the most serious government crisis of the parliamentary period, with the Hungarian SMK nearly leaving the government. As will be discussed in the next Section both the decision of the leftist parties to back the opposition amendment, and the eventual decision of SMK to remain in government with them, were heavily influenced by considerations of how Slovakia's accession to the EU could be ensured most effectively.

The role of EU accession in establishing regional self-government

When the European Commission issued a rather negative opinion on Slovakia's application to join the EU in July 1997, the country 'fell behind' its Visegrad neighbors the Czech Republic, Hungary, and Poland. Consequently,

---

88 *Ústava Slovenskej Republiky*. Zbierka zákonov č. 135/2001 (Act No. 135/2001 Coll. The Constitution of the Slovak Republic as amended).
89 Nižňanský,V., Kling,J. (2001), *'Public Administration', in G. Mesežnikov, M. Kollár & T. Nicholson (eds), Slovakia 2001: A Global Report on the State of Society, 167-188.*

when the first Dzurinda government came to power in 1998 and accession negotiations began in February 2000, there was a general perception that Slovakia needed to 'catch up' in the accession negotiations, and as accession approached, much essential legislation was pushed through parliament with little regard for debate and scrutiny. This sense of urgency also propelled the reform of self-government in Slovakia. While Slovakia's politicians had themselves recognized the need to create local democracy as early as 1990, and, as discussed, there was a heated debate about establishing regional self-government throughout the 1990s, the situation became more critical when the European Commission issued its 1997 opinion on Slovakia and stated that 'Regional policy decision-making is overly centralized with all major decisions taken directly by the Government...' This was particularly important because, as the opinion went on to state:

> Special attention needs to be focused on strengthening Slovak capacity to programme, manage, evaluate and control Community funding (AGENDA 2000).[90]

In Slovakia, as in the whole of Central and Eastern Europe, EU accession was not merely a political goal of 'returning to Europe' but also an instrumental step to gain economic advantage, and in this respect while the free movement of persons and labor was highly attractive, the prospect of receiving structural funds was arguably even more enticing. Moreover, the recognition both within Slovakia and the EU that regional disparities – with the west and the Bratislava region in particular enjoying far more prosperity, economic development, and foreign direct investment than the east – also reinforced the need for a complex regional development policy.

The paradox was that despite Slovakia's traditional top-down policymaking, the country had never developed an integrated national policy of regional development. There was also a clear link between speeding up the process of decentralizing power and institutionalizing regional self-government, and fulfilling the European Framework Agreement on cross-border cooperation among communities and territorial authorities. In addition, the creation of NUTS II regions – crucial for EU statistics and the allocation of EU funding – impacted on debates about the creation of regions. NUTS II criteria favored the creation of four regions (as in communist-era Slovakia), but in the end the eight regions finally agreed (corresponding to NUTS III regions) could be clustered to form the four necessary NUTS II regions.

The development of the regional level in Slovakia was also assisted by the adoption in 2001 of the Act on State Service and the Act on Public Service, which defined the status of state and public employees and launched a system for training public-sector workers (Law No. 312/2001).[91] This was

---

90 AGENDA 2000 – Commision Opinion on Slovakia's Application for Membership of the European Union, DOC/97/20, Brussels, 15th July 19997, p.129.
91 Act No. 312/2001 Coll. On Civil Service. Act No. 323/2001 Coll. On Public Service.

significant with regard to developing the quality of human resources at the central, regional, and local level of policymaking. The new institutional structure based on three levels of self-government opened up the policymaking process, which required the creation of implementation structures and social and political networks with new tasks based on problem-solving methods.

However, EU conditionality in regional issues, and the need to build the structures necessary to access EU funds, were not the only political pressures from the EU that affected the decision made (rather chaotically) in 2001 to accept eight self-governing regions. In a profoundly divided political community, where successive governments tended to view opposition parties as enemies rather than opponents, EU accession became, after 1998, the only uncontested goal and symbol of Slovak national interest. The need to join the EU was accepted as an overriding priority by all political actors. Although the Mečiar government is generally considered to have been a failure in furthering Slovakia's desire to join the EU, it should be noted that it was this government coalition – whose parties were in opposition in the 1998-2002 period – that submitted Slovakia's application to join the EU in June 1994. Despite the hostility the more nationalist parties often displayed towards the EU, they were never in a position to renege on the desirability of EU accession. As a consequence of the cross-party consensus that joining the EU was in Slovakia's vital national interest, in the years leading up to accession in May 2004 it was frequently possible for governments to push through radical legislative reforms needed for EU accession without extensive criticism from the opposition.

The imperative of EU accession was also an important factor in the 2001 parliamentary decision that accepted the opposition's amendment reducing the number of regions to eight. Consequently, the decision also got the support of the leftist government parties (Nižňanský 2001).[92] Although the EU had no specific requirements in terms of the number of self-governing regions there should be, by 2001 resolving the issue had become a pre-requisite for deciding many other outstanding details of public administration that were essential for achieving EU accession. In addition, the governing party which was most deeply concerned with the issue of defining regional boundaries – the Hungarian SMK – was also strongly in favor of EU accession, which would, particularly after joining the Schengen zone, help dilute the Slovak-Hungarian border which separated the Hungarian-speakers in the

---

[92] Nižňanský,V., Kling,J. (2001), 'Public Administration', in G. Mesežnikov, M. Kollár & T. Nicholson (eds), Slovakia 2001: A Global Report on the State of Society, 167-188.

two states. Consequently, the party had to consider whether its continued opposition to eight regions might precipitate early elections and thus delay the country's acession to the EU.

Openness to reform in post-communist Slovakia

In attempting to explain why a radical rearrangement of regional structures took place in Slovakia in the first decade of the new millennium, it is necessary to look at the broader context of democratic politics. The openness to reform in Slovakia was determined both by the post-communist fluidity of the political system, and by the exigencies of achieving EU accession. While the instability of the political and party system in the early years of democratic transition often slowed the decision-making process with regard to determining the shape of regional self-government, the urgent goal of achieving EU membership, and the solving of multiple tasks this required, eventually accelerated it. In this respect, a number of factors should be emphasized.

First, the decision to create self-governing regions in Slovakia was intrinsically linked both to the need to devolve the highly-centralized power structures of the communist period to local self-government bodies, and to the need to reform public service as a whole. The lack of stakeholders at local level who were skilled in lobbying for their policy preferences to some extent simplified the process, although the 'multiple agendas' of post-communist reform complicated it. The only major non-party actor which impacted on decision-making was ZMOS – although here both the small average size of the municipalities, and their tendency to be represented both by independents or by individuals supported by non-typical party coalitions – reduced their effectiveness. Powerful party politicians operating at a sub-national level were only created by the first elections to the regional self-governments at the end of 2001.

Second, party politics was complicated by the plural nature of the Slovak party system, with no government after 1994 comprising less than three parties. In particular, during the crucial 1998-2002 parliamentary period when the self-governing regions were created, the government initially comprised a broad 'pro-reform' coalition which stretched economically from the left to the right of the party system, with post-election party fragmentation increasing the number of individual actors within the government. Additionally, the two Dzurinda governments that achieved EU accession (1998-2002, 2002-2006) did not have a single dominant party. The complexity of consensus-building within such governments complicated clear decision-making within the government coalition, and thereby probably enhanced the importance of achieving EU accession in eventually creating new self-governing regions.

The decision to create eight self-governing regions represented one of the clearest examples of division within the right-left governing coalition.

Third, ethnic issues complicated both the functioning of the Dzurinda governments which introduced regional self-government, and permeated the entire debate about the number and shape of self-governing regions. The rights of indigenous ethnic minorities had never been discussed in a complex fashion during the communist period, and the multiple decision-making burden of post-communism militated against any rational debate of the subject after 1990.

NORWAY

The question

Why did the reform of regional governance, initiated in 2005 by the Norwegian government, come to (almost) nothing? Reforming regional governance was an important plank in the political platform of the red-green coalition that entered office after the parliamentary elections of 2005. A vision of large-scale regions possessing more important functions and powers than the existing county councils was outlined in the coalition's political program. Far-reaching territorial reorganization of the country was announced to the public. Such a program was politically controversial, with the parties on the right regarding an intermediary layer of government as superfluous 'bureaucracy'. However, the red-green coalition government had a comfortable parliamentary majority, and could expect to command the necessary support for its project. Still, the reform initiative resulted in only tinkering with the existing system. Nothing resembling large-scale regions was to emerge from a long and arduous process. Why?

Background to the regionalization reform – the evolution of the county councils

Norway has a two-tier system of local government, with 430 municipalities and nineteen county councils. This structure dates back to 1837 when local government legislation was first introduced. Local government carries out a dual function: they are organs of implementation of important national welfare services, and autonomous bodies of local self-government under the direction of directly elected councils. The importance of local government is illustrated by the fact that it accounts for approximately half of all public expenditure and employs around two-thirds of all public-sector personnel.

Around half of local budgets is financed though transfers, the rest stems from local sources (taxes and charges) (Baldersheim/Rose 2010a).

The number of municipalities was reduced during the 1960s from 738 to around its current number. Initiatives during the 1990s and the 2000s to further reduce that number came to nothing, however. In 1995 parliament adopted a motion that made municipal amalgamations a voluntary decision of the municipalities concerned; this principle of voluntarism blocked strong national initiatives regarding amalgamations and was also later to have a bearing on the potential establishment of regions insofar as larger regions required the amalgamations of county councils (Baldersheim/Rose 2010b).

The fortunes of the county councils peaked in the 1980s, while in the following decades they lost functions. The most serious setback occurred in 2002 when the Labor government decided to make hospitals a state rather than a county responsibility. Sixty per cent of county council budgets disappeared and 100,000 employees were transferred to state bodies. The dominant cleavage in the battle over hospitals was that of territorial Norway versus corporatist Norway. The county councils and the Association of Local Authorities defended county ownership of hospitals while associations of doctors and nurses supported the state takeover, as did the Federation of Labor and the Employers' Association (Baldersheim 2003). This hollowing-out of county councils was accompanied by an erosion of political legitimacy. Political parties of the right began to campaign for the abolition of the county councils. 'Two levels of government are enough', the argument ran.

Preparations for regional reform

As the new millennium dawned, attitudes to regional governance had crystallized into those of abolitionists (parties of the right) and revivalists (parties of the left and center). The precise options of the latter group were not yet clearly outlined. A coalition of center-left parties won the 2005 election and formed a 'red-green' government, after which the Minister for Local Affairs and Regional Development immediately started preparations for regional reform. Based on these efforts, a white paper was presented to Parliament (St.meld. nr. 12 (2006–07)) in December 2006. The paper indicated three options regarding future regional governance: (1) 'enhancement' of the present county councils, meaning a certain extension of functions; (2) enlargement of counties (for example reducing the number from nineteen to fourteen or fifteen) along with some new functions; and, (3) large-scale regions (five to nine in number) with extensive new powers. The paper stated quite clearly that the transfer of functions and powers to regions would depend on the

scale of the new regions. The minister's preferred option was clearly that of large regions, while the intermediate model was ruled out as an alternative. The objectives of reform were stated as:
- the enhancement of regional and local democracy through decentralization of state functions and a more transparent division of responsibilities between levels of government
- better coordination of public administration across levels of government
- contribute to economic development by drawing more effectively on local and regional resources and advantages
- ensure better implementation of national goals such as sustainable development, equitable access to public services, and the protection of the legal rights of citizens.

Organizing choice

Legally, the final decision concerning political-administrative boundaries – both municipal and county – is a parliamentary prerogative. Central government has been delegated the authority to make decisions regarding municipal amalgamations when all of the municipalities concerned agree. Under current legislation municipalities and counties may initiate processes of amalgamation if they so desire, and so may the Ministry of Local Government Affairs. The first step in the process is to initiate an inquiry. Municipalities are obliged to consult their inhabitants as a part of this, but there is no similar obligation for county amalgamations (LOV 2001-06-15 nr. 70).

There is thus legal room for initiating top-down as well as bottom-up procedures to amalgamate municipalities and counties. In 2006, the 1995 parliamentary decision on voluntary amalgamations blocked the option of unilateral top-down decision-making. With this in mind, the 'principle' of voluntary amalgamations was also the point of departure for the process of regional enlargement. Hence at the outset county councils were invited, first, to specify their preference for one of the two main options and, second, to indicate where they stood regarding the other option and their views regarding regional divisions. During these considerations county councils were encouraged to consult with other regional and local actors, especially regional state agencies and municipalities. The Association of Local Authorities was enlisted as a facilitator of the discussions in this regard. If these processes did not result in an overall structure that was acceptable from a national point of view, however, the central government reserved the right to intervene and present a more suitable solution for consideration by Parliament.

But how would central authorities decide the form of a suitable solution? The white paper outlined three main criteria for the determination of the appropriate scale of regions: size, functionality, and identity. Though not specified very precisely, size seemed to refer to ideas about advantages of scale, underlying fiscal capacity, and requirements of catchment areas for various public functions. Functionality by comparison meant trying to create regions that formed integrated economic zones, although commitment to this goal was attenuated by statements suggesting that scattered populations might be well served by multi-core regions. Finally, the criterion of identity emphasized feelings of belonging, and established patterns of political cooperation across geographical–institutional borders.

In sum, the central government presented an unusually open-ended proposal on regional reform. A decidedly bottom-up procedure was initiated, at least at the second stage of the reform process. County councils were given opportunities to influence the scope of functions as well as new regional borders. Hospitals, however, were not among the functions they were invited to choose; these were to remain under state control, despite intentions to the contrary expressed by one of the coalition parties (the Centre Party) before the election. The Labor Party was not willing to reverse a reform it had carried through only three years earlier. But the commitment of the Center Party to transfer hospitals back to the regions was repeated as late as March 2007 by the party's national convention. Thus, a latent cleavage existed even within the governing coalition.

Battlefronts in 2007

Reception of the white paper by the public at large was mixed, as ascertained by the analysis of newspaper clippings[93]. Adherents of large-scale regions were disappointed that this option was not more forcefully pursued at the outset. Opponents of any regional government, on the other hand, were relieved that the white paper was so vague and expected the reform initiative to come to nothing. Larger cities that had hopes of becoming the centers of enlarged regions supported the regional option, while cities that could lose out in the realignment of regional borders were negative. Commentators from peripheral areas of potentially enlarged regions tended to view the new constructions as instruments of centralization. However, there were no clear-cut

---

93 Analysis carried out by Audun Randen Johnson for the project "Territorial Choice", June 2007.

differences in attitudes between counties close to the capital (Eastern Norway) compared to those located farther away, say in Northern Norway or on the West Coast.

The outcome – continuity, no super-regions

The parliamentary debate of the white paper on regions revealed the expected cleavages with regard to the establishment of potentially enlarged regions (Innst. S. Nr. 166 2006-2007). The red-green coalition parties supported the government's proposal for stronger regions, and so did the center parties (the Liberals and the Christian Democrats), while the parties on the right (the Conservative Party and the Progress Party) were against. The spokesperson for the Christian Democrats hoped, however, that more substantial tasks would be transferred to the regions than those already outlined in the white paper, and proposed a motion to this effect. The motion, which requested the government to consider further functional transfers to regions, gained the support also of the coalition parties and was thus passed with a significant majority. The National Association of Local Authorities, having championed stronger regions over the last five years, followed up this motion and sent a letter to the minister suggesting a list of additional functions that should be transferred to regions (KS Letter 23rd May 2007).

In the summer of 2007, it was the turn of the county councils to consider the proposal. As mentioned above, a letter from the Minister for Local Affairs and Regional Development requested the councils to consider enlargement versus functional enhancement of the existing councils inside their present borders. Early in the process spokespersons for a few county councils declared a willingness to amalgamate with neighbors, while others declared against. Most councils, however, deplored the limited scope of functions that the central government had at this stage proposed for the new regions/councils, and stated that their attitude toward amalgamation would hinge on the transfer of more functions.

By July 2007 eight county councils had stated they were prepared to unite with a neighbor, while the remaining ones had expressed strong reservations or were against any amalgamations. The 'no' counties were geographically distributed in such a way that most amalgamations were impossible if the 'principle of voluntarism' were to be respected. Clearly, there was not enough support among the existing county councils for the envisaged super-regions. The councils that supported amalgamation were mainly those that expected to constitute the core of the new enlarged regions, such as Hordaland or South Trøndelag. Councils that feared they might become a periphery of the new regions were against uniting with their neighbors, e.g. Sogn &

Fjordane to the north of Hordaland and Rogaland to the south, or Finnmark in the High North. In February 2008, the Minister for Local Affairs and Regional Development therefore chose to bury the option of regional reform. A few new functions regarding highways, environmental protection, and economic development funds were scraped together for the existing county councils so that the reform would not look completely empty, but the outcome was a far cry from the ambitious visions the red-green coalition government had set out in 2005. By now only six county councils supported the option of amalgamating with neighboring ones to establish enlarged regions. Two councils had changed their position from the spring of 2007 from supporting regions to supporting the functionally enhanced county council option.

First, the way in which the decision-making procedure was set up made the central government dependent upon the agreement of the county councils. This was, however, a procedure of the government's own making. It apparently felt bound by the parliamentary motion on voluntarism regarding amalgamations;[94] although the motion was intended to cover municipalities, it seems to have been interpreted as applying also to county councils. Thus establishing larger regions could only occur if the councils agreed to this. Theoretically, an asymmetrical structure could have emerged, establishing a few large regions composed of the willing councils and allowing the recalcitrant ones to continue as before. This was in fact hinted at in the government white paper. And such a solution was in fact near at hand and could be studied just across the border in Sweden in the two recently enlarged regions of Skåne and Vestra Götaland. However, in the Norwegian case this was not practically feasible. Although a number of councils did agree to amalgamations they were distributed geographically in such a way that there were no natural neighbors with whom to unite (a possible exception was East and West Agder).

---

94 "Det har vært en forutsetning for forvaltningsreformen at kommunesammenslutninger skal være frivillige, slik det ble vedtatt av Stortinget i 1995". Ot.prp. nr. 10 (2008–2009), p. 15.

Table 10.1: The decisions of the county councils regarding structural options, in the second round of decision-making, autumn 2007/winter 2008

County council (listed north to south)	Preferred option: enlarged region vs. remaining 'enhanced' county	County with largest city of potential region (regional center)
Finnmark	County	
Troms	Region (3 northern counties)	x
Nordland	County	
North Trøndelag	County	
South Trøndelag	Region (with N. Tr.)	x
Møre and Romsdal	County	
Sogn and Fjordane	County	
Hordaland	Region (with Sogn & F. and Rogaland)	x
Rogaland	County	
West Agder	Region (with East Agder)	x
East Agder	Region (with West Agder and Telemark)	
Telemark	Shifted position from region to county	
Vestfold	County	
Buskerud	Shifted position from region to county	x
Oppland	County	
Hedmark	County	
Akershus	Region (with Oslo, and possibly Østfold)	x (Oslo as seat of regional center)
Østfold	From region to county	
Oslo (the capital city)	County (as capital region)	

Source: Ot.prp. nr. 10 (2008–2009) Om lov om endringer i forvaltningslovgivningen mv. (gjennomføring av forvaltningsreformen). Oslo: The Ministry for Local and Regional Affairs, p. 16.

Second, the county councils behaved as the self-interested, rational actors posited by the theory of joint-decision traps. They regarded the reform mainly from the point of view of "what's in it for me?" Many county councils decided that the scope of new functions was too limited to make amalgamation worthwhile. Furthermore, a number of councils that felt they might lose out and become marginalized districts in an enlarged region said no to enlargement. Fear of losing out did not only hinge on geographical considerations. Some county councils had amassed considerable assets over the years in terms of finances, buildings, and infrastructure, and they were uncertain as to what might happen to these. The county of Sogn & Fjordane was a case in point, having profited from long-term investments in electricity generation plants, the control over which it was reluctant to relinquish. Finally, the minister was unable to compensate potential 'losers' with additional, interesting functions. She was also unable to console those who said 'too little' or to allay the fears of those who feared marginalization or the loss of control over financial assets.

Discussion

In the introduction we asked whether the outcomes of the regional reform initiatives in the two countries could be accounted for by *forces of region-building* or by features of the *reform processes*? What was the significance, in Norway and Slovakia respectively, of region-building forces, such as identity politics, competitive imperatives, European integration, and democratic ideals? And what was the significance, in Norway and Slovakia respectively, of features of the reform process?

a) Identity politics was clearly a factor of some significance in the Slovak case as representatives of the Hungarian community pressed for a solution that would establish a Hungarian regional enclave. This was strongly opposed by other actors, however, and in the end the claim of the Hungarian community was not heeded. So identity politics marked to some extent the process but not the outcome. In the Norwegian case, specific regional identities played little or no role for the outcome. On the West Coast resentment to what was regarded as a too dominant capital region gave some energy to experiments in cross-border cooperation among the county councils of the area, but in the end a possibly common West Coast identity was not strong enough to overcome traditional competition between existing counties, and so no large West Coast region emerged.

b) It is also hard to see that the competitive imperative impinged differently on regions or potential regions in the two countries. The need for instruments for development policy was accepted in both countries as an overarching rationale for establishing regions.

c) European integration was clearly a paramount factor in the Slovak case; and despite the numerous cleavages that emerged in the process leading up to the reform, actors agreed that establishing regions was in the national interest; not reaching agreement was regarded as slowing down accession to the EU and made actors, for example the Hungarian minority, play down misgivings over the actual outcome. No one wanted to take the blame for slowing down the "return to Europe". In contrast, European integration played little role in the Norwegian case. Little mention was made of the role of regions in European integration, which potentially could have been played as a card for Norway to emulate. However, the most pro-European party of all, the Conservative Party, was against the idea of regions per se, while the most ardent proponents of the regional reform were strongly anti-EU. Consequently, the European dimension was not brought into the debate.

d) In both cases, ideals of democracy, transparency, and good governance were invoked by proponents of the reforms. The Slovak reform could probably be presented more convincingly as a case of democratic progress than the Norwegian one, since the reform would establish directly elected regional assemblies where none existed before, while Norway had a long history of county councils. In fact, in Norway the proposed enlarged regions were in some cases opposed because they were said to represent centralization with regard to some of the more distant parts of the new regions. However, the outcome of the reform initiatives in Slovakia and Norway had little to do with the democratic merits of the respective proposals.

e) In both countries *the processes of decision-making* had top-down as well as bottom-up features. The Norwegian process was the one most decidedly of a bottom-up nature. The Norwegian debate took place under the constraints of 'voluntarism' imposed by a parliamentary decision twelve years earlier. This amounted to giving the county councils veto powers over the outcome of reform. The county councils behaved in accordance with the expectations of rational self-interest formulated by the joint-decision trap model, i.e. they took into account only what appeared to be the best outcome seen from their own local point of view. The outcome was a reform that corresponded to the lowest common denominator of the county councils, i.e. what they could all agree on.

The contrast to Slovak decision-making is striking. There were certainly bottom-up elements and local and sectarian self-interest at play in the Slovak case too. But in the end the actors bowed to what was seen as an overriding national interest – the quickest route possible to EU membership. There was, of course, no EU demand that dictated the outcome to be eight regions instead of twelve, as proposed by the government of the day; this last-minute shift has to be understood in the light of an unstable parliamentary situation and electoral calculations by an opposition party. But the actual outcome made the reform more radical in terms of regionalization than it would otherwise have been. Compelling outside incentives combined with a parliamentary accident contributed to the final Slovak outcome. The Norwegian case was also marked by a parliamentary accident, the adoption of the voluntarism principle, introduced by a parliamentary back-bencher who probably had little idea of the long-term consequences of his initiative. Nevertheless, this 'principle' and the absence of an overriding national interest such as Slovakia's much-wanted EU accession amounted to the construction of a trap from which the proponents of regional reform were not able to extricate the reform.

References

AGENDA 2000 – Commission Opinion on Slovakia's Application for Membership of the European Union, DOC/97/20, Brussels, 15th July 19997

Annoni, Paola/ Kozovska, Kornelia (2010): *EU Regional Competitiveness Index 2010*. European Commission: Joint Research Centre Institute for the Protection and Security of the Citizen.

Baldersheim, Harald (2003): Det regionpolitiske regimet i omforming – retrett frå periferien; landsdelen i sikte! In: *Norsk Statsvitenskapelig Tidsskrift*, 19: 276-307.

Baldersheim, Harald/ Rose, Lawrence E. (2010a): Norway: The Decline of Subnational Democracy? Chapter 12. In: John Loughlin/ Frank Hendriks/ Anders Lidström, eds. *The Oxford Handbook of Local and Regional Democracy in Europe*. Oxford: Oxford University Press.

Baldersheim, Harald/ Rose, Lawrence E. (2010b): The Staying Power of the Norwegian Periphery. Chapter 5. In: Harald Baldersheim/ Lawrence E. Rose, (eds.): *Territorial Choice.The Politics of Boundaries and Borders*. London: Palgrave.

Boekema, F./ Morgan, K/ Bakkers, S/ Rutten, R eds. (2000*): Knowledge, Innovation and Economic Growth. The Theory and Practice of Learning Regions*. Cheltenham: Edward Elgar.

Harvie, Christopher (1994): *The Rise of Regional Europe*. London: Routledge.

Hooghe, Liesbeth/ Schackel Arjan H. / Marks Gary (2008). Appendix A: Profiles of regional reforms in 42 countries (1956-2006),In: *Regional and Federal Studies*, 18 (2-3): 183-258.

Keating, Michael/ Loughlin John (eds.) (1997): The Political Economy of Regionalism. London: Frank Cass.

Nižňanský,V./, Kling,J. (2001): Public Administration, In G. Mesežnikov/, M. Kollár/ T. Nicholson (eds): *Slovakia 2001: A Global Report on the State of Society*, 167-188.

Marks, Gary/ Hooghe, Liesbeth/ Schackel, Arjan H. (2008a): Measuring regional authority, In: *Regional and Federal Studies*, 18 (2-3): 111-121.

Marks, Gary/ Hooghe, Liesbeth/Schackel Arjan H. (2008b): Patterns of regional authority, In: *Regional and Federal Studies*, 18 (2-3): 167-181.

Ot.prp. nr. 10 (2008–2009) Om lov om endringer i forvaltningslovgivningen mv. (gjennomføring av forvaltningsreformen). Oslo: The Ministry for local and regional affairs.

Rokkan, Stein/ Urwin, Derek W. (1983): *Economy, territory, identity: politics of West European peripheries*. London: Sage

Scharpf, Fritz W. (1988): The joint-decision trap: lessons from German federalism and European integration In: *Public Administration*, 66: 239 – 278.
Scherpereel, John A. (2010): EU cohesion policy and the Europeanization of Central and East European regions, In: *Regional and Federal Studies*, 20 (1): 45-62
Scully, Roger/ Jones, Richard Wyn (eds.) (2010): *Europe, Regions and European Regionalism*. Basingstoke: Palgrave.
St.meld. nr. 12 (2006-2007) Regionale fortrinn – regional framtid. Oslo: The Ministry for local and regional affairs.
Surazska, Wisla/ Buček, Jan/ Malíková, Ľudmila/ Daněk, P. (1997). Towards regional government in Central Europe: Territorial restructuring of postcommunist regimes. Environment and Planning C: In:*Government and Policy*, 15, 437-462.
Ústava Slovenskej Republiky (v znení neskorších predpisov). Zbierka zákonov č. 135/2001 (Act No. 135/2001 Coll. The Constitution of the Slovak Republic as amended).
Wollman, Hellmut (1997): Institution-Building and Decentralization in Formerly Socialist Countries: The Cases of Poland, Hungary and East-Germany. Environment and Planning C: In :*Government and Policy*, 15, 463-481.

Chapter 11
Good local governance:
What is it? How can it be promoted?

Lawrence E. Rose

Introduction

Monitoring, assessing, and stimulating good governance and democracy has become a "growth industry" in recent years[95] The reasons for this are many. The collapse of the Soviet regime and the push to (re)establish democratic government in the countries of Eastern and Central Europe (not to mention developments in other parts of the world), is one noteworthy reason. Another has been the decline in voter turnout experienced in many countries (cf. Franklin 2004; Pinter/Gratschew 2004). Combined with a drop in political party membership (cf. Wattenberg 2000) and an apparent decline in public confidence in political actors and institutions in many countries (cf. Norris 1999; Putnam/Pharr 2000) these developments have led many – laymen, political pundits, public authorities and scholars alike – to raise questions about the character of democracy in their respective countries. This applies at both the national and the local level.

The situation in Norway is no exception in this regard. As Figure 11.1 makes clear, despite a slight upturn in 2007, the long-term trend in turnout for municipal council elections has been one of decline, dropping from over 70 percent in the early post-war years to roughly 60 percent in recent elections.[96] A turnout rate of roughly 60 percent is higher than that found in many countries (cf. CoR 2001), but it is nonetheless a cause of concern. Low and declining turnout is typically interpreted as a sign of weakness, indeed, even a threat to the well-being of democracy, whereas high participation is seen as a sign of health and an indication of the political system's legitimacy.[97]

---

95 See, for example, Beetham et al. 2008; Campbell/Pölzlbauer 2010; International IDEA 2010; Kaufmann et al. 2008; Pröhl 2002; Wegener 2002.
96 Turnout for county council elections has been slightly lower than that for municipal council elections.
97 Such a perspective lies at the heart of Lijphart's APSA presidential address (1997) and is found in many other discussions of democracy (see, for example, Patterson 2002; Piven/Cloward 2000; Wattenberg 2002).

Figure 11.1: Electoral turnout in municipal and county council elections in Norway, 1910-2007, per cent

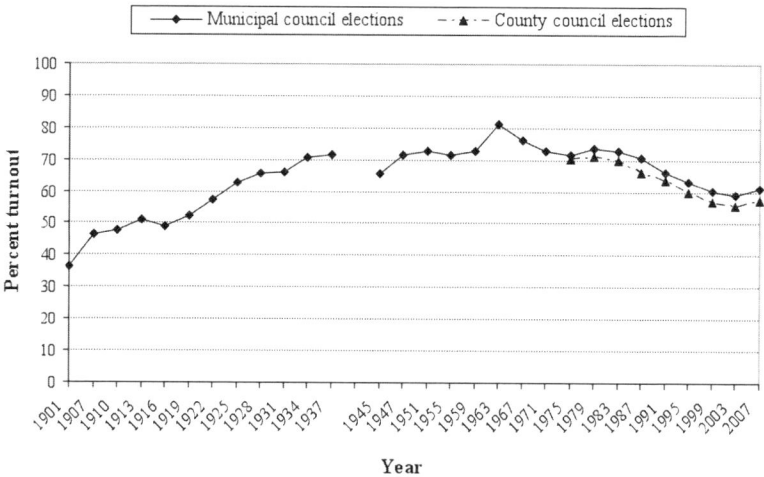

Expectations of higher turnout levels at local elections and difficulties reported by political parties in finding people who are willing to stand as candidates for office in local elections led many commentators to be concerned about the well-being of local democracy in Norway. Hence, following the 1995 elections in which aggregate turnout for municipal council elections was just below 63 percent, a sharper focus on the character and quality of local democracy emerged and the issue moved up on the national political agenda. The official response came from two prominent players – the Norwegian Association of Local and Regional Authorities (known in Norwegian as KS) and the Ministry of Local Government and Regional Development (abbreviated in Norwegian as KRD). In what follows the major efforts pursued by these two players from the mid-1990s up to the present are outlined and briefly discussed. At many junctures these efforts have overlapped and been coordinated. The efforts, moreover, have been the basis for a pronounced Norwegian role in work undertaken by the Council of Europe regarding local democracy, especially most recently in the Council's efforts in developing a label of "good local governance". This and other "ripple effects" of the Norwegian efforts will also be briefly presented. The chapter then concludes with some reflections about the nature and possible implications of efforts to evaluate and stimulate local democracy in Norway and elsewhere.

Efforts by the Norwegian Association of Local and Regional Authorities (KS)

Following the 1995 local elections, the national conference of the Norwegian Association of Local and Regional Authorities (KS) decided to make "Democracy, participation and government" a major area of work for the 1996-2000 period. In doing so the intent was to increase popular involvement in local self-government. To achieve this end KS set aside earmarked funds for a national research and development program. Three areas of emphasis were identified: (1) increased participation in local politics; (2) improved dialogue between residents and local authorities; and (3) increased involvement in the development of sustainable local communities. Municipal and county governments were then invited to submit proposals to conduct local projects within any of these areas. Proposals submitted by 15 local authorities were eventually selected for the program, and an independent research team was given responsibility to follow up and report on these projects.

It is important to stress that whereas the invitation to take part in the program was issued by KS, responsibility for developing project proposals rested with local authorities. The program was not a "top heavy" nationally directed effort; it was instead a program that provided a genuine opportunity for "grass root" innovation and development. The proposals submitted and subsequently selected reflected this fact, with projects concerning

1. Political parties
2. Initiatives aimed at specific groups
3. Community processes
4. Participation for sustainable development
5. User surveys as tools of democracy
6. Information and communication technology (ICT) in local democracy
7. Deliberative hearings

Results from the projects were summarized midway (Aars 1998) and at the end of the program, providing the basis for a set of pamphlets that offered a popularized presentation of what had been done along with advice on how similar projects might be undertaken and conducted in other locations.[98] These pamphlets received wide circulation, but no effort was made by KS or other central authorities to promote adoption of similar projects in other municipalities.

As part of the same effort, KS undertook a campaign entitled "Renew local democracy" prior to the 1999 local elections. A special supplement to *Kommunal Rapport* – the weekly newspaper published by KS – appeared in the fall of 1998, and a special letter encouraging local action was sent to

---

98 In addition to a pamphlet devoted to each of the seven categories, an eighth pamphlet (Øvrum 2000) provided an overview and some suggestions with respect to the implications and possibilities highlighted by experiences from the relevant projects.

mayors of all municipalities and counties. Again the intent was to encourage innovative thinking about how local democracy operated at the grassroots level and to stimulate higher electoral turnout. An expansion of possibilities to vote by mail was one measure adopted in this connection. In the same spirit KS also endorsed an experiment introduced by the Ministry of Local Government and Regional Development that allowed for the direct election of mayors in 20 selected municipalities.[99]

Despite these efforts, electoral participation fell further in the 1999 elections. For municipal council elections the aggregate turnout was roughly 60 percent, whereas for county council elections turnout was under 57 percent. Then in the 2003 local elections, notwithstanding further experimental efforts sanctioned by the Ministry of Local Government and Regional Development intended to stimulate higher electoral participation, this decline continued unabated. At this point KS opted for a new tack. The organization's governing body decided to pursue a strategy designed to create a platform of "Good local democracy" for use internally and by its members in their respective localities. A first step involved commissioning a set of working papers devoted to a discussion of what characterizes good local democracy.[100] These working papers provided a basis for KS's further work with the platform. As eventually adopted in 2007, the platform stipulated three overarching considerations, each of which was elaborated in a set of more specific characteristics (see Box 11.1).

---

99 Details regarding this experiment are found in the following section of this chapter.
100 In all five papers were commissioned – three from various Norwegian research environments, the other two from Denmark and Sweden respectively.

Box 11.1. Norwegian Association of Local and Regional Authorities' platform on good local democracy – summary excerpt

Good local democracy is achieved when…

Citizens have confidence in their local politicians

This implies

- High voter turnout
- That citizens have a good basis on which to vote and are motivated to use their voting rights
- Providing people with good information about rights, policies and services
- The rule of law
- That people must know how to raise issues at the political level in the municipal authority
- Allowing people to participate apart from elections
- Open public political debate
- Active voluntary groups and organisations
- Safeguarding the rights of minorities
- A high level of activity in local party organisations
- That political parties secure good recruitment to local politics

Those elected set the agenda, control the use of resources and are ombudsmen for citizens

This implies

- Clarifying roles and procedures between elected representatives and the administration
- Good cooperation and relations within municipal councils
- Balanced gender representation
- Good conditions for elected representatives to perform their role
- High ethical standards and the absence of corruption
- Active ownership and governance of municipal and inter-municipal enterprises
- Clarifying the roles of the municipal councils and representatives in non-municipal bodies and partnerships (for example regional boards)

There is delivery on promises

This implies

- Results in relation to promises
- Good services
- Development of society and use of room for action
- Supervision and control of own activities

The driving idea behind the platform is stated in the document's opening paragraph:

> In Norway, democracy at the local level is well developed – but can and should be improved. KS believes that a platform document will be a useful *tool for further development of democracy* at the local level. A platform will provide a common starting point, it will indicate the direction for development of local democracy, and it will provide a standard for comparison. (Author's translation, emphasis added).

In keeping with this preamble, KS sought to develop means of assessing the status of local democracy in different municipalities. Rather than attempting to identify a set of *objective criteria* for evaluating the character of local democracy, the intent was instead to create a device that could tap important *subjective perceptions* of how local democracy functioned in specific settings. It was recognized, in short, that despite similar outcomes in terms of objective measures, perceptions of local conditions may vary substantially among citizens and elected officials alike. Thus, as a springboard for reflection and action to improve the functioning of local democracy, subjective perceptions were deemed to be more critical than objective assessments.

The development of a subjective assessment device was turned over to external consultants who worked in close cooperation with a KS project team.[101] After consideration of different alternatives, it was decided to carry out a pilot project involving a combination of sample surveys among residents and written questionnaires completed by all municipal council members in six municipalities.[102] The surveys of residents were carried out by telephone,[103] whereas the surveys of council members were written questionnaires handed out and in most cases completed at a council meeting following a presentation of the project. This procedure meant that virtually all council members completed and returned the questionnaires.

The items included in the questionnaires were designed to tap different facets of local democracy found in KS's local democracy platform. In addition to this platform, however, a number of other international efforts regard-

---

101 The author of this chapter was one of the team, the others being Professor Harald Baldersheim and Associate Professor Jostein Askim from the University of Oslo, and Associate Professor Morten Øgård from the University of Agder.
102 KS announced the pilot study and solicited interested municipalities among its members. Based on responses to this announcement, six municipalities found in different parts of the country and with otherwise different characteristics were selected for participation in the study. All costs of participation were born by KS, but the municipalities chosen were expected to facilitate the work in their own municipalities. The foremost obligations in this respect were the collection of survey responses among council members and a follow up of the study results.
103 The number of telephone interviews completed varied from 250 to 400 depending on the number of inhabitants in the municipality. The smallest municipalities, in which only 250 interviews were completed, had between 4,000 and 5,000 inhabitants, while the largest municipality where 400 interviews were completed, had nearly 80,000 residents.

ing the assessment of (local) democracy were also consulted (e.g. Beetham 2004; Beetham, et al. 2002; Council of Europe 2007; UNDP 2007). Considerations found in these various approaches were ultimately grouped and summarized in terms of four dimensions of good democratic government. These dimensions were:

- *Reliable governance* – i.e. governance characterized by political integrity and equal treatment of all residents
- *Responsible governance* – i.e. governance characterized by transparency and accountability
- *Citizen-oriented governance* – i.e. governance characterized by receptiveness and responsiveness to citizen interest and input
- *Effective governance* – i.e. governance characterized by an ability to provide services in accordance with the needs of residents within the means available

In order to facilitate comparison of resident and councilor perceptions, some of the items included in both surveys were identical. Insofar as possible, moreover, both survey instruments used a common format whereby respondents could answer using a 4-point agree/disagree scale. This response scale permitted ready calculation of percent difference index (PDI) scores based on differences between the percentage of respondents agreeing versus the percentage disagreeing with a specific statement. These index values were then used to provide a visual summary of perceptions among residents and elected councilors either separately or, when identical items were available, in the same figure. Figures 11.2 and 11.3 provide examples of this approach.

Figure 11.2: PDI index values for responses from citizens in six municipalities to the statement indicated

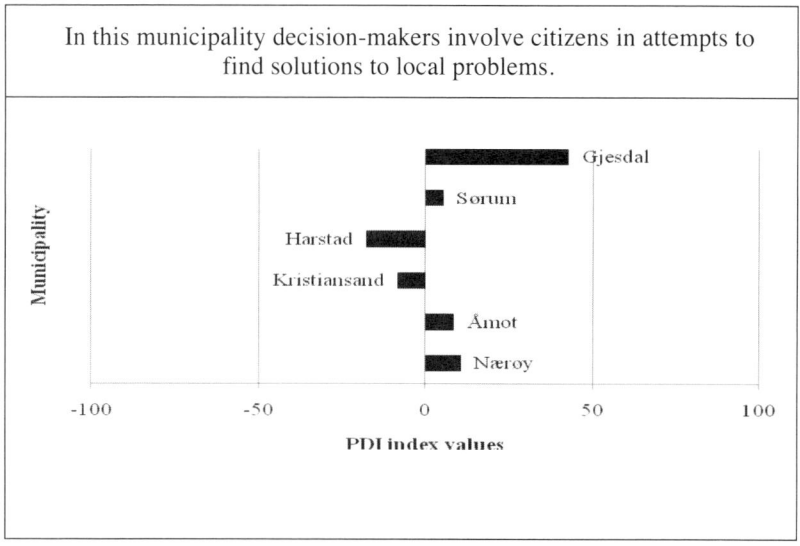

Figure 11.3: PDI index values for responses from citizens and local council members in four municipalities to the statement indicated

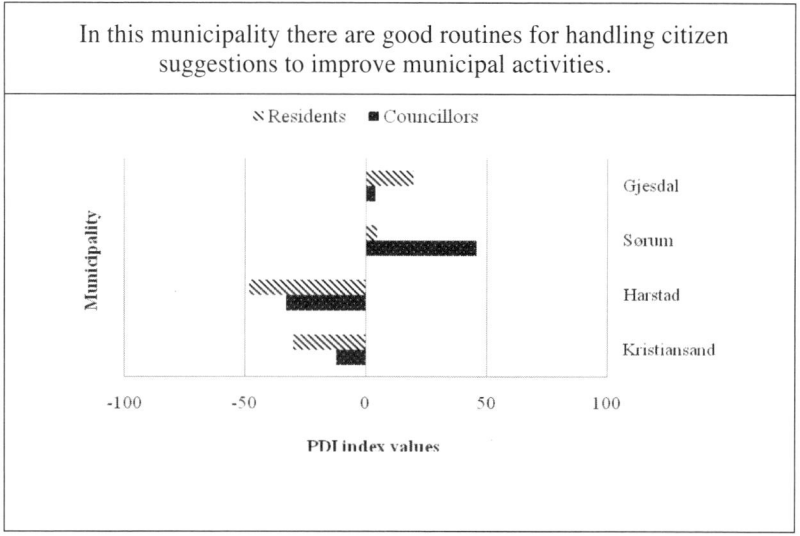

Results from the pilot studies were compiled in a set of reports – one for each municipality and one comprehensive report for use by KS. Reports to the municipalities were presented at a meeting of either the entire municipal council or the executive committee of the council as a matter of information and potential follow up. It was then up to the individual municipalities to decide how, if at all, the results were to be used in efforts to improve the character of local democracy in the municipality.

The impact the project had at the local level varied. In Kristiansand, a municipality of roughly 80,000 inhabitants located on the southern coast of Norway, for example, the report was presented to the executive committee of the municipal council. In the eyes of both residents and elected representatives alike, the municipality had scored fairly well in terms of the indicators of reliable and effective governance, but was perceived less favorably in terms of responsible and citizen-oriented governance. When presented with the results, the executive committee decided to establish an ad hoc committee that was asked to prepare suggestions for measures that could improve the situation. This committee reviewed the results in greater detail together with the results of other investigations and earlier efforts made to improve local democracy in Kristiansand. The committee also invited local political parties, interest groups, the media, educational institutions and residents to make suggestions that could contribute to how local democracy functioned in the municipality.

In preparing its recommendations, the committee placed special emphasis on measures that could enhance the quality of local democracy, and with this the reputation of elected representatives and the municipality more generally. The suggestions ultimately submitted contained eleven points for subsequent action (see Box 11.2). This recommendation was passed upon by the executive committee in its meeting in June of 2010 and sent to the mayor, chief administrative officer and local political party groups for evaluation and incorporation in the municipal's annual plan of action and budgetary process for 2011.

> **Box 11.2: Measures recommended to improve local democracy in Kristiansand**
>
> 1) Implement plans for a "virtual city hall"
>
> 2) Make clear how residents and groups can influence and gain insight into planning documents on the homepage of the municipal website
>
> 3) Secondary school pupils can teach older residents how to use the internet
>
> 4) Enhance service and customer contact capabilities of municipal employees
>
> 5) Make clear methods for participation in (municipal) planning processes
>
> 6) Strengthen the paticipatory competence of elected representatives, planning personnel and other municipal employees
>
> 7) Use municipal organs more actively in participatory processes and dialogues with groups of residents who face a democratic deficit
>
> 8) Extend theme meetings held by the municipal council executive committee in different areas of the town
>
> 9) Use instruments of measurement (benchmarks) found and used in other municipalities, and integrate these in programs of action and annual reports
>
> 10) Review existing user surveys with respect to the information they provide about residents' confidence in the municipality as a whole
>
> 11) Invite relevant expert groups to provide analyses and suggestions for what can be done to improve confidence in local democracy in Kristiansand
>
> Source: Document 200909457-4 dated May 12, 2010 prepared for the municipal executive council meeting held on June 9, 2010 (Author's translation)

Other municipalities that took part in the pilot project responded in a similar if not identical manner, considering the findings and setting in motion various processes to follow up. The extent to which suggestions emerging from such processes have been adopted and implemented, and if so whether they will ultimately lead to more positive perceptions of how local democracy functions in the individual municipalities, is not known at this point. On the surface, however, it would seem that the exercise contributed to heightened *awareness of* and *reflection about* the nature of local democracy and how it was perceived to operate in each of the participating municipalities.

Even without more detailed evidence of the longer-term consequences of the exercise, results from the pilot project were judged by both KS and the Ministry of Local Government and Regional Development to be sufficiently positive that a decision was reached to proceed and create a more comprehensive local democracy database. The idea for such a database was set forth in the second report issued by the Local Democracy Commission (NOU 2006:7), a national commission created in 2004 with a mandate to investigate the condition of local democracy in Norway and to make recommendations as to how local democracy could be strengthened. (More details concerning the creation and results of this commission are found below.) It was expected that the database would – especially if it were to be maintained and extended to cover many if not all municipalities in the country and multiple points in time – constitute an important benchmarking device allowing municipalities to assess and seek to improve the quality of local democracy.[104]

Negotiations between KS and the ministry led to an agreement in which funding was provided to establish a preliminary version of such a database with a broader sample of municipalities. A letter of invitation to take part in the project was sent to all municipalities in the summer of 2009. Of the municipalities that responded favorably, 50 were selected and data collection took place in late 2009 and early 2010. The municipalities selected constituted a diverse group, ranging in demographic size from less than 1,000 inhabitants to more than 250,000 inhabitants and being spread out geographically throughout the country. Again data collection among residents occurred by telephone interviews among a representative sample of the population 18 years or older, whereas data for elected councilors was gathered by means of written questionnaires that were for the most part completed in connection with a municipal council meeting. In all over 14,000 residents were interviewed, and 1,374 councilors completed the questionnaire.[105] A subsidiary of KS was given responsibility for registering the data for both residents and elected councilors in a common database and subsequently generating standardized reports with summary information that was sent to each municipality. Municipalities participating in the program were also given the opportunity to use the database for additional analyses of responses in their own municipality and to undertake comparisons with results from other municipalities. The initial phase of this project was completed in the spring of 2010 and a second phase expanding the database was completed in early 2011.

---

104 This type of benchmarking and inter-municipal comparative analysis is in keeping with other efforts of KS in recent years using a common internet portal entitled "A better municipality" (http://www.bedrekommune.no/).

105 The number of residents interviewed in each municipality depended on the population size of the municipality. In the smallest municipalities 150 were interviewed while in the largest municipalities 400 were interviewed. For most municipalities, however, the number was either 250 or 300.

Efforts by national authorities

The local democracy database is only one of several measures which the Ministry of Local Government and Regional Development has pursued in attempting to curb the decline of turnout for local elections and to stimulate local democracy more generally. Following 1995 the first effort focused on experimenting with the direct elections of mayors. Traditionally the Norwegian system of local government has been characterized by a form of consensual democracy whereby the municipal council is elected through a system of proportional representation based on party lists after which the municipal council elects an executive board composed proportionally of councillors from all parties represented in the council. The mayor is also elected by and amongst the council members. The primary function of the mayor is to chair meetings of both the council and executive committee, but the mayor has no special powers in this regard. The position is more of symbolic and ceremonial character in which the mayor represents the municipality on official occasions.

With this procedure for selecting the municipal council, executive committee and mayor, the Norwegian electoral system has not typically been characterized by a strong personal focus. It has rather been a more anonymous party-dominated system.[106] In introducing a more direct form of electing mayors, it was believed that local elections would generate greater interest and serve to bring more voters to the polls. After some debate, a decision was reached to test this presumption in connection with the 1999 elections. But instead of adopting a sweeping reform permitting direct elections of mayors in all municipalities, an experimental approach was chosen.[107] A letter inviting municipalities to submit applications for participating in such an experiment was sent to all local authorities, and 20 municipalities were selected from among the applications received. Once again it is important to note that local authorities were, within relatively broad guidelines, permitted to formulate their own rules for the experiment and submit them for ministerial approval.[108] Consequently the rules adopted varied substantially from

---

106 The electoral system does contain an element of preferential voting whereby voters are able to give extra votes to a number of candidates and cross out others. Use of these provisions may have an impact on which persons are elected to represent specific parties, but for the most part election outcomes are a function of how parties create their electoral lists.

107 The use of experiments to "test the waters" rather than jumping in with comprehensive local government reforms has been a frequently used strategy in Nordic countries since the beginning of the 1980's (cf. Rose 1990 and Baldersheim/Ståhlberg 1994).

108 In particular six points that were open for local variation and specification: (1) requirements for the election result to be valid; (2) requirements for a candidate to be declared a winner; (3) the mayor's place in the local council and executive committee; (4) the means of selecting the vice mayor; (5) the means of determining a winner in the event of a tie; and (6) how candidates were to be nominated. In addition to these matters, municipalities were

municipality to municipality, the only common denominator being that the elections were carried out on the same day as elections for municipal and county councils, but on a separate ballot.

Results of the experiment were not a resounding success. Compared to the 1995 elections, turnout did increase in four of the 20 municipalities and was stable in one, but declined in the other 16 municipalities. The average decline in the 20 experimental municipalities was, to be sure, slightly less than the national average (a drop of 2.4 per cent in contrast to 2.8 percent), but participation in the *direct election of mayors* was in general lower than that for the *regular council elections*.[109]

Despite these disheartening results, the ministry decided to continue and even expand the experiment in the 2003 local elections. In 1999 the municipalities involved were all relatively small, having an average of less than 3,000 eligible voters. Elections in these municipalities could therefore be said to be characterized by a stronger element of personal familiarity and focus among the electorate in any event. For this reason KRD was interested in involving some larger municipalities in the experiment as well. Thus, following a new round in which municipalities were again invited to submit proposals, 21 new municipalities were selected to take part, seven of which had more than 10,000 eligible voters. At the same time, five of the municipalities that had taken part in the experimental program in 1999 withdrew and reverted to the traditional indirect manner of selecting a mayor.

The outcome of the 2003 elections was no more successful than that of 1999. On the contrary, for the 36 municipalities using one experimental scheme or another for the direct election of mayors, aggregate turnout was three percent *lower* than it was for the country as a whole. In only five municipalities that took part in the program for the first time did turnout increase, whereas for the others turnout decreased. Just as in 1999, moreover, participation in elections for mayors tended to be lower than turnout for council elections. The principal conclusion to be drawn, in short, was that even if the direct election of mayors did add an element of increased personal focus, it failed to achieve the primary goal identified by national policy makers – namely to stimulate greater electoral participation.[110]

Despite this unfavourable result, the ministry extended the experiment to yet a third election in 2007. Yet once again the outcome failed to live up to expectations, and after further consideration the experiment has been

---

also able to decide on special rules relating to the mayor's position (cf. Buck et al. 2005 for a discussion of these points).
109 For additional information and comments on results from the 1999 direct elections, see Larsen 2002:126-7.
110 Results from more detailed investigations of conditions at the local level, especially of how voters viewed the experiment, however, were in general more positive (cf. Buck et al. 2005).

abandoned; the 2011 local elections were held without any direct elections of mayors.

The direct election of mayors was not the only experiment aimed at improving conditions for local democracy that proved disappointing. According to some critical voices, one of the reasons for declining turnout was that local elections, due to the fact that they were all held on the same day, had become an arena in which national parties competed for attention; local elections had become a type of "trial run" for the national parties in preparing for subsequent parliamentary elections. As such, they diverted attention from important local issues, thereby undercutting some of the motivation for people to participate in local council elections. Based on this reasoning, in 2003 one municipality sought and was granted the right to arrange the local council election more than two months prior to the date on which all other local elections were to be held.[111] In the tradition of experimentation, the logic was again that the municipality would provide a testing ground for the idea that separate election days would make local elections more genuinely *local*. A separate election would place local issues and local politicians in the limelight, something that would generate greater interest and have a mobilizing effect with respect to electoral participation.

Once again hopes were dashed. Rather than increased electoral participation, turnout dropped by over 16 percent to a record low of just over 46 percent. Inasmuch as permission to hold elections on a special day had been granted with relatively short notice, and the election campaign was carried out in a period (at the end of the school year) when there are typically many other activities that competed for the voters' attention, some had anticipated a decline in turnout, but nothing quite so dramatic. Despite this unexpected outcome, local officials were not totally dejected. From their point of view the primary intent of the experiment was not so much one of increasing turnout, but rather one of placing greater emphasis on local issues and stimulating local debate about these. The results were more positive in this respect. Elder care, school and child day-care, local culture and opportunities for young people, planning and transportation issues all occupied a central place in the election campaign, and in a survey conducted after the election voters identified three of these as being important for how they voted. A majority also agreed with statements suggesting that local issues and local politicians had characterized the election, whereas only a small minority responded that the campaign had been boring or uninteresting due to the absence of national political figures (cf. Skålnes 2005:90-1, 96-97).[112]

---

111 Elections in Norway, both national and local, are generally held on the first weekend of September. In this case the municipality was permitted to arrange the election in mid-June.

112 It is worthy of noting, however, that several national politicians did make appearances in the municipality during the campaign in support of their local compatriots, but in some instances this drew negative commentary.

While a heightened local electoral focus provided an element of satisfaction for some, the general mood among commentators and politicians following the 2003 local elections was rather one of increased dismay and alarm. And a reaction was not long in coming. In October 2003, just a month after the election, two parliamentary representatives from the Liberal Party introduced a private members' proposal to create a national commission to investigate conditions relating to local democracy and its development. Following normal parliamentary procedures, this proposal was submitted to committee consideration, endorsed by the committee and then unanimously adopted in February of 2004, after which a national commission was created by a cabinet resolution passed in March of the same year.[113] The commission was given a mandate to carry out investigations concerning two principal issues: (1) what consequences developments in central-local relations have for realizing a vibrant local democracy; and (2) what is the nature and status of local democracy within different local authorities?

The commission's work, carried out over a two-year period, resulted in two official reports (NOU 2005:6; NOU 2006:7). A definitive answer as to just what stimulates electoral turnout and other forms of local participation was not given, but the reports did touch upon a broad spectrum of factors thought to have some relevance, and contained a number of suggestions for further action. One such suggestion was the creation of a national database on local democracy – a suggestion that was endorsed in the parliamentary white paper submitted in June of 2008 and subsequently pursued in cooperation with KS as previously noted.

International "ripple effects"

Local democracy has not only been a matter of concern and discussion domestically; it has also been an objective which Norway has sought to facilitate in the international arena. This is true for both KS and the Ministry of Local Government and Regional Development. Through its membership in the Council of European Municipalities and Regions (CEMR) and the United Cities and Local Governments (UCLG), KS has played an active role in seeking to develop a solid foundation for local democracy in Europe and elsewhere. This role has been personified by the involvement of KS's current

---

113 The commission consisted of one member from each of the political parties represented in parliament, four members representing local government and two independent members, both of whom had done research on local government.

leader, Halvdan Skard, who for many years served as a delegate to the Council of Europe Congress of Local and Regional Authorities and was elected as president of the congress for 2006-08.[114]

Central government authorities have similarly been active in international affairs concerning local government and democracy. Most noteworthy in the present context has been Norway's role with respect to *The Strategy for Innovation and Good Governance at Local Level* initiated by the European Committee on Local and Regional Democracy (CDLR).[115] This strategy seeks to provide "a practical instrument for improving governance at the local level and the quality of local life as a result."[116] Norway has formal membership in the Stakeholders' Platform group responsible for overseeing development and implementation of the strategy, and has served as a pilot country in which the strategy instrument has been tested.

The strategy implies development of a European Label of Government Excellence (ELOGE) and a means by which local governments may qualify to receive the label, symbolized by a crystal dodecahedron – an object with 12 sides, one for each of 12 principles of good democratic governance at the local level (see Box 11.3). In discussions regarding the content of the instrument for assessing local government performance and hence whether local authorities qualified for the European label, representatives from KRD drew upon results of the KS pilot project and sought to incorporate elements of this approach in procedures for assessing local government performance.

---

114 In recognition of his efforts Skard was awarded the Emperor Maximilian Prize in May of 2010, and in June 2010 he was elected to be the leader of a newly created EFTA forum for local and regional government.
115 This strategy is an offshoot emerging from the Valencia Conference of 2007 (cf. http://www.coe.int/t/dgap/localdemocracy/Ministerial_Conferences/Valencia/default_en.asp). The text of the strategy document adopted by the Committee of Ministers is available at http://www.coe.int/t/dgap/localdemocracy/Strategy_Innovation/default_en.asp.
116 Cf. http://www.coe.int/t/dgap/localdemocracy/Strategy_Innovation/default_en.asp.

Box 11.3: Principles of Good Democratic Governance, Council of Europe

The Principles of Good Democratic Governance at local level are:

1) **Fair Conduct of Elections, Representation and Participation**, to ensure real possibilities for all citizens to have their say in local public affairs;

2) **Responsiveness**, to ensure that the local authority meets the legitimate expectations and needs of citizens;

3) **Efficiency and Effectiveness**, to ensure that objectives are met while making the best use of resources;

4) **Openness and Transparency**, to ensure public access to information and facilitate understanding of how local public affairs are conducted;

5) **Rule of Law**, to ensure fairness, impartiality and predictability;

6) **Ethical Conduct**, to ensure that the public interest is put before private ones;

7) **Competence and Capacity**, to ensure that local representatives and officials are well able to carry out their duties;

8) **Innovation and Openness to Change**, to ensure that benefit is derived from new solutions and good practices;

9) **Sustainability and Long-term Orientation**, to take the interests of future generations into account;

10) **Sound Financial Management**, to ensure prudent and productive use of public funds;

11) **Human rights, Cultural Diversity and Social Cohesion**, to ensure that all citizens are protected and respected and that no one is either discriminated against or excluded;

12) **Accountability**, to ensure that local representatives and officials take responsibility and are held responsible for their actions.

Source: *Good local and regional governance – the European challenge*, Council of Europe 2007.

Both the content and criteria for performance assessment and awarding the good governance label were the subject of extensive discussion and revision within various Council of Europe bodies, and the instrument was subject to testing via pilot projects carried out in three member countries – Belgium, Bulgaria and Norway. As currently formulated, the assessment procedure consists of two parts: (1) a fairly extensive municipal self-assessment segment based on a set of pre-defined activities and indicators relating to the 12 different principles, and (2) a smaller segment based on responses from citizens surveys containing one item pertaining to each principle. With small modifications the items on the citizen surveys are taken from the surveys conducted in Norway as part of the KS pilot project and local government database. For all of the indicators a 4-point rating scale is used and the scores on all items are added together to determine whether a local authority is qualified to receive the good governance label.

The structures and procedures for awarding the European good governance label are set forth in a document which has been approved by the Stakeholders' Platform. Any Council of Europe member country can take part in the exercise, but to do so requires a formal decision and joint commitment of national as well as local and regional authorities to adhere to a set of rules governing the assessment and award procedures. These rules seek to assure cross-national comparability and emphasize objectivity and transparency. Participating countries are expected to use the benchmarking tool as developed by the European Stakeholders' Platform group; any deviations must be justified and approved prior to implementation. Moreover, independent experts are required to validate the results of the self-assessment procedures completed by local authorities whereas the European Stakeholders' Platform group retains the right to suspend or withdraw national accreditation procedures and may, in the case of serious breaches of the regulations, retroactively invalidate awards already awarded.[117]

In passing a second ripple effect of the Norwegian efforts may also be mentioned – in this case an effect within the Nordic area. Much as in Norway, a concern with the character and quality of local democracy has also been evident in Sweden for some time. A public commission has addressed the issue (cf. SOU 2000:1), various experiments with new forms of local participation have been undertaken (cf. Olsson/Montin 1999), and the topic has occupied a prominent place on the agenda of the Swedish Association of Local Authorities and Regions (abbreviated SKL), the counterpart of KS in Norway. As part of its work, SKL has considered the establishment of a local democracy database along the lines of that initiated by KRD and KS. To this

---

117 Implementation of the strategy has begun and the status of the program as of early 2011 was summarized in a document submitted to the European Committee on Local and Regional Democracy (CDLR) for its meeting in Strasbourg 28-30 March 2011. See Council of Europe document CDLR (2011)12.

end SKL has been in contact with KS and has received information regarding the Norwegian approach and survey instruments used. It remains to be seen, however, if and just how such a database will be developed in Sweden.

Evaluating and stimulating local democracy – some concluding observations

The story told in this chapter is not unique to Norway. Similar if not identical stories can be told based on experiences in other countries (see, for example, Lowndes et al. 2006). These stories serve to raise a variety of issues that deserve further reflection, of which the following are indicative.

What is the motivation for such exercises?

Arguably efforts to evaluate and stimulate local democracy are motivated by a sincere desire to improve the character and quality of (local) democracy in practice. Without specifying more clearly what is meant by democracy in practice, however, such a suggestion constitutes a potentially naïve, if not meaningless, assertion. It fails to recognize the plural meaning of democracy – a term which encompasses various forms of direct democracy, indirect or representative democracy, and deliberative democracy respectively. Yet even should one of these more basic conceptions of democracy be held up as a standard, there is no universally agreed upon set of criteria with respect to just what constitutes a normatively – much less empirically – satisfactory realization of the envisioned state of affairs. How high does electoral turnout have to be, for example, before it may be claimed that representative democracy is functioning in a satisfactory manner? Or what is required to achieve a genuine and satisfactory form of deliberative democracy?

These questions illustrate only part of the problem. Every bit as important is recognizing that democracy, whatever its form, may serve several purposes. Robert Salisbury, in a classic article on political participation (1975), notes how political activity may have three purposes or implications – instrumental, expressive and legitimizing. By extension, the same can be said about democracy and attempts to improve democratic performance. Democracy is not only an instrumental, policy making device; it may also be an expressive mechanism through which individuals achieve self-realization, and it may offer a source of legitimacy for the political system and those responsible for public decision making.

What mix of motivations or intentions underlies efforts to evaluate and stimulate (local) democracy is a matter which can be debated. There seems to be little doubt, however, that in the Norwegian case a principal motivation for undertaking some of the experiments was a desire to strengthen the (perceived) legitimacy of the political system and how it functioned. The same can reasonably be said about many of the schemes to assess and revitalize local democracy in Norway and elsewhere, especially when these efforts have a top-down character. Findings from empirical studies in other countries support such a conclusion (see, for example, Michels/de Graaf 2010; Secchi 2010; Zittel/Fuchs 2007). Analyses show that the introduction of arrangements to provide new participatory opportunities are quite commonly built upon the premises of public authorities operating within representative democratic decision making traditions. People may be given the chance to exercise voice, but the final decisions are taken by elected representatives or other public officials. Under these circumstances the intent and hope is typically that such opportunities will serve to redress perceptions of a democratic deficit and give rise to a greater sense of system legitimacy. Whether new participatory opportunities may also indeed have instrumental and/or expressive consequences is typically of more secondary concern and relevance.[118]

Various forms of local democracy assessment or benchmarking exercises are of a somewhat different character and may therefore be cast in a slightly different light. Although they may be initiated and carried out on a top-down basis, at the outset there is generally no prescribed procedure for how the results will be put to use. Hence, for these exercises the motivational issue is relevant. But in this case it is necessary to phrase the question in terms of what if any follow up is intended. Before addressing this question, however, it is appropriate to consider the validity of such assessment exercises themselves.

How valid are local democracy assessment schemes?

Here the crux of the matter relates to the classical and well-known issue of measurement validity. What are the relevant dimensions of local democracy and what are proper (as well as cross-nationally valid) indicators of these dimensions? Do assessment instruments include indicators of all significant dimensions, or are some dimensions noteworthy for their absence? Answers to these questions are likely to be influenced not only by theoretical and empirical considerations; in many cases they will also be founded upon underlying normative perspectives and understandings of democracy. Virtually all assessment schemes, for example, take representative democracy as a point of reference and departure. In addition, such schemes typically skirt the difficult issue of local autonomy (cf. Goldsmith 1995) and what this implies for

---

118 For a useful discussion of this issue in connection with the Norwegian program of experimental projects sponsored by KS, see Aars 2007.

the character of local democracy in different settings. Can citizens living in authorities operating within narrow limits of local autonomy be said to have the same potential for experiencing and benefitting from local democracy as those living in municipalities endowed with a broader scope of legal discretionary power? How are comparisons to be made?

Similar questions can be raised about how other differences in political arrangements complicate comparison of assessment results, especially on a cross-national basis. The relative importance or weight attached to different dimensions of democracy when attempting to establish a summary assessment measure further complicates the issue. At the same time, every bit as critical is the frequent need (if not desire) to "simplify" assessment instruments due to cost considerations and the implications for measurement validity this has. In developing the Norwegian local democracy database, for instance, this problem has been most evident in the reduction of the number of indicators used to measure various dimensions of local democracy. The problem is even more apparent in the Council of Europe labeling enterprise in which only a single item is used in the citizen surveys intended to tap each of the 12 principles of good democratic governance. A simplification of this sort defies all of the prescriptions laid down by the multi-trait, multi-item measurement philosophy that has strong roots in the relevant research literature (cf. Campbell/Fiske 1959; Adcock/Collier 2001).

What are the consequences of local democracy assessment schemes?

A third question that can be raised here concerns the use – or misuse – of the results from democratic assessment exercises. The essence of this issue is again one of motivation, but motivation in a slightly different light. Are those responsible for initiating the assessment process committed to follow up on the results, and if so how? The key idea underlying assessment and benchmarking endeavors is that results will provide a basis for subsequent action; assessment exercises are presumed to be a tool for identifying strengths, weaknesses, opportunities and threats for the actors involved. Whether the instrument is used in this manner, however, is an empirical question. The pitfalls are many, two being particularly noteworthy. One is passivity due to a sense of congratulatory self-satisfaction following in the wake of positive results. The other is also passivity, but one of different velour brought on by the potentially enervating effects of poor results, a sense of dejection and resignation.

These pitfalls may be avoided by thoughtful actors who are prepared for all eventualities and who are committed to use assessment results to move forward in any case. But the situation and conditions confronted in the follow up process are often complicated by how other actors – the (local) media and the general public in particular – react. For example in Harstad, the municipality that came out poorest among the four municipalities that took part in the Norwegian pilot project, the local press carried news of the results under bold headlines on the front page. This response, however, did not deter the mayor and municipal council from confronting the challenge and seeking to find means of improvement. The same was true in the case of Kristiansand as already mentioned.

More problematic are efforts to declare a "winner" in a type of local democracy contest where results from many municipalities are compared and presented to the public in a superficial fashion. Such was the case in a recent issue of *Kommunal Rapport* when Bærum, a municipality that constitutes a large suburb of Oslo, was said to be a "hot candidate" to be Norway's best municipality with respect to local democracy. The fact that this suggestion was based on results emerging from the first round of data collection (in which only 50 of the 430 municipalities in Norway were included in the database) was not made explicit. Nor was more detailed information on the methodology underlying the results presented. Interestingly enough, Halvdan Skard, leader of KS who has his political roots in Bærum, was quoted as being more restrained and reflective in his interpretation of the results. In Skard's eyes, while Bærum may have some reason to be satisfied, he suggested there is more that could be done to further strengthen local democracy in the municipality. Involving citizens in the budgetary process was one such possibility mentioned by Skard.

This example serves to illustrate the lesson emerging from the well-known question about whether a glass of water is half empty or half full. Results of local democracy assessment procedures, much as is the case with respect to electoral turnout statistics, may be interpreted in different ways, all depending on the perspective of who answers the question. This is not to say that local democracy assessment endeavors are without merit; it is merely that they may be subject to both use and misuse, and hence deserve to be treated with caution. When so treated, such efforts may well prove to offer a useful means for stimulating and maintaining vibrant local democracies.

References

Aars, Jacob (1998): *Underveisrapportering fra satingsområdet "Demokrati, deltakelse og styring": Hva skjer i prosjektkommunene?* Bergen/Oslo: SEFOS/Kommunenes sentralforbund.
Aars, Jacob (2007): Democratic Renewal in Local Government? Top-down Strategies for Bottom-up Involvement. In: Zittel, Thomas/Fuchs, Dieter (eds.): *Participatory Democracy and Political Participation: Can Par-*

ticipatory Engineering Bring Citizens Back In? London: Routledge, pp. 202-222.

Adcock, Robert/ Collier, David (2001): Measurement Validity: A Shared Standard for Qualitative and Quantitative Research. In: *American Political Science Review 95*, 3, pp. 529-546.

Baldersheim, Harald/ Ståhlberg, Krister (eds.) (1994): *Towards the Self-Regulating Municipality: Free Communes and Administrative Modernization in Scandinavia*. London: Dartmouth Publishing Co.

Beetham, David (2004): Towards a Universal Framework for Democracy Assessment. In: *Democratization 11*, 1, pp. 1-17.

Beetham, David/ Bracking, Sarah/ Kearton, Iain and Weir, Stuart (2002): *International IDEA Handbook on Democracy Assessment*. Haag: Kluver Law International.

Beetham, David/ Carvalho, Edzia/ Landman, Todd and Weir, Stuart (2008): *Assessing the Quality of Democracy: A Practical Guide*. Stockholm: International IDEA.

Buck, Marcus/ Larsen, Helge O./ Willumsen, Tord and Lanes, Mikal (2005): Direktevalg av ordfører: Demokratisk nyvinning eller mislykket eksperiment? In: Saglie, Jo/Bjørklund, Tor (eds.): *Lokalvalg og lokalt folkestyre*. Oslo: Gyldendal Akademisk, pp. 102-121.

Campbell, David F. J./ Pölzlbauer, Georg (2010): *The Democracy Ranking 2009 of the Quality of Democracy: Method and Ranking Outcome. Comprehensive Scores and Scores for the Dimensions."* Vienna: Democracy Ranking
http://www.democracyranking.org.

Campbell, Donald T./ Fiske, Donald W. (1959): Convergent and Discriminant Validation by the Multitrait-Multimethod Matrix. In: *Psychological Bulletin, 56*, 1, pp. 81-105.

CoR (2001): Voter Turnout at Regional and Local Elections in the European Union, 1990–2001. Brussels: Committee of the Regions, European Union. CoR-Studies 1–3/2001.

Council of Europe (2007): Good local and regional governance – the European challenge. Valencia: Conference of European ministers responsible for local and regional government, 15th Session, October 2007.
http://www.coe.int/t/dgap/localdemocracy/Ministerial_Conferences/Valencia/default_en.asp.

Franklin, Mark N. (2004): *Voter Turnout and the Dynamics of Electoral Competition in Established Democracies since 1945*. Cambridge: Cambride University Press.

Goldsmith, Mike (1995): Autonomy and City Limits. In: Judge, David/Stoker, Gerry and Wolman, Harold (eds.): *Theories of Urban Politics*. London: Sage Publications, pp. 228-252.

International IDEA, Institute for Democracy and Electoral Assistance (2010): 15 Years Supporting Democracy Worldwide. Available at http://www.idea.int/publications/15_years_supporting_democracy/index.cfm.

Kaufmann, Daniel/ Kraay, Aart and Mastruzzi, Massimo (2008): *Governance Matters VII: Aggregate and Individual Governance Indicators, 1996-2007*. Washington, D.C. World Bank Policy Research Working Paper No. 4654. Available at http://ssrn.com/abstract=1148386.

Larsen, Helge O. (2002): Directly Elected Mayors: Democratic Renewal or Constitutional Confusion? In: Caulfield, Janice/Larsen, Helge O. (eds.): *Local Government at the Millennium*. Opladen: Leske + Budrich, pp. Xxx-xxx

Lijphart, Arend (1997): Unequal Political Participation: Democracy's Unresolved Dilemma. In: *American Political Science Review, 91*, 1, pp. 1-14.

Lowndes, Vivien/ Prachett, Lawrence and Stoker Gerry (2006): Diagnosing and Remedying the Failings of Official Participation Scemes: The CLEAR Framework. In: *Social Policy & Society 5*, 2, pp. 281-291.

Michels, Ank/ de Graaf, Laurens (2010): Examining Citizen Participation: Local Participatory Policy Making and Democracy. In: *Local Government Studies 36*, 4, pp. 477-491.

Norris, Pippa (1999): *Critical Citizens: Global Support for Democratic Government*. Oxford: Oxford University Press.

NOU 2005:6. Samspill og tillit. Oslo: Kommunal- og regionaldepartementet.

NOU 2006:7. Det lokale folkestyret i endring? Oslo: Kommunal- og regionaldepartementet.

Olsson, Jan/ Montin, Stig (ed.) (1999): *Demokrati som experiment: Försöksverksamhet och förnyelse i svenska kommuner*. Örebro: Novemus.

Patterson, Thomas (2002): *The Vanishing Voter: Public Involvement in an Age of Uncertainty*. New York: Knopf.

Pinter, Rafael López/ Gratschew, Maria (2004): *Voter Turnout in Weestern Europe since 1945*. Stockholm: International Institute for Democracy and Electoral Assistance.

Piven, Francis Fox/ Cloward, Richard A. (2000): *Why Americans Still don't Vote: and Why Politicians Want it that Way*. Boston: Beacon Press.

Pröhl, Marga (ed.) (2002): Good Governance Für Lebensqualität Vor Ort. Gütersloh: Verlag Bertelsmann Stiftung.

Putnam, Robert D./ Pharr, Susan J. (eds.) (2000): *Disaffected Democracies: What's Troubling the Trilateral Countries*. Princeton: Princeton University Press.

Rose, Lawrence E. (1990): Nordic Free-Commune Experiments: Increased Local Autonomy or Continued Central Control?" In: King, Desmond E./Pierre, Jon (eds.): *Challenges to Local Government*. London: Sage Publications, pp. 212-241.

Salisbury, Robert H. (1975): Research on Political Participation. In: *American Journal of Political Science 19*, 2, pp. 323-341.

Secchi, Leonardo (2010): Entrepreneurship and Participation in Public Management Reforms at the Local Level. In: *Local Government Studies 36*, 4, pp. 511-527.

Skålnes, Sigrid (2005): Uklar diagnose og tvilsom medisin? Erfaringer med eigen valdag i Nittedal i 2003? In: Saglie, Jo/Bjørklund, Tor (eds): *Lokalvalg og lokalt folkestyre*. Oslo: Gyldendal Akademisk, pp. 83-101.

SOU 2000:1. En uthållig demokrati! Politik för folkstyrelse på 2000-talet. Demokratiutredningens betänkande. Stockholm: Fritzes Kundservice.

UNDP (2007): Governance Indicators: A Users' Guide. 2nd edition. New York: United Nations Development Programme.

Wattenberg, Martin (2000): The Decline of Party Mobilisation. In: Dalton, Russell J./ Wattenberg, Martin P. (eds.): *Parties without Partisans: Political Change in Advanced Industrial Democracies*. Oxford: Oxford University Press, pp. 19-36.

Wattenberg, Martin (2002): *Where Have All the Voters Gone?* Cambridge, MA: Harvard University Press.

Wegener, Alexander (2002): "Die Kriterien Zu Good Governance" In: Pröhl, Marga (ed.): *Good Governance* Für Lebensqualität Vor Ort. Gütersloh: Verlag Bertelsmann Stiftung.

Zittel, Thomas/ Fuchs, Dieter (eds.) (2007): Participatory Democracy and Political Participation: Can Participatory Engineering Bring Citizens Back In? London: Routledge.

Øvrum, Rolf (2000): En del hovedresultater fra Demokrati, deltakelse og Styring: Smakebiter fra idéhåndbøkene fra KS' FoU-satsing 1996-2000. Oslo: Kommuneforlaget.

Chapter 12
Prospects for two small countries in a turbulent world

Harald Baldersheim and Jozef Bátora

Key findings

The book has sought to compare politics and policy choices in two small European democracies in turbulent times. The analyses presented here exemplify options and constraints that small countries face and the solutions they explore. While being contrasts in terms of system maturity Norway and Slovakia are subject to many of the same pressures and tribulations arising from international as well as from domestic forces. In responding to these pressures the two countries seem less narrowly scripted by outside forces and their own history than is often assumed as regards small countries.

Security and sovereignty: smallness as an adaptational advantage

A key finding related to security is that the crisis of military spending combined with the multiple crises of NATO as a basic security framework in Europe have left small European states highly vulnerable and highly exposed. The study of the responses of Norway and Slovakia indicates two parallel patterns of adaptation to this situation: a) the modernization of armed forces, the adaptation of security strategies, and the development of crisis response measures on a national basis; and, b) the development of regional frameworks for cooperation and coordination in the realm of security policy. The former pattern indicates a growing need in small states in Europe to take on a higher level of responsibility for their own security and sovereignty than the peaceful development in the two decades following the end of the Cold War might have suggested. However, as the costs of the newest defense technologies have been soaring, even wealthy small states such as Norway can hardly afford to stand alone. This is one of the main driving forces behind the development of regional defense frameworks. In the sphere of defense cooperation, the Nordic region has been among the most advanced, and has been a source of inspiration and learning for others, including the Visegrad region. Regionalization is an emerging way of creating sustainable defense frameworks for small states in Europe during the financial crisis. This involves maitaining sovereignty by pooling strategic resources and effective multilateralism – patterns that small states like Norway and Slovakia are traditionally familiar with and prefer. Major European powers such as the UK, Germany or France face similar challenges in the sphere of austerity measures as small states (Valasek 2011)[119], but they seem less capable of adopting viable and sustainable patterns of regional cooperation and pooling of strategic resources. Smallness and the concomitant readiness to cooperate with others seem to be an advantage in times of soaring expenditures and decreasing budgets in the defense sector.

The latter observation also holds regarding the management of migration flows, where both Norway and Slovakia have been developing their national approaches to migration while adapting to a broader regional framework of rules and regulations related to their membership of the Schengen zone. While Norway has significantly higher numbers of immigrants and more experience in managing their societal integration, Slovakia shows similar patterns of policy adaptation in the realm of immigration. Undeniably, in some respects Slovakia also demonstrates a certain reluctance, viz. the adoption of fairly restrictive precedures for obtaining citizenship in comparison to Norway. However, as indicated by the preceding analyses of populism and New Politics (see chapters 7 and 8) immigration policy engenders opposition also in Norway and has become a component of the new cleavage structure (see below). We wish to emphasize that both countries have so far managed to tackle issues of immigration and integration through the procedures of 'normal' politics[120].

National and international responses to the financial crisis: competition and complementarity

As the case of Slovakia shows, small states combine in-depth domestic reforms with openness to a number of supranational solutions offered by the EU and other international actors. Slovakia's responses to the financial crisis were constrained by its membership of the eurozone, which denied it the option of monetary measures (e.g. devaluation), and also placed limits on public spending, i.e. deficit budgeting. However, EU membership also

---

119 Germany is to cut its defense budget by 25 per cent between 2010-2015. France had its defense budget cut by 3 per cent in 2010, The UK is to have its budget cut by 7.5 per cent between 2011-2015 (Valasek 2011:7).

120 The massacres in Oslo on July 22 2011 are not likely to signal a more polarized climate on immigration issues in Norway but are rather the expression of the marginality of hostile opposition in this regard. The massacres resulted in the loss of 77 lives in a bomb explosion in Oslo and a shooting incident at Utoya carried out by the same person. These acts of terror were aimed at government buildings in the center of Oslo and at a youth camp organized by the Labor Party, the senior party in the governing coalition. At the time of writing these seem to have been the acts of an isolated, possibly deranged individual of Norwegian stock, not the coordinated attacks of an organized group.

opened up access to cheap credit through the EIB and assistance from the structural funds to help overcome obstacles to competitiveness, which hamper the Slovak economy. These obstacles will need to be addressed persistently in the coming years. At the same time, Slovakia was called upon to demonstrate solidarity with other eurozone countries in more dire circumstances than itself, especially Greece, a call that Slovakia resisted. While such resistance may demonstrate space for independent action in a time of crisis, it may not necessarily represent the most statesmanlike attitude.

Financial and economic reforms prompted by the crisis have been reflected in political party programs in electoral campaigns for national parliaments and the EU parliament. The Slovak case indicates that the impact of the crisis on party competition was quite profound. This relates primarily to politically loaded controversies about whether solutions to the crisis should move along the national axis or include concerted EU-wide actions driven by considerations of solidarity. Parties at the conservative end of the political spectrum promoted national solutions and were skeptical of EU-wide actions, while parties with leftist leanings were more open to joint EU-coordinated efforts to combat the crisis. A new cleavage line concerning visions of an emerging political order in the EU could be discerned in Slovakia. This was new in two senses. First, relations to the EU have traditionally been among the most consensual issues in Slovak politics – all parties supported close relations to the EU, and a positive and proactive approach to EU policies. The fact that relations to the EU have now become a source of political cleavage lines breaks with that tradition which had been valid for about two decades since the Velvet Revolution in 1989. Second, the center-right and liberal-conservative parties in Slovak politics have traditionally been the pro-EU force in Slovak politics, driving EU integration efforts and the EU-oriented modernization of the country in the last two decades. The fact that these parties have now come to represent the euroskeptic side of the EU-related political cleavage is a new pattern prompted largely by the crisis.

While financial crises and crises of the economic performance of countries may have profound effects on patterns of party competition in some small states, this is not always the rule. The study of the electoral performance of governments in Norway shows that while economic performance is an important factor, it may not be decisive. This is related to a number of contextual factors, where in a small and open economy such as Norway, voters do not necessarily hold the government responsible for the development of the economy which they see as highly dependent on developments in the global economy. Another factor is that in a well-developed welfare system such as Norway's, voters simply do not automatically perceive the need to reward or punish the government for plummeting or growing economic performance. Hence, societal factors ensure that financial crises have only a limited impact on the electoral performance of governments, despite the openness and global inter-connectedness of the Norwegian economy.

Political cleavages in flux:
the social structure of politics and its implications

While Norway is a settled democracy with well-established political cleavages, and Slovakia is a post-communist country with a party system still under development, the explanatory power of social structure in party choice was found to be similar in both cases. Patterns of classical left-right class voting were weak in both countries (weakened by the advent of 'New Politics' in Norway while cleavages were not as yet fully crystallized in Slovakia). The crystallization of classical left-right patterns in Slovakia was found to be hindered by the dominance of the tension between democratic politics, and authoritarian and nationalist tendencies. This cleavage related to nation-building was, however, expected to decline over time. 'New Politics' in Norway, related to conflicts regarding immigration and growth-oriented policies was found to be the reason for the left-right dealignment in the country.

These shifts in the political structures were also reflected in the rise in populist politics in both countries. Populism was observed in various parties, but most vividly it was represented by the Progress Party (FRP) in Norway, and in the nationally oriented parties in Slovakia (SMER, HZDS, and SNS). The populist appeals in the two countries within the context of the financial crisis were also found to be correspondingly different. As the crisis did not affect Norway too severely due to its oil and gas reserves and their rising prices, the FRP has been calling for spending more money on public services and the like, while limiting immigration. In Slovakia, the appeals of populist parties have varied, but in general they have called for policies that would help protect "the people" from the effects of the unaccountable elites of global financial capitalism. As a parallel to FRP's restrictive immigration policies much of the populist agenda in Slovakia concentrated on more restrictive policies toward the Roma population in the country.

As a general rule democratization could be expected to lead to more representative politics, and especially so in a small state. Why are there, then, so few women in Slovak parliaments? On average, female representation in Slovak parliaments since 1989 is less than half that of the last communist National Council elected in 1986, and it has not increased much since the turn of the millennium. In the 2010 election, fifteen per cent of the MPs in Slovakia were women, while the Nordic average is forty-two per cent, and the European average without the Nordic countries is twenty per cent. An insufficient supply of eligible and willing female candidates is not a credible explanation for the low share of female MPs in Slovakia, and certainly not for the variation between parties. Factors associated with the nomination process seem to explain much of the difference in average female representation between communist and democratic parliaments in Slovakia, as well as between Slovakia and the Czech Republic in the 2000s. Most importantly, the Communist Party of Czechoslovakia – and from the mid-1990s its successor, the Communist Party of Bohemia and Moravia – employed gender quotas. In contrast, such quotas have been absent across the left-right divide in Slovakia since the transition to democracy. The territorial spread of electoral strongholds and weak spots may, furthermore, explain some of the present variation across parties. Parties with more support in cities and among the well-educated social strata seem to send more women to parliament than do parties with predominantly rural roots. The general lesson is that democratization does not automatically lead to better representation of all social groups in national politics; and as long as the representation of women is not an issue on the reform agenda of Slovak political parties, women will remain underrepresented.

Institutional transformation:
changing patterns of regional and local governance

Both countries sought to reform their overall structures of territorial governance in the 2000s. Slovakia introduced eight regions of self-governance in 2001-2002. In Norway, directly elected county councils have a long history, and an initiative to transform them into larger, more powerful regions was launched in 2005 but resulted only in modest change. In both cases controversy and resistance surrounded the initiatives. Why was Slovakia able to overcome or accommodate resistance and establish regions, while Norway's regional initiative came to (almost) nothing?

European integration was clearly a paramount factor in the Slovak case and despite the numerous cleavages that emerged in the process leading up to the reform, actors agreed that establishing regions was in the national interest; not reaching agreement was regarded as slowing down accession to the EU and made actors, for example the Hungarian minority, play down their misgivings over the actual outcome. No one wanted to take the blame for slowing the "return to Europe". In contrast, European integration played little role in the Norwegian case.

In Norway the nature of the decision-making process took on a momentum of its own. Decision-making took place under the constraint of 'voluntarism' imposed by a parliamentary decision a decade earlier. This amounted to giving the county councils veto powers over the outcome of reform. The county councils behaved in accordance with the expectations of rational self-interest formulated by the joint-decision trap model (Sharpf 1988), i.e. they took into account only what appeared to be the best outcome seen from their own local points of view. The outcome was a reform that reflected the lowest common denominator of the county councils, i.e. what they could all agree on, which ruled out any mergers of county councils into larger regions.

In Norway growing concern about the state of local democracy has emerged against a background of declining voter turnout in local elections. How can the quality of local democracy be enhanced? This is the question posed by the central government as well as by representatives of local governments. A two-pronged strategy is being tested in local authorities around the country. By measuring the quality of local democracy and publishing the result, the hope is that municipalities will try to improve their interface with the public as well as open up to a greater degree their processes of decision-making to public scrutiny. The quality-of-democracy indicators cover aspects of local decision-making and service provision as well as citizens' attitudes to and experiences of their respective municipalities. In developing the latter type of indicators Norway is spearheading a parallel initiative launched by the Council of Europe, the aim of which is to establish a "label" of good governance to which local authorities may aspire. It is still somewhat early to judge the results of the Norwegian initiative. But so far the interest in Norwegian municipalities has been overwhelming – nearly one hundred municipalities have taken the citizen-focused good governance test, and a database has been established which allows citizens and the media to assess the performance of their own municipality compared to others. This again has prompted the municipalities involved to put democracy issues on the agenda of the local councils, and has given birth to a variety of measures. The results of these measures are not known yet. Overall, however, it has to be said that the ripple effects of these initiatives seem promising.

Conclusions

Referring back to the concepts of system maturity and political integration introduced in Chapter 1 some of the findings are as expected, while others are quite surprising. The lower levels of system maturity in Slovakia compared to Norway led us to expect more volatility in external adaption, and more conflict in internal processes of decision-making in the former case. The parallels found between the two states suggest, however, that there are a number of general patterns regarding the adaptability of small European states.

First, it seems that the sustainable adaptability of small states is fostered by *cooperation in regional integration clusters*. The difference between broad-based integration projects such as the EU and regional integration processes such as those in the Nordic region and in the Visegrad region is that the latter connect small states with similar experiences, close cultural backgrounds, and similar societal challenges. These conditions help small states integrate resources and allow for their more efficient use. They also support knowledge transfer, the sharing of reform experiences, and foster learning in ways which are often less likely in complex multi-level political frameworks such as the EU. The pattern of *regional binding* that the Norwegian and Slovak experiences with tackling the recent wave of global turbulences indicates is not a process undermining broader integration frameworks such as the EU or NATO. On the contrary, it may serve as a vehicle for making these broader frameworks more efficient. Hence, the general observation here is that small states do multiple and layered kinds of binding.

Second, binding in governance frameworks can work as a way of protecting a small state from turbulences and make it more stable, but it can also be *a source of limits in adaptation*. Slovakia's membership of the eurozone has been regarded as a stabilizing mechanism for the country's economy in the initial phases of the financial crisis. But the inefficient institutional set-up of eurozone governance has led to severe inefficiencies in decision-making in tackling the debt crises of several member states in 2010 and 2011, and Slovakia found itself dealing with tough political dilemmas. These related primarily to the issue of whether the costs of maintaining a common approach to tackling the debt crisis of eurozone members outweighed the benefits. The dilemmas were demonstrated very clearly in October 2011, when the Slovak Parliament was to vote on the ratification of the increase of guarantees in the European Financial Stability Facility. Prime Minister Radičová connected this with a vote of confidence, but one of the coalition parties – Freedom and Solidarity (SAS) – voted against the package and the government had to leave office. The bill was eventually passed two days later with the help of the Social Democratic party (SMER) in opposition. This event demonstrated that Eurozone governance was suffering from serious inefficiencies if a small member state with a fragmented governmental coalition could hold the rest of the 16 member states hostage to the will of one of its political parties. The episode also demonstrated that EU's normative power, which previously worked in Slovakia as a unifying force of modernization has in the context of the financial crisis acquired the characteristics of a divisive force.

In general, as several of the contributions to this volume show, small states' strategies of binding themselves in multi-lateral frameworks (cf Steinmetz and Wivel 2010) may lead to profound effects of external factors on restructuring the domestic political game, the creation of new political cleavages as well as on the development of governance reforms. Here, the comparison of Slovakia and Norway is useful as an indicator, where the former due to its status as an EU and eurozone member seems to have been more exposed to external factors than the latter. This has had both limiting and enhancing effects on adaptability. As the study by Baldersheim and Malíková of local governance reforms shows, while Slovak reforms were driven by EU guidelines and deadlines, Norwegian reforms were more informed by local concerns and moved slowly.

Third, surprising parallels between the two countries were also found as regards processes of political integration and disintegration. Patterns of political dealignment could be discerned in both countries, meaning that the strong connections between socio-political interests and party choices were being attenuated in Norway, while they were never very strong in Slovakia in the first place, so that in both countries at the start of the twenty-first century post-modern features of political behavior could be said to be emerging. An interesting aspect to this picture is the persistent position of populist appeals in both countries, although more so in Slovakia than in Norway. Growth of populism often signals deep splits at the elite level, since the essence of populism is attempts to capitalize on resentment to elites – whoever happens to be in power. Typically, Norway's main populist party has refused to join the consensus reached by the other parties on major issues such as pension reform, constraints on the use of oil revenues, and so on. In Slovakia, a populist stance seems to be the standard strategy of almost any party in opposition with ensuing low levels of political integration and elite consensus, with the exceptions of issues related to the EU and NATO. Even the elite consensus on the EU may be fragile and may be breaking down under the present financial turmoil.

In general, small states with their relative cultural and social homogeneity have a propensity for *exploitation* (cf. March 1991) in reaction to external change, that is, they make use of options with which they are already familiar. However, as March (ibid.) argues, an excessive focus on exploitation may lead to gradual irrelevance, and there is a need to balance this with processes of *exploration* – seeking new solutions by re-combining and innovating existing procedures. As a number of studies in this volume show, excessive exploration seems to be the rule of the day in newly established small states such as Slovakia, which generates somewhat instable patterns of adaptation. One of the solutions allowing for finding a proper balance between exploration and exploitation seems to be the setting up of regional cooperation frameworks between small states. As the Nordic experience with governance reforms on various levels in recent decades indicates, learning and benchmarking in regional settings are an effective way for small states to test and develop new ideas while maintaining the relative stability of domestic processes.

References

March, James G. (1991): "Exploration and Exploitation in Organizational Learning" in *Organizational Science,* 2(1): 71-87

Steinmetz, Robert/ Anders Wivel (2010). *Introduction*, chapter 1 in Robert Steinmetz/ Anders Wivel, eds.: *Small States in Europe: Challenges and Opportunities*. Farnham: Ashgate.

Scharpf, Fritz W. (1988): The joint-decision trap: lessons from German federalism and European integration, In: *Public Administration*, 66: 239 – 278.

Valasek, Tomas (2011): *Surviving Austerity: The Case for a New Approach to EU Military Collaboration*. London: Centre for European Reform.

Index

Adaptation
- as exploitation 261
- as exploration 261

Amalgamation 208, 220, 222, 224
Authoritarian 4, 125-130, 166, 257

Banking system 9, 12, 64, 66
Big Brother 3, 6, 12
Budget deficit 69, 81, 87

Center-periphery 127
Charismatic leader 14, 159, 172
Citizen effectiveness 4
Citizen-oriented governance 235, 237
Class voting 128, 130, 146, 152, 257
Cleavages
- ethnic 180
- religious 1
- political 11, 13, 257, 260
- social 23, 128, 135, 152
- structural 127

Clientelism 5
Cold War 1, 8, 22, 37, 210, 254
Comparative approach 1
Competitiveness 3, 63, 71, 227, 257
Corporatism 7
Corruption 5, 11, 70, 126, 170, 233
Cyber attacks 8, 19, 22-23, 29

Dealignment 14, 123, 152, 153, 257, 261
Democratization 125, 187, 257, 258

Economic crisis 66
- in Slovakia 80-81
Economic openness 3, 63, 66
E-governance 5
Elections
- European Parliamentary 82-84
- national Slovak 86-90
- national Norwegian 115

Elite 3, 5, 14, 157, 171, 188, 261
Emigration
- from Norway 40-41
- from Slovakia 39-40

Ethnic
- conflict 129
- identity 13
- minority 137, 165, 218

European cooperation 7, 167
European integration 2, 7, 13, 35, 82-90, 161, 210, 213, 225, 258
European Stability Mechanisms 68
Euroskeptic 83, 91, 161, 256
Eurozone 65, 68, 225, 260

Financial crisis
- forms of exposure 64-65
- regulatory institutions 67-68
- regulatory legislation 68
- margin for national action 70

Five-party system model 124
Foreign policy 2, 31, 84
Fragmentation 7, 97, 217

Gender differences/gap 136,
Gender quotas 196, 206, 258
Globalization 12, 158, 210

263

Good governance 2, 210, 226, 246, 259

Ideological space 128, 130
Immigration
- access to nationality 55-56
- anti-discrimination 57-58
- education of migrants 49-50
- family reunion 48-49
- integration policies 44-45
- labor market policies 46-47
- legal regulation 42-43
- long term residence 54-55
- populist political parties 164-166
- political participation 52-53
- statistics 44
Incumbency effect 95, 96, 103
Institutional nimbleness 5
Institutional transformation 11, 15, 258
Institutionalization 6, 39
Integration, political 4, 5, 7, 13, 259, 261
Issue ownership 99, 117, 120

Joint-decision trap 18, 211, 226, 258

Leadership 1, 4, 25, 198
Learning 1, 4, 210, 254, 260, 261
Left-right dimension 126, 146
Local authority 245-246

Military dependence 3
Modernization 14, 20, 254, 260
Municipality 234, 236, 237, 239, 250

Nationalism/nationalistic 91, 126, 129, 162, 165, 179

NATO
- institutional crisis of 21-26, 254
- Article V 19-20
- regionalization of 34-35
New Politics 128, 146, 153, 257
Nordic cooperation 12, 27, 28, 37

Oil fund 102, 105, 112, 118

Political cost-effectiveness 3
Political culture 6, 180-181, 203
Political integration 4, 13, 30, 259, 261
Political party system
- in Norway 124-125
- in Slovakia 125-127
Political stability 7, 13
Post-modern politics 14

Quality-of-democracy/indicator 251, 259

Regional framework 31, 255
Regionalization 15, 34, 208, 226, 254
Regional security integration
- in clusters 259-260
- in the Nordic region 26-30
- in the Visegrad region 31-33
Resource curse 101, 119,
Right-wing parties 82, 85, 99, 162
Roma population 257

Scripted 7, 15, 254
Security
- and sovereignty 254-255
- pooling strategic resources 255
Solidarity 22, 256
Sovereign debt crisis 67

Sovereign fund 10
Stoltenberg report 20, 27-28, 30
Subprime loan 9
System capacity 4
System maturity 6, 7, 254, 259

Territorial governance 15, 208, 258
Transitional democracy 6, 181
Tyranny by majorities 5

Veto 33, 89, 163, 226, 258
Velvet Revolution 158, 187, 256
Vulnerability 4, 17, 64, 67

Warfare 8
Welfare 1, 10, 95, 99, 101, 118, 159, 164, 218, 256

Eigene Notizen

Democracy after the financial crisis

Ursula van Beek
Edmund Wnuk-Lipinski (eds.)
Democracy under stress
The global crisis and beyond
2012. 244 pp. Pb.
29,90 € (D),
30,80 € (A),
41,90 SFr,
US$45.95, GBP 26.95
ISBN 978-3-86649-453-4

This book focuses on the global financial crisis of 2008-2009 and its implications for democracy. Why and how did the crisis come about? Are there any instructive lessons to be drawn from comparisons with the Great Depression of the 1930s? What are the democratic response mechanisms to cope with serious crises? Do they work? Is China a new trend setter? Do values matter? Are global democratic rules a possibility? These are some of the key questions addressed in the volume.

> Wissen, was läuft: Kostenlos **budrich intern** abonnieren!
> Formlose eMail an: info@budrich.de – Betreff: budrich intern

Direkt bestellen: www.budrich-verlag.de

Verlag Barbara Budrich • Barbara Budrich Publishers
Stauffenbergstr. 7 • D-51379 Leverkusen Opladen • Tel +49 (0)2171.344.594 •
Fax +49 (0)2171.344.693 • info@budrich-verlag.de • www.budrich-verlag.de

The new Journal
Politics, Culture & Socialization

PC&S publishes new and significant work that report on current scientific research, discuss theory and methodology, or review relevant literature. It welcomes the following types of contributions on topics which fall within our aim and scope:

- Empirical research articles
- Theoretical articles which analyze or comment on established theory or present theoretical innovations
- Methodological articles
- Book reviews

The journal is published four times a year for an international audience. It relies on a wide range of subjects, compiled by scholars from around the world.

Editors: Prof. Dr. Christ'l De Landtsheer (University of Antwerp, Belgium), Prof. Dr. Russell Farnen (University of Connecticut, USA), and Prof. Dr. Dan German (Appalachian State University, USA).

Rates: Individual subscription (print) 59.00 €, (print + online) 69.00 €; institutional subscription 100.00 € (for institutional online, please contact publisher (josef.esser@budrich.eu); reduced rates (students, members of certain IPSA RCs) (print) 49.00 €. Postage added.

Verlag Barbara Budrich • Barbara Budrich Publishers
Stauffenbergstr. 7. D-51379 Leverkusen Opladen
Tel +49 (0)2171.344.594 • Fax +49 (0)2171.344.693 • info@budrich-verlag.de

www.barbara-budrich.net